FINANCIAL MARKETS
— AND —
FOREIGN DIRECT INVESTMENT
— IN —
GREATER CHINA

Hung-Gay Fung and Kevin H. Zhang, editors

AN EAST GATE BOOK

M.E.Sharpe
Armonk, New York
London, England

Financial markets and
foreign direct investment

An East Gate Book

Copyright © 2002 by M. E. Sharpe, Inc.

Library of Congress Cataloging-in-Publication Data

Financial markets and foreign direct investment in greater China / edited by Hung-gay
Fung and Kevin H. Zhang.
    p. cm.
    Based on an international symposium organized by the Center for International
Studies and College of Business Administration of University of Missouri-St. Louis in
March 2000.
    "An East gate book."
    Includes index.
    ISBN 0-7656-0804-9 (alk. paper)
    1. Finance—China—Congresses. 2. Investments, Foreign—China—Congresses. I.
Fung, Hung-gay. II. Zhang, Kevin H.

HG187.C6 F556 2001
332′.0951—dc21   2001020960

Printed in the United States of America

The paper used in this publication meets the minimum requirements of
American National Standard for Information Sciences
Permanence of Paper for Printed Library Materials,
ANSI Z 39.48-1984.

BM (c)   10   9   8   7   6   5   4   3   2   1

Contents

Part III. Foreign Direct Investment

Part IV. Business Environment and Policy Issues

FINANCIAL MARKETS
—— AND ——
FOREIGN DIRECT INVESTMENT
—— IN ——
GREATER CHINA

1

Introduction

Hung-Gay Fung and Kevin H. Zhang

For the last two decades, China has witnessed dramatic changes in financial reforms and inflows of foreign direct investment (FDI). In light of the recent East Asian financial crises and China's entry into the World Trade Organization (WTO), a study on policy and practice of China's financial market and FDI is warranted. The quality of the papers and the expertise of the authors should make the book a timely contribution to an understanding of the processes and prospects of China's financial reform and foreign investments.

Chinese financial market reforms have removed many economic activities from state control and have helped build a basis for a civil society. Recent economic developments, inside and outside China, have made Chinese policymakers especially cautious about the potential for financial crises to destabilize the national economy. It remains the top priority for Chinese policymakers to reform the financial system so that a risk-control mechanism, compatible with the evolving Chinese economy, may be established. International lending institutions, such as the World Bank, are also greatly concerned that the financial reform in China is successfully carried out.

Financial market reforms enable Chinese state-owned enterprises (SOEs) and private firms to raise capital in domestic financial markets and offshore markets. The new sources of funding are important for China's continued efforts to expand and grow. At the same time, the financial market reforms raise new issues and concerns for China as it becomes a more market-oriented economy. This edited volume will highlight some of these financial issues, which include reforms in stock and bond markets, banking and nonbank financial institutions, and the importance of corporate governance.

Since the economic reforms were initiated in the late 1970s, China has emerged as the most dynamic FDI-host country, and the role of FDI in the Chinese economy has burgeoned in ways that no one anticipated. FDI flows into China in 1997 totaled US$45 billion, which constitutes over 30 percent of total FDI in all developing countries. By 1999, the total FDI into China reached as much as US$311 billion. Inward FDI flows in 1995 constituted 26 percent of gross fixed capital formation. The foreign-invested firms employed 18 million Chinese by the end of 1996, constituting 18 percent of the total nonagricultural labor force. In 1997, 19 percent of total gross industrial output was produced by the foreign affiliates, and foreign-invested firms produced almost half of China's total exports. Thus, FDI plays an important role in China's economy.

This book is based on, and extended from, a recent international symposium on Challenges and Opportunities in the 21st Century for the Greater Chinese Economy, convened by the Center for International Studies and the College of Business Administration of the University of Missouri–St. Louis in March 2000. It is hoped that this book will provide readers with a better understanding of the processes and prospects of China's reforms in financial markets and inward FDI, one of the most urgent tasks in the current stage of the economic reform in China. Successful establishment of a modern financial market and full utilization of FDI will provide an extremely important assurance that China's economic reform will continue; it will also be instrumental in solving the dilemma of the state-owned enterprises through efficient allocation of domestic and foreign capital. To say that the ultimate success of the conversion of China's centrally planned economy to a market-oriented economy turns on this single dimension—the financial market reform and use of FDI—is an understatement.

Three goals of the book are as follows. First, it provides a forum for academic research on China's reforms in financial markets and the pattern of inward FDI. The rigorous theoretical modeling, statistical testing, and in-depth case studies in the book will not only lead to better understanding of China's financial reform, but also provoke heated academic discussion on the most fundamental aspect of the economic transition in China.

Second, it provides policy guidance to China's financial market reforms and regime for shaping multinational firms' activities, as well as investment guidance to foreign investors. Policy-circle readers may utilize the book to enhance policy formulation, and investors may improve their opportunities based on the analysis in the book.

Third, the book could be used as a textbook in graduate or training programs at major universities in courses focusing on International Finance, International Business, International Economics, International Political Economy, and area studies on China or Pacific Asia.

The main body of the book consists of fifteen chapters on various aspects of China's financial markets and FDI inflows, which fall into four parts: (1) Financial Markets: Institutions, Regulation, and Policy; (2) Recent Developments in Stock Markets; (3) Foreign Direct Investment; and (4) Business Environment and Policy Issues.

In the first part—Financial Markets: Institutions, Regulation, and Policy, there are four chapters. Specifically, Chapter 2, Financial Liberalization: Implications for Corporate Governance, explains the process of the financial liberalization in China by focusing on the development of the financial markets and the banking reforms. The discussion of the critical aspects of financial liberalization then leads to policy implications on corporate governance.

Chapter 3, on the stability of the RMB in the post–Asian crisis period, argues that the Chinese government is able to and will defend the Chinese currency (RMB) in the near future, but not for the long run. The cost for China to defend the RMB is not formidably high for the time being. However, as China implements an expansionary macroeconomic policy, causing changes in the macroeconomic environment, it will be economically unacceptable to peg the RMB to the U.S. dollar.

The next two chapters, Banking Reform in China and the Development of Nonbank Financial Institutions, examine different stages of banking and nonbank institution reforms under the gradual approach toward the market economic system. The problems and accomplishments in banking reforms are analyzed and the main characteristics of Chinese banking systems before and after 1978 are also compared. After providing a summary of the development of nonbank financial institutions in China, Chapter 5 urges that careful consideration and resources must be given to the guidance, regulation, and supervision of nonbank financial institutions in China, because they are important segments of the financial system but have been overlooked for a long time.

In the second part, Recent Developments in Stock Markets, there are three chapters dealing with the issue of Chinese stock markets. The opening of stock exchanges in Shanghai and Shenzhen in 1989 and 1991, respectively, symbolized a key step of financial reform in China. Chapter 6, The A- and B-Share Chinese Equity Market: Segmentation or Integration, takes a close look at the two types of shares traded: A shares available to domestic investors, and B shares to foreign investors. The evidence presented in the chapter suggests that A- and B-share markets are trending toward integration, based on the increasingly similar link of return volatility with the bid-ask spread and trading volume across the two markets, and decreasing differences in risk behavior of A and B shares.

In Chapter 7, on Ownership Restrictions and Stock Price Behavior in China, the stock price behavior of the Shanghai and Shenzhen Stock Exchanges is investigated under the two-tier trading systems of A and B shares. The A and B share prices tend to be driven by their own economic forces because of differences in the ownership distribution, liquidity, and financial characteristics of the firms.

Chapter 8 (Market Structure, Volatility, and Performance of H shares) compares the market structure and pricing of A and H shares issued by the same Chinese companies. H shares are highly liquid, extremely volatile, and traded at a large discount to corresponding A shares. Yet the share discount has increased dramatically over the years due to listed firms' lack of financial transparency, poor management, improper usage of funds in noncore businesses, and deteriorating profitability.

In the third part, issues relating to foreign direct investment are discussed. The two most prominent characteristics of FDI inflows in China are the dominant position of Hong Kong and Taiwan in FDI sources, and the growing role of FDI in the Chinese economy. This part of the book focuses on the two issues to provide readers with a broad picture of foreign capital in China in the past two decades.

Chapters 9 (China's Inward FDI Boom and the Greater Chinese Economy) and 10 (Taiwan's Outward Investment in Mainland China) explore the link between China's FDI boom and the greater Chinese economy, and factors that influence such capital flows. The large amount of investment from Hong Kong and Taiwan has been associated with the greater Chinese economy and Chinese connections. Like investments from Hong Kong, the Taiwanese investments were motivated primarily by cheap labor, incentive policies, market access, and cultural and linguistic affinities that provide Taiwanese investors with operation advantages over other investors.

In Chapter 11, on Changing Trends of FDI Patterns in China, the author discusses the impact of FDI in terms of sales, tax revenue, and assets on the Chinese economy, focusing on primary industry, secondary industry, and tertiary industry. The analysis sheds light on industrial structural change resulting from FDI and potential effects of FDI after China's accession to the World Trade Organization.

Chapter 12 (Location Advantages, FDI, and Technology Advance: Evidence of China) explores the importance of location advantages, which are considered critical by MNCs when they decide where to invest. The chapter first develops a theoretical location advantage framework and then applies the multilevel analytical methodology to empirical analyses. The paper thoroughly examines the international factors, intranational factors, and their relationship. The results are considered robust and more compatible in studies on the relationship between location advantages and FDI.

The last part of the book is on business environment and policy issues. Chapter 13, on United States-China-Taiwan: A Precarious Triangle, focuses on the interesting issues related to economic relations, on political relations, and military relations among the United States, China, and Taiwan. Although business environmental issues are domestic, that basic difference in national treatment generates serious political difficulties in the United States in maintaining good trade relations with China. The United States should welcome the development of improved relations with China and further progress in the day-to-day interactions of its people. However, the United States should be prepared for more pragmatic relationships and less happy outcomes.

Chapter 14, International Business and Multinational Corporations in China, applies Porter's theory of entry strategy to develop a congruency model that depicts the interrelationships among entry strategies and environmental determinants. The model suggests that design of entry strategies should be treated as an ongoing and dynamic process to allow for maximum flexibility and adaptability. The model has implications for multinational corporations to develop effective entry strategies for successful ventures in China.

The next two papers are written by government representatives of Hong Kong and Taiwan in the United States. In Chapter 15 (Taiwan' s Recent Economy and Business Environment), the author not only demonstrates that Taiwan has undergone remarkable economic growth for several decades, but also discusses Taiwan's recent economic performance in terms of trade, foreign investment, and trade partners. The future challenges facing Taiwan in the context of the greater Chinese economy are discussed.

Chapter 16, on Opportunity and Challenge of Hong Kong in the New Millennium, is devoted to discussing the opportunities and challenges facing Hong Kong after its reversion to China in 1997. The focus is on Hong Kong's business environment, its role after China's accession to the World Trade Organization, and policy implications for its future development.

Part I

**Financial Markets:
Institutions, Regulation, and Policy**

2

Chinese Financial Liberalization: Implications for Corporate Governance

Hung-Gay Fung and Wai Kin Leung

Chinese economic policies have been viewed as models for developing countries because of China's remarkable economic growth rate since 1978. This success is attributable primarily to various sound economic plans. They include economic reforms such as different economic zones, provision of government incentive packages that promote exports, opening up the economy to foreign investors for joint ventures and investment, and the restructuring of numerous unprofitable state-owned enterprises (SOEs).

Bank credit and government-issued treasury bills and bonds are the traditional sources of financing to SOEs. Because government-controlled banks lack incentives to monitor credit, bank loans are largely policy loans. That is, lending decisions are a matter of government *policy* whose purpose is to maintain employment and national security. Alternatively, bank loans can be the result of the bank's *guanxi* (connections) with the borrowers. Although Chinese banks have been motivated to lend on a more rational basis in recent years, about 75 percent of bank loans are still channeled to state enterprises. Estimates indicate that at least 20 percent of bank loans are nonperforming.

The Chinese government also set up stock markets to allow SOEs to raise money by forming stock companies that can issue shares to the public. Our study discusses the process of financial liberalization in China. We primarily focus our analysis on the development of financial markets and banking reforms. These two aspects of financial liberalization are critical to China's reforms that will stimulate its future growth. We analyze the implications of these financial reforms on corporate governance.

The Domestic Stock Market

In the 1980s, the Chinese government allowed SOEs to become stock companies. That is, these companies could issue shares to their employees and to other companies. In 1989, the State Council of China (the executive branch of the Chinese government) decided to establish two stock exchanges to allow SOEs to raise money from the public. The first, the Shanghai Stock Exchange (SSE), was opened in December 1989. The second, the Shenzhen Stock Exchange (SZSE), was opened in April 1991, allowing companies in the southern part of China to raise external equity capital.

Established in 1992, the China Securities Regulatory Commission (CSRC) is a special interagency committee of the State Council Securities Policy Committee which approves listings of shares on exchanges. The recent Securities Law enacted in July 1999 regulates the stock market and provides a consistent legal framework for the securities industry.

Types of Domestic Shares

There are several types of shares on stock exchanges in China. The first type is *state shares*, which are held by authorized central and local government agencies. Of course, the ultimate owner of these state shares is the State Council of China. *Legal-person shares* are the second type, which can be purchased by domestic companies and nonbanking financial institutions. The third type is *employee shares*—only an insignificant fraction of the total number of shares. The fourth type is shares issued to the public. These shares are called "A shares." A shares are common stocks that can be held only by Chinese residents, including state institutions (legal person), and public shares (including employee shares).

There is another type of share called "B shares," which are issued to foreign investors only. Both the SSE and SZSE trade both A and B shares. A shares are denominated in local currency and are only for domestic Chinese residents while B shares on the SSE are denominated in U.S. dollars on the SSE and in Hong Kong dollars on the SZSE. While A and

B shares are different in terms of ownership, they enjoy equal rights.

The companies listed on the B-share market are typically large and export-oriented because they need to fulfill dividend payments either in Hong Kong or U.S. dollars. The listing requirement for firms in the B-share market is more stringent than for the A-share market. The B-share market cannot exceed a ceiling of 25 percent of the total shares. This restriction serves as a control for foreign ownership in these companies.

There are more than one thousand companies listed on the two exchanges, with total market capitalization equal to about 50 percent of China's gross domestic product (GDP). The growth of the stock market is phenomenal. The size of the Chinese stock market has become comparable to those of the industrialized countries and thus cannot be ignored (Allen and Gale 1995).

Although shares similar to these A and B shares are traded in other countries (Domowitz, Glen, and Madhaven 1997; Bailey and Jagtiani 1994), pricing behavior in the China A- and B-share market is unique as compared to other countries. While in other countries B-share prices are typically higher than the prices of the corresponding A shares, the prices of China B shares are generally traded at a discount to A shares (Wo 1997; Bailey 1994). Market segmentation and liquidity have been suggested as the explanation for the price differential in these markets (Fung, Lee, and Leung 2000; Poon, Firth, and Fung 1998; Wo 1997).

Table 2.1 shows the percentage of ownership for different types of shares on the two exchanges. The results indicate that state shares will be about 40 percent, institutional shares 20 percent, public shares 33 percent, and foreign shares 7 percent on both exchanges. It is likely that the percentage of state shares will decline over time, as the government wants to reduce its ownership in these companies.

In recent years, it seems that the prices of A and B shares are coming closer together. This result is probably due to the following two reasons. First, it is believed that the government is consolidating the two markets. Second, Chinese residents are investing in B shares via nominal accounts in Hong Kong and elsewhere.

Types of Offshore Markets

Chinese companies have issued new shares in external (offshore) markets to raise capital during the past several years. Hong Kong, New

Table 2.1

Ownership Structure of Chinese Firms (by value of shares, including listed shares only)

Exchange	Year	No. of obs.	State	Institution	Public	Foreign
Shanghai	1991	6	0.66940	0.03407	0.29653	0.00000
	1992	30	0.53784	0.15194	0.10461	0.20561
	1993	105	0.50357	0.22275	0.14832	0.12536
	1994	170	0.42523	0.25743	0.16638	0.15096
	1995	187	0.40285	0.25760	0.18360	0.15596
	1996	291	0.40767	0.23352	0.22970	0.12910
	1997	382	0.39122	0.24213	0.27549	0.09115
	1998	434	0.41322	0.22447	0.28769	0.07462
	1999	479	0.41583	0.22403	0.29261	0.06753
Shenzhen	1991	6	0.10887	0.42301	0.46812	0.00000
	1992	24	0.20155	0.34372	0.30928	0.14545
	1993	76	0.30479	0.29207	0.31447	0.08866
	1994	119	0.29027	0.30997	0.32989	0.06987
	1995	131	0.31165	0.26896	0.31326	0.10614
	1996	231	0.35726	0.23792	0.29879	0.10603
	1997	357	0.39753	0.20652	0.32380	0.07214
	1998	410	0.41356	0.19822	0.32667	0.06154
	1999	459	0.41003	0.20422	0.33371	0.05204

Source: Taiwan Economic Journal, China Database.
Note: Value of shares is the closing price times the number of shares.

York, and other markets represent important markets for Chinese initial public offerings (IPOs).

Chinese companies started to issue shares in Hong Kong in 1993. Shares of mainland Chinese firms issued in Hong Kong are called "H shares." The shares of Chinese companies incorporated in Hong Kong and controlled by mainland government entities are listed on the Hong Kong Stock Exchange as "red chips." The H-share and red-chip markets have grown dramatically during the last few years. As more Chinese companies are planning to raise capital in Hong Kong, they will become dominant in Hong Kong's financial markets. One interesting result is that H shares are also traded at a deep discount to their A-share counterparts, similar to the discount pattern between A and B shares.

There are also several Chinese companies that for the past several years have raised capital in U.S. stock markets such as the New York Stock Exchange. Table 2.2 displays the number and names of Chinese

Table 2.2

Number of N Shares Listed and Capital Raised on the New York Stock Exchange

Panel A: Chinese IPOs on the New York Stock Exchange							
Year	1993	1994	1995	1996	1997	1998	1999
Number of IPO	1	2	1	1	3	1	0
Number of Companies	1	3	4	5	8	9	9

Panel B: Names of companies listed on the NYSE as of 1999

1. APT Satellite
2. Beijing Yanhua Petrochemical Co. Ltd.
3. China Eastern Airlines Corp. Ltd.
4. China Mobile (Hong Kong) Limited
5. Guangshen Railway Company Limited
6. Huangneng Power International Inc.
7. Jilin Chemical Industrial Company Ltd.
8. Asia Satellite
9. Shanghai Petrochemical Company

Source: NYSE homepage.
Note: All are year-end data, except 1999 from July 16, 1999.

companies listed on the New York Stock Exchange. Chinese companies list in U.S. markets in the form of American depository receipts (ADRs), while shares of some Chinese companies list on other exchanges such the Canadian and London exchanges in the form of global depository receipts (GDRs).

The Corporate Bond Market

Before 1986, the only debt securities traded in China were treasury bills. In 1986, corporate bonds were issued for the first time when their amounts averaged about RMB 8 billion (Kumar et al. 1997, 5). The total issue of corporate bonds increased to about RMB 13 billion in 1995 (Holmes 1997). There are three types of Chinese corporate bonds: state investment company bonds, financial bonds, and enterprise bonds.

The Chinese corporate-bond market is relatively underdeveloped as compared to its equity market. It is unlikely to have a significant increase in corporate-bond issues in the future for the following reasons. First, investors are not really excited about bonds because bond-coupon rates are low and stipulated by the government. Second, corporate bonds suffer from a bad image problem because some bond-interest payments are not paid according to schedule. Third, legal rights of bondholders are not properly defined in case of bankruptcy.

China is in the process of reforming its sluggish domestic-bond market by (a) creating an over-the-counter market, (b) encouraging participation of foreign institutions as underwriters, and (c) unifying the two existing bond markets—one run at the country's two stock exchanges and the other at the interbank market. The planned OTC market will enable individuals to gain easier access to the bond market; insurance companies, brokerages, investment funds, and other nonbanking financial institutions were allowed to participate in the market after 1999.

Banking Reforms

China's central bank is the People's Bank of China (PBOC), which has restructured its organization along the lines of the U.S. Federal Reserve Bank system. The number of provincial branches of the PBOC has been reduced substantially from thirty-one to twelve. The purpose of such reorganization is to maintain a greater centralization of control. The PBOC has largely deregulated bank-loan rates, giving the banking sector flexibility in lending. Deposit rates, however, are still very much under the control of the government. More deregulation is still required in the years to come for banks to be competitive in a market economy.

The four state-owned banks (Bank of China, Agricultural Bank of China, Industrial and Commercial Bank of China, and China's Construction Bank) control about 80 percent of the banking business. These four banks are now struggling to become real banks with full responsibility for their own bottom line (profitability) as the Chinese economy is becoming more market oriented. These banks face many challenges in the process of reform. They require substantial amounts of additional capital and significant internal restructuring. Because the four big banks are all overstaffed and deficient in account- and internal-information management, they need to upgrade their management systems and downsize their organizational structure. At the same time, changes in attitude, management style, and ways of handling business are necessary.

The PBOC has implemented several policies to reduce the amount of bad loans on the banks' balance sheets. Five steps have been or need to be taken. First, additional capital has been injected into the banks to improve their capital adequacy by issuing government bonds. Second, banks need to assess nonperforming loans on a risk-adjusted basis into a five-category classification: pass, special mention, substandard, doubtful, and loss. Third, more loan-loss provision is required to offset potential bad loans. Fourth, some bad bank loans are written off. Finally, the government set up four asset-management companies (AMCs) to buy bad loans from the four major state-owned banks. These AMCs will convert some of the bad debts of the SOEs into ownership shares of the companies.

The following example illustrates the working of an asset-management company. Cinda Asset Management Corporation, set up in April 1999, took over the compromised assets (RMB 220 billion in nonperforming loans) of China's Construction Bank. Cinda funded its purchase via bond issues. Some of the available funds were used for debt-for-equity deals.

The three other AMCs that were set up are: China Orient Asset Management, a subsidiary of the Bank of China; the Great Wall, a subsidiary of the Agricultural Bank of China; and Huarong, a subsidiary of the Industrial and Commercial Bank of China. The four asset-management companies (Cinda, China Orient, Great Wall, and Huarong) have bought about RMB 1.4 trillion of bad assets from banks and have signed debt-to-equity contracts with 587 state-owned companies (*South China Morning Post*, November 20, 2000).

The AMCs collect funding either by issuing corporate bonds that are guaranteed by the minister of finance or by applying for loans from the PBOC. They may also borrow money from domestic and foreign corporations or financial institutions.

The city of Shanghai and other city governments have also launched their first state-owned asset-management companies as a part of state-enterprise reform. It is expected that some of these badly managed companies have been sold for cash. For instance, Cinda recently published a list of thirty-eight projects for sale to foreign investment. In some cases, Cinda may not have ownership of 25 percent of the badly managed firms after the debt-equity swap. Thus, it is not clear if these sales to foreign investors are legitimate, because, according to Chinese law, at least 25 percent ownership stake in a company is required by foreign investments under Sino-foreign joint-venture arrangements (*South China Morning Post*, September 25, 2000).

The Issue of Corporate Governance

Corporate governance is an important issue because it is related to efficient allocation of resources within corporations and also means proper protection for stockholders and debt holders. Corporate governance describes the institutional arrangements that govern relationships among shareholders, creditors, and managers. Corporate governance defines and is associated with control of the firm, selection of officers within the firm, and the agency costs that arise from conflicts of managers and other stakeholders.

In the United States and other developed countries, market forces, bank-monitoring processes, and legal enforcement are effective to ensure the integrity of corporate governance. Below we discuss each of these factors to shed light on corporate governance in China.

Financial Markets

Given the competitiveness and efficiency of the stock market, stock prices will be depressed if managers act to deviate from the interest of the stockholders. As a result, the value of these firms will be seen as undervalued because of the agency-cost problem. The managers are likely to face the threat of being acquired by raiders. In the case that they are acquired, most of the managers in the acquired firms will be thrown out. As a result, market forces will force managers to act in the proper manner.

In China, corporate structure and culture are vastly different from those in the West. In China, market forces will not be such an effective form of discipline on managers. First, many big SOEs package some profitable units of their companies to satisfy the listing requirements on the exchanges. Then, these units form into a corporation to be listed on the exchanges to raise capital. The appointment or removal of a top manager of a listed company is controlled by the parent company. As a result, the top managers of such companies work closely with the parent firm and are not necessarily responsible to the stockholders at large.

The debt-swap case of Cinda is an illustration of the argument. In cleaning up the bad-debt program, Cinda Asset Management filed a court petition to liquidate the Zhengzhou Baiwen Company (a government-owned wholesaler and retail concern) because Cinda holds more than $180 million in Baiwen debt. Shandong Sanlian Group, a government retailer (SOE) and also the parent of Zhengzhou Baiwen, will pay $36 million to take control of its ailing Baiwen subsidiary and assume its public listing on the Shanghai Stock Exchange (*Wall Street Journal*, December 4, 2000). The Baiwen rescue illustrates two of the thorniest problems facing China: how to deal with dozens of unprofitable government firms listed on the exchanges, and how to impose sound corporate-governance practices.

Second, investors are not necessarily looking at company fundamentals. Stock prices are very much influenced by politics and rumor. They are volatile and not necessarily driven by fundamental economic factors. The deep discount in price between A and B shares and between A and H shares of the same company illustrates the point. Furthermore, it is widely believed that over 50 percent of these companies are likely to give either inflated or manipulated financial figures. Moreover, the financial market may not be efficient enough in reflecting accounting information or other economic fundamentals of the firms, given its short history.

The lack of a well-developed corporate-bond market in China has important implications, especially for corporate governance. First, a liquid bond market enables corporations to raise debt money in public; they do not necessarily depend on policy loans to avoid misguided credit plans. Resources can then be ensured an efficient allocation in the market.

Second, a well-informed rating agency gives proper signals to the market regarding the riskiness of these bonds. This in turn disciplines corporate managers to behave properly. Otherwise, they have to pay a higher premium in issuing these corporate bonds.

Finally, a smoothly functioning bond market enables bondholders to have efficient reorganization in the case of default or bankruptcy. For example, there is a mechanism for plans to work out a rehabilitation or liquidation through a voluntary reorganization or under court supervision. Thus, there are legal ramifications for corporate managers to behave properly.

A transparent legal system such as this will certainly improve the issue of corporate governance in the event of conflict. In many cases, stockholders (especially minority stockholders) and debt holders can sue the managers if they feel their rights are not properly protected and managers are not acting in the best interest of these stakeholders.

Bank Monitoring

In European countries like Germany, banks that sit on corporate boards monitor corporate governance. Banks are a major source of finance to corporations. In order to ensure that managers in corporations behave properly, banks will tend to monitor the activities of these companies to reduce agency cost.

In China, banks are not necessarily independent of government policies. If their lending policies are not based on risk-return criteria, it is impossible for them to monitor the activities of companies. Thus, an urgent task of the Chinese government is to deregulate the banking sector. Banks should be allowed to make their decisions independently and should be accountable for their activities. If they do not perform their jobs properly, they have to face the consequences.

For the banks to effectively monitor companies, the financial reports of companies need substantial improvement. It is widely understood that the financial statements of Chinese companies are not reliable and that many of them are manipulated. Thus, the banks' role in corporate governance cannot be isolated from other regulations in China.

Summary

This paper has described the process of financial liberalization in China. In particular, the reforms in financial markets and banking were illustrated. These two aspects of financial liberalization are crucial for China's future economic success.

The liberalization in the financial markets and the banking sector has tremendous implications for corporate governance. The critical issue of corporate governance in China is not completely resolved under the current financial liberalizations because market forces cannot work effectively under the current structure. One of the key factors in market discipline is to weed out the weak through mergers and acquisitions. However, it is currently difficult for other companies to take over the weak ones.

Second, banks cannot properly monitor the behavior of the firms if bank loans are policy loans. Banks need to act independently and lending should be primarily based on risk-and-return analysis. Furthermore, corporate financial statements are not properly prepared for banks to accurately evaluate the performance of loans.

Finally, the legal structure needs to be reformed to reflect the need of a market-oriented economy where conflicts of interest can be resolved via a transparent legal system. The legal system should properly define the rights of stakeholders (stockholders and debt holders), the proper procedure of claims in case of bankruptcy, and the appropriate penalty for those who do not act properly.

References

Allen, F., and D. Gale. 1995. "A Welfare Comparison of Intermediaries and Financial Markets in Germany and the United States." *European Economic Review,* 39: 179–209.

Bailey, W. 1994. "Risk and Return in China's New Stock Markets: Some Preliminary Evidence." *Pacific Basin Finance Journal:* 243–60.

Bailey, W., and J. Jagtiani. 1994. "Foreign Ownership Restrictions and Stock Prices in the Thai Capital Market." *Journal of Financial Economics* (August): 57–87.

Domowitz, I.; J. Glen; and A. Madhaven. 1997. "Market Segmentation and Stock Prices: Evidence from an Emerging Market." *Journal of Finance* (July): 1059–85.

Fung, H.G.; W. Lee; and W.K. Leung. 2000. "Segmentation of the A and B Chinese Equity Markets." *Journal of Financial Research:* 179–95.

Holmes, W. D. 1997. "China's Financial Reforms in the Global Market." *Law and Policy in International Business* (spring): 715–77.

Kumar, A.; K. Jun; A. Saunders; S. Selwyn; U. Sun; D. Vittas; and D. Wilton. 1997. *China's Emerging Capital Markets.* London: Financial Times.

Poon, W.; M. Firth; and H.G. Fung. 1998. "Asset Pricing in Segmented Capital Markets: Preliminary Evidence from China-Domiciled Companies." *Pacific Basin Finance Journal* (August): 307–19.

Wo, C. S. 1997. "Chinese Dual-Class Equities: Price Differential and Information Flows." *Emerging Markets Quarterly* (summer): 47–62.

3

The Stability of the RMB in the Post-Asian Financial Crisis

Gene Hsin Chang

I. Introduction

The Chinese economy has been reasonably stable during the Asian financial crisis. However, there is widespread speculation about the stability of the yuan, the Chinese currency. Will the renminbi (RMB), the Chinese currency, depreciate in the near future? The subject is still receiving attention across the world, even in the post–Asian-financial-crisis period. The crisis was characterized by currency depreciation followed by an economic recession (Table 3.1). During the crisis period (1997–1999) China and Hong Kong were the only two regions that maintained currency stability (Figure 3.1). Since China is the tenth largest trader in the world, and as the size of the Chinese economy is estimated as the second largest in the world by the purchasing power parity standard,[1] if the yuan depreciates, it will inevitably cause a confidence crisis and trigger a new round of currency devaluation in Asia. Consequently, the global economy will be greatly affected.

In their early conversations with overseas guests,[2] Chinese leaders have repeatedly promised that there will be no devaluation of the yuan.

*The author thanks readers at Harvard University and the University of Michigan, participants in the 1999 AEA session "Can China Catch Asian Flu," and Dr. Zhi Wang for their help and comments.

Table 3.1

Basic Indicators of Economic Performance of the Concerned Asian Countries in the Crisis Period (1997–1998)

	GDP growth rate %	Inflation rate (cpi) %	Unemployment rate %	Trade balance $bn	Current account balance $bn	Foreign reserves $bn	Exchange rate change %	Stock price change, Dec. 31, 1997– Dec. 31, 1998 %
China	7.8	–0.8	3.1–20.0?	43.6	24.6	145.0	+0.09	–4.8
Taiwan	5.2	0.9	2.37	5.1	5.7	84.0	–18.00	–16.8
Philippines	1.7	10.6	13.30	–6.8	–3.5	9.3	–29.00	–31.0
Singapore	1.6	–0.4	2.20	–0.5	13.5	72.0	–15.00	–39.5
Thailand	–0.4	10.0	3.70	4.8	2.9	27.0	–19.00	–39.0
Malaysia	–1.8	5.8	2.90	6.4	–4.8	19.7	–33.00	–45.4
Japan	–3.7	0.4	4.10	113.2	106.4	222.0	–24.00	–3.6
Hong Kong	–5.0	3.2	4.20	–16.8	–6.1	96.0	0.00	–26.9
Indonesia	–6.2	52.0	20.0?	17.7	–5.8	18.0	–74.00	–10.2
South Korea	–6.6	7.3	6.90	24.7	23.4	40.8	–31.00	–15.6

Source: The Chinese figures are from the recent release of the State Statistical Bureau, Feb. 26, 1999, for the year 1998; the only exception is the current account figure which is for the year 1997. Statistics for other regions are from *The Economist*, August 29, 1998; adjustments are made by the recent 1999 report for the figures in Hong Kong.

Figure 3.1 **Currency Plunge In the Crisis Period**

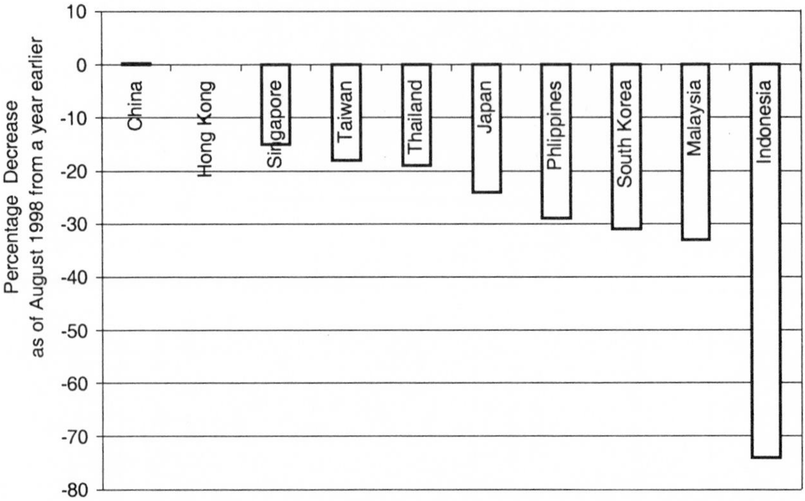

Source: The Economist, August 29, 1998, Emerging Market Indicators.

In response to widespread concern over the stability of the renminbi, Dai Xianglong, the president of the central bank, and Xiang Huicheng, the finance minister, reiterated that the renminbi will be stable in 1999 and 2000 (Dai, 1999). Dai and Xiang Huicheng reiterated their belief in the stability of the RMB at the World Bank and IMF meetings in October 1999 (*People's Daily,* Oct. 6, 1999). In his speech at the World Bank on October 4, Xiang indicated that depreciation of the RMB would trigger a new round of currency devaluation in Asia, hence he ruled out the RMB depreciation in the shortrun. The market, however, has remained suspicious. As observed, "fear of a yuan devaluation has continued to roil global financial markets, and has hung heavy on confidence domestically."[3] The black market exchange rate since late 1997 has been hovering at around 8.7 yuan for one U.S. dollar, representing a 6 percent devaluation.[4] In some places such as Taishan, Guangdong province, the exchange rate once even hit a level of 11 yuan for one dollar. Standard and Poor has cut the yuan rating from stable to negative.[5]

Will China maintain yuan stability in the near future? An academic investigation of the question cannot rely on the promises of Chinese leaders for the answer. After all, governments in Thailand, Indonesia, and Malaysia all struggled hard to keep the currency stable in terms of the U.S. dollar, but all failed. The market force was more powerful than these governments' capability. However, neither is the verdict of the speculations on the exchange rate in the black markets reliable. The outcome will depend on economic fundamentals and other related factors. This article will investigate the issue from an academic perspective. We know that for the time being the Chinese government intends to maintain the stability of the yuan. Yet this is not enough. Two more issues need to be examined. First, is China able to maintain the stability of the yuan? Second, will China do it at any cost? What are the costs and how large are they? The fate of yuan stability will depend on the answers to these two questions. Our arguments are organized as follows. Section II examines the government's ability to maintain yuan stability. Section III analyzes the cost associated with maintaining yuan stability. Section IV discusses the uncertainty and the outlook of the state of the yuan. Section V is the summary.

II. Will the Chinese Government Be Able to Defend the Yuan?

Although many economists attribute the Asian crisis to some factors that include the nontransparency of the government's decisions and the corrupt financial system, the triggering cause apparently was a currency crisis. In all of the suffering Asian countries, the currency disaster started from a large sale of local currency by speculators, joined by creditors and the public in panic, and accompanied by the government's inability to meet the demand. The large scale of excess supply caused the quick fall of currency in the foreign exchange market.

A further examination reveals some more fundamental reasons responsible for the panic sale. Prior to the crisis, the affected countries had run current account deficits for a long period of time. They had accumulated a large amount of external liability that was due shortly. Their currencies were convertible. Their institutions allowed easy flow of financial capital so they were vulnerable to a sudden flight of capital. They did not have enough foreign reserves to meet the demand. The combination of all these factors caused a shortage of foreign exchange. When the shortage led to a sudden sale of local currency and quick capital outflow, the crisis started.

Yet China is quite different. The above conditions for a currency meltdown do not exist in China, and the mechanism on which a capital flight relies does not exist either. Let us examine these conditions for devaluation as they affect China.

It is true that the Chinese economy has many problems. Some of the problems are similar to those of the affected Asian countries, for instance, the problems of overinvestment and a large number of bad loans in the banking system. It is estimated that in the Chinese banking system, more than 20 percent of the total outstanding loans are either bad or nonperforming, while the same indicator in South Korea was 17 percent on the eve of the crisis. Many economists attribute the Asian crisis' origin to these problems. However, it should be noted that these problems did not directly cause the currency crisis. These problems can remain domestic and be contained within the border, if there are no other necessary mechanisms to realize a currency crisis.

The currency crisis was triggered by a sudden flight of capital in the affected countries. To have a large amount of currency flight, a country must have a mechanism that allows investors and speculators to sell local currencies, securities, and other assets; to convert the proceeds to foreign exchange; and to deliver them abroad. The key link in this process is currency convertibility. The affected Asian countries permitted free exchange in capital accounts (with the exception of South Korea, which had some restrictions); hence capital flight could occur. Yet in China, such a mechanism does not exist. The yuan is not convertible in capital accounts. Foreign financial capital cannot freely flow across the border. It is not possible for foreign speculators to sell short on the yuan or Chinese securities outside China. It is equally difficult for them to sell yuan and Chinese securities inside China and deliver dollars overseas. Hence there is no mechanism for a sudden flight of capital out of China.

To be more precise, there are some legal loopholes for capital flows crossing the border. The "B" shares of stocks in Shenzhen and Shanghai, which are denominated in the U.S. dollar, are supposed to be traded by overseas investors.[6] Theoretically, overseas investors can sell the stocks and take the proceeds out of China. However, in reality, sales in the B shares can hardly generate any significant impact on the exchange rate. First, the B shares account for only an insignificant amount of the total stock shares. The market value of all B shares amounts to only US$2.1 billion, accounting for 0.4 percent of GDP. Even including A shares, which can only be traded in yuan inside China, the stock market capitalization in China is still only 7.5 percent of GDP. It is insignificant compared with the affected Asian countries, which ranges from 44 percent for South Korea to 340 percent for Malaysia.[7] Moreover, most of the B shares are actually owned by the local Chinese. Although we do not have the breakdown figures in terms of value among the nationalities of the shareholders, the 1994 Shanghai Stock Exchange Report reveals that 74 percent of the B share accounts were owned by Chinese living in China.[8] Given the tiny number of B shares owned by outsiders, even a large fluctuation in the stock market and outflow of this category of money cannot make a significant impact on the exchange rate.

The nonconvertibility of the yuan in the capital account shields China from sudden capital flight resulting from speculators' attacks. Yet this factor in itself is still insufficient for yuan stability. The equilibrium exchange rate is determined by supply and demand in the foreign exchange market: that is, the country's ability to earn foreign exchange and the need for foreign exchange by various agents in the economy. This state of supply and demand is reflected by the current account balance. A country cannot avoid a currency crisis if it runs a chronic current account deficit. South Korea also had restrictions on the capital account, but it was unable to avoid the crisis because of its inability to service the large amount of its short-term debts. Table 3.2 presents the statistics of debt service, current account balances, and other relevant information about the concerned countries.

It can be seen from Table 3.2 that there are some obvious differences between China and the affected countries. The affected countries have been running sizable deficits, but China has continuously run large trade surpluses since 1994. The current account surplus in 1997 was US$22 billion. The trend has continued through 1998. Although under pressure from the Asian crisis, China has still registered positive growth of 0.5 percent in exports in 1998 to US$184 billion. Because of the decline in imports, China had a trade surplus of US$43.6 billion in 1998, up 7.9 percent from the year before.[9] Although growth slowed down in the first half of 1999, for the first three quarters of 1999 China still registered a trade surplus of US$19.4 billion. From the continuous surplus, China has accumulated a large foreign reserve. The foreign reserve at the end of 1998 and in September 1999 was US$145 and US$151 billion, respectively, the second largest in the world.[10]

China is also safe from the demand side. China does not have a large burden from either external liability or short-term payments. China has an external debt of US$118 billion,[11] but 86 percent consists of long

Table 3.2

Debt Service versus Current Account Balances for Selected Countries (as percent of GDP)

	1990	1991	1992	1993	1994	1995	1996	1997
China								
Current account balance	3.4	3.5	1.5	-2.7	1.4	0.2	0.9	2.5
External debt service	1.7	1.7	2.3	2.5	2.4	2.2	2.0	1.9
Indonesia								
Current account balance	-2.8	-3.4	-2.2	-1.5	-1.7	-3.3	-3.3	-2.9
External debt service	8.3	8.4	8.7	8.4	8.6	8.5	9.0	10.5
Malaysia								
Current account balance	-2.1	-8.8	-3.8	-4.8	-7.8	-10	-4.9	-5.8
External debt service	6.9	5.9	5.6	6.1	5.2	6.6	5.4	8.4
Thailand								
Current account balance	-8.3	-7.7	-5.6	-5.0	-5.6	-8,0	-7.9	-3.9
External debt service	3.8	4.0	4.3	4.4	4.0	5.0	5.4	7.1
Korea								
Current account balance	-0.9	-3.0	-1.5	0.1	-1.2	-2.0	-4.9	-2.9
External debt service	n.a.	n.a.	n.a.	n.a.	n.a.	n.a.	15.3	22.0

Source: IMF, *World Economic Outlook*, Interim Assessment, 1997, pp. 49–51, and Wong, 1998, table 2.

term debts.[12] Given the large size of the Chinese economy, the external debt ratios are rather small according to international standards. The liability (debt-to-GNP) ratio, debt service ratio and foreign debt (debt-to-exports) ratio, are 14.0 percent, 11.8 percent, and 73.9 percent, respectively, according to 1997 figures.[13] The corresponding figures for 1998 and the first half of 1999 were also in line with the previous levels. For comparison, we notice that the corresponding averages of the ratios for the low-income developing countries in 1995 were 38.7 percent, 15.4 percent, and 183.9 percent, respectively. For the middle-income developing countries, the corresponding averages in 1995 were 39.9 percent, 17.4 percent, and 142.6 percent. The Chinese ratios should be well within the safety limits.

It should be indicated that, compared with the debt ratios of Latin American countries, the debt ratios of the affected Asian countries in general do not seem to be excessively large. In addition, the Asian countries were great exporters. Feldstein (1998) argues that, to a large extent, the Asian crisis is a problem of liquidity rather than insolvency. This implies that the crisis could have been avoided if the IMF and creditors had provided timely and sufficient credit relief. This argument appears to be supported by the fact that the Asian countries with large foreign reserves—including Taiwan, Singapore, and Hong Kong—have remained relatively unscathed. Given the fact that China's sizable foreign reserves actually exceed its total external debt, China should have no liquidity problems in meeting its external liability. Table 3.3 presents information on the Chinese economic fundamentals relevant to yuan stability.

We should indicate that the official figures may not reflect the entire picture of the problem China is facing. There are many unofficial and illegal channels for converting and delivering renminbi abroad. Some estimate that a quarter of the outflow through the current account is in fact disguised capital flight: dollars earned from false invoicing, illegal foreign-exchange deals, and other nefarious activities.[14] There are many unregistered external debts by domestic firms and local governments. One example is the recent closedown of the second largest trust corporation, Guangdong International Trust and Investment Corporation (GITIC). It is said that GITIC may sit on more than $2 billion in total debt.[15] And a large amount of the debt consists of bonds held by overseas creditors, without the knowledge of the State Administration for Foreign Exchange.

We do not have reliable official figures about the unofficial and ille-

Table 3.3

Chinese Economic Fundamentals for RMB Stability

	1995	1996	1997	1998	1999
GDP Growth Rate	10.2	9.7	8.8	7.8	7.1
Inflation Rate (CPI)	17.1	8.3	2.8	−1.0	−0.8(Sept)
Trade Balance (bn$)	16.7	17.2	40.3	45.0	29.1
Current Account Surplus (bn$)	1.62	7.24	21.7	29.7	—
Debt/GDP Ratio (percentages)	15.5	14.3	14	15.2	—
Debt/Export Ratio (percentages)	69.9	75.6	73.9	79.5	—
Debt Service/Exports Ratio (percentages)	7.3	6.7	11.8	9.4	—
Short-term debt as percentage of total debt	11.2	12.1	14	11.9	11.5
Foreign Reserves (bn$)	73.6	105.0	139.9	145.0	154.7

Source: Current account values, 1992–1996 are from State Information Center, Data Express, CEI data.Other data are from the State Statistical Bureau, and *Statistical Yearbooks*, various issues, and latest release.
Note: Debts referred to are all external debts.

gal leakage. Some estimate the unofficial capital flight to be as large as inward flows of foreign investment (US$35 billion–US$45 billion a year). However, compared with companies in affected Asian countries, the Chinese companies' overseas operations and their exposure to overseas creditors have been very preliminary and relatively limited. Many of the overseas accounts of so-called foreign companies are actually owned and controlled by the parent Chinese companies (now the government is calling back these accounts). Even including the estimated figures, there is unlikely to be a drastic change of the entire balance situation.[16] In addition, China is taking steps to clean up the financial system and fortify foreign-exchange control. China will spend about 40 billion yuan to recapitalize some major banks this year. Meanwhile, some deeply troubled financial institutions, including GITIC, have been ordered to close. The government claims that it will not bail out these institutions and it guarantees only the creditors whose lending has been registered in the State Administration for Foreign Exchange. It appears that the Asian crisis offers a good lesson to the Chinese government to accelerate reform in its financial system, so the crisis could even benefit China in the long run.

Given the economic fundamentals discussed above, China is capable of defending the yuan if it wishes. The conditions favorable for yuan stability are summarized as follows: In capital accounts, capital flight cannot happen because of restrictions on capital flow. In the current account, China is continuously running a trade surplus and a current account surplus. In terms of external debt and servicing debt, China has a relatively small external liability but possesses a large amount of foreign reserves. The Chinese financial system is troublesome; however, the problems largely remain domestic.

III. The Cost to Maintain Yuan Stability in the Near Future

Earlier, we argued that China has the ability to defend the yuan. This ability alone does not automatically warrant the action. A rational government should also weigh the benefits and costs associated with defending the yuan. If the implied cost is high enough to make the policy economically or politically undesirable, the Chinese government may abandon its rigid yuan policy, if it acts rationally.

So, what are the costs associated with a stable yuan? The Asian turmoil has caused real appreciation of the RMB with respect to the affected currencies. The appreciation may adversely affect China's competitiveness in the world market, especially in the long run. Thus, some Chinese economists argue that China should devaluate the yuan to stimulate exports. However, a careful investigation reveals that so far it is unclear how large a stimulus will be to exports if the yuan is devaluated.

Devaluation might lead to a decrease in foreign exchange earnings from exports in the short run, according to the J-curve theory. The J-curve theory means the currency value will depreciate initially before it appreciates later on, creating a pattern that looks like the letter "J." Besides, there are other reasons to counter the devaluation argument. First, China's export structure differs from that of other affected Asian countries (only Indonesia's appears to be close). China tends to export more low-end manufactured goods. It is estimated by some economists that only 10 to 15 percent of Chinese exports to the rest of the world overlap those from the affected Asian countries (see Fan 1998). Second, a substantial amount of the overlapping goods are textile products, which are restricted by the import quotas of developed countries. Hence, there is not much room for affected Asian countries to increase exports. Third, given the low income base in China, even after the depreciation the wage rate in the affected countries, with the exception of Indonesia, is still higher than that in China. Fourth, many export products of affected Asian countries are from the processing industry. The currency depreciation causes the imported material to become more expensive, thus largely offsetting the price advantage due to the devaluation. Fifth, China imports much more from the affected countries than it exports to them. Many of the imports from these Asian countries are used as inputs for processing exports to the U.S. and to Western Europe. About 50 percent of Chinese exports are from the processing trade. The currency devaluation in these countries has lowered the cost of Chinese exports significantly. Finally, the instability of the currency has raised the risk and cost of export finance. Hence many exporters in the affected countries lack credit and working capital to finance their exports. All these factors combined prevent the countries from benefiting from the cost advantage of devaluation. For instance, it is reported by an Indonesian organization that foreign exchange earnings from the Indonesian footwear industry, which is an overlapping area with Chinese exports, has dropped to 1 billion from 1.9 billion in 1997 due to a decline in orders. And instead, the orders have gone to China (and Vietnam), despite the fact that Chinese products now are 20 percent more expensive than Indonesia's.[17] It was largely due to the concern of American and European importers over the risks of uncertainty in the affected countries.

The Chinese export sector weathered the crisis rather well in the crisis period. The slowing of export growth, however, is mainly caused by shrinking demand from the affected Asian countries. China still maintains a healthy export growth with other regions. In 1998, exports to Hong Kong, Japan, and Korea fell by 11.5 percent, 6.7 percent, and 31.3 percent from 1997, respectively. Exports to the entire Asia in 1998 fell by 9.9 percent. However, exports to the EU and the U.S. grew 18.1 percent and 16.1 percent, respectively. Exports to Latin America and Africa grew 20.1 percent each, and to Pacific countries grew 11 percent.[18] Since exports to the affected Asian countries, which include Japan, Korea, and Southeast Asia, account for only 30 percent of total exports, the increase of exports to other regions largely offsets the decline of exports to the affected Asian countries. The overall export growth in 1998 was still positive at 0.5 percent, although it was small. As the other Asian economies started to recover, exports accelerated in the third quarter of 1999 at an annual rate of 2.1 percent.

China adopted a series of measures to minimize the adverse impact of the crisis. China encouraged the export industries to raise efficiency, to improve nonprice attributes of exports, and to diversify product lines. Starting from January 1, 1999, China further raised the tax rebate rate for exports to an average of 12.56 percent from the 10 percent average in 1998. For exports of electronic goods, machinery, transportation equipment, and instruments, the rebate rate is raised to 17 percent.[19] It is estimated the two-percentage-point increase in the tax rebate was equivalent to a 4 percent currency devaluation.[20] Moreover, China is experiencing deflation, thus resulting in a real devaluation. All these factors have lowered the costs of exports. From the performance of Chinese exports so far in the crisis period, it seems that the costs to Chinese exports by maintaining the current renminbi exchange rate are rather limited.

One major cost of the rigidity of the exchange rate is monetary dependency. A country loses its independent monetary policy in a pegged exchange rate regime. Hence the country cannot adjust its macroeconomic policy to the best, resulting in an economic cost. This is the basic argument of the optimal currency area theory. If China maintains the yuan "stability," which means pegging the yuan to the U.S. dollar, China's monetary policy will be handicapped by the policy changes of the Fed in the United States. Since the two economies are quite different, this would lead to a great cost on the macroeconomic side to the Chinese economy.

The argument is valid, however, that given the unique circumstances of China, the implied cost may not be as great as it would be otherwise. The cost would be greater for a small open market economy. But China is different. It is large in size, hence the impact from outside is relatively small. China does not have free capital flow and the yuan is not freely convertible. Hence, to a large extent China can isolate its markets, both the monetary and the real markets, from outside shocks. China does not have a developed financial market, and the public is not very sensitive to the interest rate. An interest rate differential between the yuan and foreign currencies does not induce a substantial change in the money-holding behavior of the residents. Moreover, the government controls the overwhelming portion of the economy, and it does not hesitate to intervene in the market with administrative measures. Hence, China still has enough flexibility to adjust its monetary policy even if it maintains a stable exchange rate with the United States.

IV. The Likelihood of Yuan Depreciation in the Near Future

Earlier, we argued that China is able to defend the yuan if it desires, and the costs of defending it are not substantially high for the time being. However, it would be wrong to expect the above conclusion to remain valid in the long run. As international and domestic conditions change in the future, the cost of a pegged renmimbi may increase. And such a change becomes more likely as time elapses.

As the Asian countries recover, they increase their imports from China, thus helping strengthen the yuan. However, as their currencies have depreciated against the renminbi, the Asian countries may eventually increase their competitiveness in the world market, as argued by the J-curve hypothesis. In fact, China has already encountered some challenges. In 1998, China lost a large number of orders for steel, shipbuilding, and chemical products to South Korea due to the price disadvantage. The prices of textile and shoe products from Indonesia are now 20 to 30 percent cheaper than similar Chinese products. As its situation stabilizes, Indonesia will expand its share in the world market, taking the cost advantage. As pressure mounts, the internal voices from the export sector in China calling for depreciation will get louder, and the yuan will be forced to devaluate.

Rapid change in the Chinese macroeconomic environment will force adjustments in monetary policy. A rigid yuan exchange rate can make the implementation of the monetary policy impossible or ineffective. This is a potentially great cost of the rigid yuan exchange rate in the near future.

The Chinese economy was in recession during the period of 1997–1999. In order to stimulate the economy, the Chinese central bank (People's Bank) has cut the interest rate three times within a short period of only nine months since October 1997.[21] The bank further imposed a tax on interest payments starting from November 1, 1999. However, these policies may have a limited impact as long as China is mired in a liquidity trap like Japan's.

In response to the recession and the ineffective monetary policy, the Chinese government turned to expansionary fiscal policies by increasing the fixed asset investment. In April 1998, it announced a series of increases in fixed asset investment.[22] The additional increase in infrastructure alone amounts to ¥150 billion each year. The scale of investment in various sectors increased from 1.4 to 17 times that of the original plans at the beginning of the year.[23] The source of the increase includes bank credits from state banks and bonds issued by the government. In July, M0, M1, and M2 increased by 10 percent, 10.5 percent, and 15.5 percent from the year before. In the same month, bank credits increased by ¥75.64 billion, representing an additional increase of 24.45 billion yuan from the year before.[24] An additional 100 billion yuan of government bonds is to be issued to finance investment.[25] It is reported that as a result industrial output bottomed out in August and has started to accelerate. Meanwhile, the trend of the prices of construction materials has also turned around from fall to increase.[26]

What are the implications of these macroeconomic policies for the stability of the yuan? First, monetary expansion, which includes a cut in interest rates, will inevitably add pressure to the yuan. At this moment, yuan deposits in the banks are still stable even though there is an interest differential between the yuan and foreign exchanges, because of the restrictions on currency convertibility. Yet such a system can be operated only within certain limits. China allows the domestic public, including firms and residents, to hold a certain amount of foreign currency. If the differential gets too large, a large-scale selling of yuan by the public, including individuals and firms, on the black market or through other channels, would be inevitable.[27] As the economy develops and China becomes more open, it will be more difficult to isolate the domestic financial market from the rest of the world, and the cost of enforcement will increase. The Chinese government will eventually find that it is impossible to maintain the fixed interest rate.

In addition to the monetary aspect of the problem, in the real sector, the expansionary fiscal policy will cause the current account balance to deteriorate. A regression analysis finds that the imports will be significantly affected by the increase in fixed-asset investment. In particular, each 100–yuan increase in investment will induce 30 yuan of increase in imports.[28] The current account surplus in 1997 was 204 billion yuan. Hence China may run a current account deficit, other things held constant, if capital investment rises by more than ¥680 billion (9 percent of GDP). The deficit may arrive even sooner if we take into account the real appreciation of the yuan.

In addition to the above reasons, there is an important factor that will affect yuan stability. That is the political and economic link between the yuan and the Hong Kong dollar. Although the pressure of the Hong Kong dollar on the yuan has been felt by Chinese economists and bankers, as reported by the *Wall Street Journal* in September, overseas observers seem to overlook this factor.[29] Hong Kong is unlike China. It is small and dependent. It is highly open. It has a very liquid capital market with few restrictions on capital flow. And it has run current account deficits for a long time. All these factors make the cost to defend the Hong Kong dollar much higher than the cost of defending the yuan. Although the Hong Kong monetary authority so far has successfully maintained the Hong Kong dollar stable against the U.S. dollar, relying on their huge foreign reserves and high interest rate to attract Hong Kong dollar deposits, the cost to defend the Hong Kong dollar has been very high. The government spent 13 percent of its foreign reserves to prop up the stock market in August with a very limited success. Even worse, because of the tight monetary policy used to defend the Hong Kong dollar, the interest rate has surged, resulting in a shortage of credit in the economy. This threw Hong Kong into recession during that period. In the second quarter of 1998, Hong Kong experienced a 5 percent fall in GDP, the first time it had had negative growth since 1968. That implies a loss of GDP of US$7.5 billion. Meanwhile, the unemployment rate rose to more than 4.2 percent, also the worst in the last two decades. By maintaining the pegged-rate regime, Hong Kong does not have an independent monetary policy. Hence Hong Kong is handicapped in adopting a more expansionary monetary policy to stimulate the economy. Hong Kong has had a real appreciation of 43 percent against the U.S. dollar since 1990 because it had much higher inflation than the U.S during the seven-year period. Hence, Hong Kong has lost much of its competitiveness; thus the trade balance has deteriorated. As the Hong Kong dollar has now experienced a new round of real appreciation against other regional currencies, it will be even more difficult for Hong Kong to turn to a current account surplus in the near future. Although it is still controversial, an increasing number of economists question the wisdom of sticking to a fixed exchange rate system. The opportunity cost is high and will be even higher as time moves on.[30]

If Hong Kong is going to abandon the fixed exchange rate system, it will make it difficult for the yuan to stand alone. A confidence crisis for yuan stability may occur, the Chinese external trade balance will deteriorate, and so forth. Yet above these reasons, there is a more important reason. Around 50 percent of the basic food in Hong Kong comes from mainland China. If the Hong Kong dollar falls against the yuan, the resulting price increase in basic food and other necessities will hurt low-income families. As China is very sensitive to any possible sentiments of residents in Hong Kong and to any element that could destabilize Hong Kong, China will make adjustments to minimize the impact. Then yuan devaluation would probably be the easiest way to solve the problem.

In addition to the above reasons, many other factors emerge as time moves on. The changes in the environment will make it more and more costly to maintain a rigid yuan. In the long run, it is impossible for a country as large as China to peg its currency to a foreign currency. The yuan can move in either direction, but it cannot be fixed to the U.S. dollar. It is only a matter of time before the switch to a more flexible exchange rate regime, although in the near future the Chinese government will still claim its commitment to yuan stability.

V. Conclusion

The subject of the stability of the Chinese currency (yuan) has been widely discussed as the world currency market is still unstable. Although Chinese officials have repeatedly promised not to devaluate the yuan, the market and speculators continue to show their lack of confidence in the yuan. This article argues that the Chinese government is able to defend the yuan and that the cost to defend it is not substantially high, for the time being. Hence in the near future, the yuan will remain stable. However, as China implements expansionary monetary and fiscal policies, the resulting changes in the economic environment will make it more costly to maintain a fixed exchange rate regime. China is promising to make its currency more convertible into the capital account after it enters the WTO. As time elapses, the necessity for adjustment of the yuan rate will increase. In the long run, it is unlikely that China will maintain a rigid exchange rate.

Notes

1. IMF. 1998. *World Economic Outlook*. Washington, DC: IMF, p. 133.
2. Zhu Rongji, Jiang Zemin, and others have all made such a statement on various occasions. See AFX News, quoting Xinhua News Agency, on August 28, 1998.
3. Karby Leggett, "China's State Banks Fortify Control on the Yuan Market." *Wall Street Journal*, Asia Section, September 11, 1998.
4. Karby Leggett, "Hong Kong's Peg to U.S. Dollar Is Impeding Confidence in Yuan." *Wall Street Journal,* Asia Section, September 9, 1998.

5. "Hopes for China Revival in '98 Recede." *Asian Wall Street Journal*, July 20, 1998, p. 3.

6. A small number of Chinese companies are publicly listed in Hong Kong—termed "H" shares in the Hong Kong stock market—and listed in New York—termed "N" shares in the New York stock exchange market. However, their transactions are restricted only to Hong Kong dollars or U.S. dollars outside of China, so no money can be delivered crossing the border. Recently China further tightened control of "illegal" stock transactions crossing the border.

7. See Wong, 1998, table 3.

8. Theoretically, the B shares must be owned by non-Chinese citizens. However, because of many loopholes, such as special accounts given by the security companies to preferred customers, many local people own the B-share accounts.

9. Xinhua News Agency, quoted in "China's Exports Rose 0.5 percent in 1998 to 183.76 Billion." *Wall Street Journal Interactive Edition*, January 12, 1999.

10. "Mending China." *Economist*, Feb. 13–19, 1999, p. 69.

11. This is the 1997 figure; the 1998 figure is not available but should be soon.

12. State Statistical Bureau, September 23, 1998.

13. Estimates from Dai Xianglong, chairman of the Central Bank (People's Bank). *People's Daily*, December 29, 1997, p. 1.

14. "Reading Their Lips." *Economist*, October 27, 1998.

15. "China Bank Fails to Pay Bondholders." *Wall Street Journal*, October 28, 1998, p. A15.

16. See "Reading Their Lips." *Economist*, October 27, 1998. Including this figure still cannot change the sign of the external balance, as we witness the increase in foreign reserves held by the government. In addition, the government is taking steps to plug foreign-exchange leaks.

17. *Jakarta Post*, July 15, 1998, p. 8.

18. Chinese Statistical Bureau, *Statistical Report on the National Economy and Social Development of P.R.China in 1998*, Feb. 26, 1999; "Foreign Trade Hit 320 Billion Dollars Last Year." *People's Daily*, January 12, 1999, p. 1.

19. "Raising Tax Rebate for Some Exports to Stimulate Sustainable Growth." *People's Daily*, Jan. 30, 1999, p. 3.

20. Report by Xinhua News Agency, Sept. 11, quoted by *Security Times*, September 11, 1998, Shenzhen, China.

21. The most recent cut was made on July 1, 1998. It is said that the central bank will cut the interest rate again in the near future.

22. State Information Center, *Economic Analysis*, July 9, 1998.

23. They include a fourfold increase in the agricultural infrastructure, a 1.43-time increase in transportation and communications, a 2.8-time increase in urban infrastructure, a fourfold increase in urban residential housing, and a 17.5-time increase in grain storage capacity. Reported by the *People's Daily*, September 2, 1998.

24. The Central Bank, August 13, quoted by *People's Daily*, August 14, 1998, p. 2.

25. Reported by *People's Daily*, September 9, 1998, p. 1.

26. State Statistics Bureau, quoted by *Shanghai Security News*, September 8, 1998.

27. Karby Leggett, "China's State Banks Fortify Control on the Yuan Market." *Wall Street Journal*, Asia Section, September 11, 1998, reported some of the chan-

nels for buying: "Foreign-invested firms and trade companies were cited as heavy dollar buyers. But traders also said some of those firms were acting on behalf of individuals who were trying to convert assets into dollars as a hedge against the yuan. Much of that capital was moving through loopholes that exist in the market regime, such as phony joint venture companies that are set up to transact a financing deal."

28. The structure, data, and results of the regression analysis by the author are available on request.

29. See note 4.

30. We are again facing the two questions: first, can Hong Kong defend its dollar? Maybe, if the mainland intervenes by using its foreign reserves. Second, will Hong Kong be willing to do so at any cost? If the recession continues for a couple of more years, the public protest against the rigid monetary policy will force the government to abandon the current policy.

References

Dai, Xianglong. 1999. "On the Monetary Policy of the Central Bank," *People's Daily*, January 28, 1999, p. 1.

Fan, Gang. 1998. "Impacts of Asia Economic Shake-up on China's Reform and Development," Working paper series, no. 98–01. Beijing: National Economic Research Institute, China Reform Foundation.

Feldstein, Martin. 1998. "Refocusing the IMF," *Foreign Affairs,* vol. 77, no. 2; *People's Daily*, various issues.

State Information Center. Various issues, in 1997 to 1998. *Economic Analysis.*

————. 1998. *Chinese Statistical Abstract—1998.*

————. February 26, 1999. *Statistical Report on the National Economy and Social Development of the People's Republic of China in 1998.*

Wang, Zhi. 1998. "Should RMB Depreciate or Not—A Perspective from China's Export Structure and Its Trade Relation with Major Partner Countries." West Lafayette, IN: Purdue University, and Washington, DC: Department of Agriculture, mimeo.

Wei, Shang-jin, Ligang Liu, Zhi Wang, and Wing T. Woo. 1998. "The Chinese Money Puzzle: Will a Yuan Develuation Help or Hurt the Hong Kong Dollar?" Cambridge, MA: Kennedy School, Harvard University, mimeo.

Wong, John. 1998. "Will China be the Next Financial Domino?" *EAI Occasional Paper*, no. 4. Singapore: World Scientific Publishing Co. and Singapore University Press.

4

A Retrospect on China's Banking Reform

Wai Chung Lo

China's banking system has undergone substantial changes in the past two decades, and it has been transformed from an institutional setup for central planning to a banking system in a market-oriented economy. The reform strategy is consistent with the overall economic reform in China, which, unlike many transitional economies in Eastern Europe, has taken a gradual or incremental approach. This approach enables the banks in China to progress in phase from the accounting units of the central planner to a modern commercial banking system consistent with the price system which aims at efficient allocation of financial resources. The first phase of the reform (1978–92) created a banking system that was oriented to a market economy but imprinted with the legacy of central planning. The second phase of reform (1992–present) has removed the remnants of central planning and established a full-fledged modern banking system. The purpose of this paper is to delineate the banking reform's gradual approach, with the focus on the achievements and problems of each stage.

The Monobank System Before 1978

Economic activities in a centrally planned economy are under direct government control, with physical resources allocated to various units according to the material plans formulated by the central planner. The banking system, subordinated to the central planner, merely provides accounting means to match the allocation of physical resources. The instruments for allocation of financial resources are different for the state sector and the nonstate sector, the former comprising state-owned enterprises (SOEs) and government organizations, while the latter consists of households and non–state-owned enterprises. The allocation of credits between SOEs and government organizations is arranged through the banking system according to the credit plan, which is prepared in the form of a source-and-use-of-funds balance statement to match the estimation of the demand for physical resources. The cash plan is restricted to wage payments, daily petty cash transactions, and subsequent procurement of farm products. The banking system, structured in accordance with the centrally planned economy, can best be characterized as an all-inclusive monobank. Its major function is to implement the credit plan and cash plan designated by the planning authority.

The major banking institutions in the early 1950s were the People's Bank of China (PBOC), the Bank of China (BOC), the Bank of Communications (BOCOM), the Agricultural Bank of China (ABC), and the rural financial cooperatives, with the PBOC in the dominant position as both a central bank and a commercial bank. The BOCOM, which before 1949 had specialized in banking for the industrial sector, maintained this role during the early years of the new regime. As the PBOC evolved into an all-inclusive bank, the BOCOM functioned only in managing appropriations for infrastructure investments. It was restructured as the People's Construction Bank of China (PCBC) under the Ministry of Finance (MOF) in 1954. Strictly speaking, the PCBC was not a bank. It was merely a cashier for the MOF in allocating funds for investments in infrastructure. The BOC specialized in foreign exchange. However, for the entire period before 1978, it served only as a branch of the PBOC for managing foreign exchange, because foreign trade in the 1950s and 1960s was mostly restricted to the former Soviet Union, and the system of foreign trade was highly centralized. The original settings of the ABC and the rural cooperatives were to establish a network in rural areas to absorb deposits and finance investment. In practice, the ABC and its bank branches had to strictly follow the guidelines of the PBOC and submit the deposits they received to the PBOC. It was virtually a branch under the PBOC for managing deposits and loans in the rural sector. The bank functioned only briefly in the 1950s before being abolished in the 1960s.

By the mid-1960s, the PBOC had become the only all-inclusive bank. It was structured in accordance with the nationwide administrative hierarchy, with bank branches established at the province, county, and city levels. Credits were allocated through the bank branches to various units within the state sector, and all transactions were to be settled through the accounts with the banking system. It was estimated that about 95 percent of the PBOC's transactions on the eve of the economic reform that began in 1979 were in the form of transfers from one account to another.[1] The PBOC was also nominally responsible for ensuring the SOEs' effective use of funds. In practice, the bank branches of the PBOC simply followed instructions from banks at a higher level in the hierarchy and had no incentive for efficient monitoring of the SOEs' use of funds. Besides being an executive branch of the State Council for fulfilling credit and cash plans, the banking system was also enlisted as a network for amassing saving deposits from households. However, under the highly centralized banking system whose major function was to implement the credit plan formulated by the state, bank branches just passively received deposits from households. The state sector accounted for more than 70 percent of total deposits in the banking system from 1958 to 1978, as indicated in Table 4.1.

Establishing a Two-Tier Banking System (1978–92)

The reform of the banking sector, in line with reform in other sectors of the economy, took the approach of "crossing the river by feeling the pebbles beneath." There was no specific foresight for the direction of the reform, other than the general principle that banking operations should be more market oriented. The first step of the reform was to revitalize the specialized banks. The ABC was re-established in 1979 as the commercial bank that served the rural sector. It was responsible for overseeing the operation of rural credit cooperatives. In the same year, the PCBC was separated from the MOF and was positioned as a specialized bank in charge of the fixed-asset investments of state enterprises, and the BOC was separated from the PBOC, specializing in loans and deposits in foreign exchange and international settlements. The banking reform was aimed at transforming the monobank system into a two-tier system, with the PBOC playing the role of central bank. The State Council issued a directive in September 1983 to establish the PBOC as the central bank of China. A new specialized bank, the Industrial and Commercial Bank of

Table 4.1

Components of Deposits in the Banking System, 1958–78, Selected Years

Year	Government	Enterprises	Urban households	Rural	Total
1958	154.8	77.6	35.1	27.8	388.4
	(52.2)	(26.3)	(14.4)	(9.4)	(100.0)
1960	272.8	86.0	51.1	49.9	550.9
	(59.3)	(18.7)	(13.0)	(10.9)	(100.0)
1965	196.4	181.9	52.3	50.1	574.9
	(40.9)	(37.8)	(15.5)	(10.4)	(100.0)
1970	330.4	226.1	64.5	83.3	796.0
	(46.9)	(32.1)	(12.6)	(11.8)	(100.0)
1975	360.9	362.7	114.6	136.9	1066.9
	(37.0)	(37.2)	(17.6)	(14.0)	(100.0)
1978	456.8	368.4	154.9	154.4	1226.6
	(40.3)	(32.5)	(19.4)	(13.6)	(100.0)

Source: Almanac of Banking and Finance in China, 1990.

Note: "Government" refers to deposits from the treasury, deposits for investment in infrastructure, and deposits from various governmental organizations. The numbers in parentheses are percentages of total deposits.

China (ICBC), was established in 1984 to take over the household and enterprise deposits that were previously handled by the PBOC. The ICBC was responsible for providing working capital and settlement for urban industrial and commercial enterprises. Thus, in total, there were four specialized banks, all solely owned by the state, under the supervision of the PBOC.

In 1979, in order to extend the network for raising funds from foreign sources, the State Council established under its control China International Trust and Investment (CITIC), which was the first nonbank financial institution in China to target international financial investments.[2] The BOCOM was reestablished as a shareholding bank in 1986.[3] It was positioned as a universal bank, with financial services extending throughout the world. Both the BOCOM and CITIC Industrial Bank (CITICIB), a universal bank solely owned by CITIC, were permitted to compete with the four specialized banks for domestic business.

In the first phase of the banking reform, the authorities aimed at improving the efficiency of the banking sector without substantially diminishing the role of the government as central planner. The 1984 regulation that governed credit management in the banking sector clearly revealed the government's intention. On the one hand, specialized banks were allowed a certain freedom in the use of funds and were responsible for profits and losses. On the other hand, the regulation stipulated that banks were obliged to submit projections on loans and deposits to the PBOC, which, after considering the nationwide economic condition, would compile the aggregation and submit it to the State Council for approval. The approved credit plan would specify credit quotas to the specialized banks that were strictly forbidden to make credits that exceeded the ceilings.

The specialized banks were obliged to support the state in "policy lending" which had never been clearly defined by the Chinese authorities. Mehran et al. (1996) delineate policy lending as follows: power and transport investments with long-term repayment periods, fixed-asset loans to improve the technology of SOEs, loans for improving the well-being of rural areas, working capital for prioritized SOEs, and loans for subsidized sectors such as education and health. Before the economic reform, funds were directly allocated to SOEs through the MOF to finance investment in infrastructure and even working capital. During the reform era of the 1980s, the authorities gradually implemented the *bogaidai* policy; that is, the MOF ceased allocating funds to SOEs, which had to borrow from banks instead. It was estimated that 20 percent of the ICBC's total lending in 1994 was in policy loans, compared with 30 percent for the ABC, 15 percent for the BOC, and 45 percent for the PCBC.[4] In order to finance priority loans, the specialized banks borrowed substantially from the Central Bank, a practice referred to in the Chinese literature of banking and finance as *zaidaikuan* (relending).

Besides the policy lending assigned by the state, state banks were also under pressure from local governments for credit. The 1984 banking regulation stipulated that branches of the specialized banks be under double leadership: bank headquarters were responsible for leadership in banking operations, whereas local governments were responsible for branch organization of the Chinese Communist Party within the banks. In practice, this double leadership created opportunities for local government intervention in banking operations. Specifically, although the headquarters were empowered with the authority to appoint officials for local bank branches, it was crucial that such nominations obtained the approval of local governments. Given the role of local government in personnel matters, banking officials would submit to the requests of local governments, granting loans which they could have no hope of recovering. This consequently further eroded the effectiveness of the bank branches' efficient use of credit quotas.

Table 4.2

Deposits in the State Banks, 1979–96 (RMB billion, %)

Year	RMB billion	% of GDP
1979	113.9	28.2
1980	116.1	25.7
1981	202.7	41.7
1982	237.0	44.8
1983	278.9	47.0
1984	358.4	50.0
1985	426.5	47.6
1986	535.5	52.5
1987	651.7	54.5
1988	742.6	49.7
1989	901.4	53.3
1990	1,164.5	62.8
1991	1,486.4	68.8
1992	1,889.1	70.9
1993	2,323.0	67.1
1994	2,932.8	62.7
1995	3,878.3	66.3
1996	4,959.3	73.1

Source: Finance Year Book of China, 1996 and 1997.
Note: The figures include the deposits of the BOCOM and CITIC Industrial Bank.

In retrospect, the reform in the 1980s burdened state banks with the conflicting objectives of policy lending and profit seeking. The proliferation of trust and investment companies (TICs), mostly formed under the state banks to bypass credit quotas, was in fact a reflection of the impasse.[5] Nonetheless, despite all the difficulties and problems of the state banks, the 1980s saw a decade of rapid expansion in the banking sector, as evidenced by the higher growth rate of banking deposits (Table 4.2). Bank loans increased from RMB 18.5 billion, or 51 percent of GDP in 1978, to RMB 180.6 billion, or 92 percent of GDP in 1991.

Banking Reform Since 1992

On the basis of the rapid expansion of the financial sector, the State Council announced the blueprint for the second phase of reform in 1993. The Decision on Reform of the Financial System stipulated three objectives in regard to the banking reform: (1) to transform the PBOC into a modern central bank to implement monetary policy under the leadership of the State Council; (2) to transform the state banks into genuine commercial banks by separating policy lending from commercial lending; and (3) to create a commercial banking sector in which the state banks and other forms of banking institutions could coexist and compete under regulations set forth by the Central Bank.

To separate policy lending from commercial banking activities, three policy-lending banks were created in 1994 to take over government-directed policy lending from the four specialized banks that were repositioned as state-owned commercial banks. The State Development Bank of China (SDBC) was responsible for financing national infrastructure; the Export-Import Bank of China (EIBC) was for financing international trade; and the Agricultural Development Bank of China (ADBC) was for financing agriculture development.

To supplement the state banks and to encourage competition in the commercial banking sector, a number of shareholding banks were established in the 1990s. Two nationwide commercial banks,[6] Hua Xia Bank (HXB) and China Everbright Bank (CEB), were established in 1992, and the China Minsheng Bank (CMSB) was founded in 1996. Nationwide commercial banks do not have geographical restrictions on the locations of bank branches, although they must have approval from the Central Bank. The CMSB is the most notable among the five nationwide commercial banks. It was formed in 1996 by the All-China Federation of Industry and Commerce, a nongovernment industry group, and unlike other shareholding banks that are jointly owned by central and regional governments, CMSB's major shareholders are private enterprises. The bank was one of three banks that went public in China.[7] Regional commercial banks, alongside nationwide commercial banks, have also developed rapidly. The difference between regional and nationwide commercial banks is in the restriction on geographical location. Figure 4.1 shows the banking structure in the 1990s.

State banks and shareholding banks are governed by the Commercial Bank Law of 1995. The Commercial Bank Law plus the Central Bank Law issued in the same year complete the regulatory backbone of the transformation of the banking sector from a centrally planned economy to a market-oriented economy. The Central Bank Law stipulates that the PBOC is responsible for formulating and implementing monetary policy, as well as supervising the operations of commercial banks. Its duties include receiving deposit reserves from financial institutions, providing rediscount services, providing liquidity to commercial banks, executing open-market operations, and acting as a clearinghouse for commercial

Figure 4.1 **Structure of the Banking Sector**

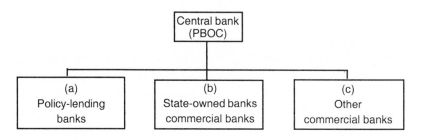

(a) Policy-lending banks:
      State Development Bank of China (SDBC)
      Agricultural Development Bank of China (ADBC)
      Export-Import Bank of China (EIBC)

(b) State commercial banks:
      Industrial and Commercial Bank of China (ICBC)
      Agricultural Bank of China (ABC)
      Bank of China (BOC)
      People's Construction Bank of China (PCBC)

(c) Other commercial banks:
      Nationwide commercial banks
          Bank of Communications (BOCOM)
          CITIC Industrial Bank (CITICIB)
          China Everbright Bank (CEB)
          Hua Xia Bank (HXB)
          China Minsheng Bank (CMSB)

      Regional commercial banks:
          China Merchants Bank (CMB)
          Guangdong Development Bank (GDB)
          Shenzhen Development Bank (SDB)
          Shanghai Pudong Development Bank (SPDB)
          Fujian Industrial Bank (FIB)
          China Investment Bank (CIB)
          Yantai Housing Savings Bank (YHSB)
          Bengbu Housing Savings Bank (BHDB)

financial institutions. The Commercial Bank Law put much emphasis on the management of the quality of loans. The law provides clear guidelines on liability management, such as capital sufficiency and ratios in the balance of loans and deposits. The law also stipulates that banks are not to be interfered with by any work unit or individual.[8] This is clearly a response to the unfortunate fact that banks had been frequently pressured by regional governments for loans. As a further measure to shield the banking sector from local government intervention, and also to better monitor the operation of the commercial-banking sector, the PBOC was reorganized into nine regional branches. In 1999, it formally abandoned the quota management on credits, replacing it with asset-to-liability management.

Unfinished Reform

Despite the rapid development of shareholding banks, state-owned commercial banks are still dominant. At the end of 1999, total assets of state-owned commercial banks amounted to RMB 8.854 trillion, which is almost eight times the total of other commercial banks.[9] The performance of the state-owned banks, however, has been lagging. As shown in Table 4.3, the four state-owned commercial banks have distinctly lower efficiency compared to other commercial banks. The average profit-to-capital ratio of the four state banks is 3.2 percent, which is significantly lower than the 11.9 percent of the sampled shareholding commercial banks. The state-owned commercial banks also have a lower capital-adequacy ratio, ranging from 9 to 10 percent, compared with approximately 20 percent for other commercial banks. Table 4.4 shows the liability positions of state-owned commercial banks and other commercial banks. State-owned commercial banks borrowed heavily from the Central Bank, which accounts for 20 to 30 percent of the banks' total liability, whereas the figures for shareholding commercial banks ranged only from 1 to 5 percent. The state-owned banks' reliance on the Central Bank is in fact a reflection of the practice of *zaidaikuan* (relending).

The most pressing problem of state banks, however, was the quality of their assets. The Chinese authorities estimated that nonperforming loans in state banks amounted to 20–25 percent of total loans.[10] Up to the end of 1998 the balance of outstanding loans in the four state-owned commercial banks totaled RMB 6.844.2 billion,[11] implying that their nonperforming loans were as much as RMB 1,700 billion and that the amount that needed to be written off would be RMB 540 billion. Lardy pointed out that the size of nonperforming loans should be much larger because official figures significantly underestimate the liabilities of state

Table 4.3

Efficiency Indicators of Top Ten Banks in China, December 1999 (RMB billion, %)

Bank	Tier-one capital	Total assets	Capital asset ratio	Pre-tax profits	Profit/ Capital	Employees	Branches	BIS ratio
ICBC	18,147.8	353,986.6	5.13	412.6	2.27	5,490,387	36,898	8.98
ABC	13,446.6	227,583.5	5.91	-35.5	-0.26	n/a	n/a	n/a
BOC	12,643.2	290,392.2	4.35	660.3	5.22	208,792	312	9.8
CCB*	10,925.4	220,106.5	4.96	736.6	6.74	324,360	38	n/a
BOCOM	2,506.8	59,805.0	4.19	268.5	10.71	n/a	72	n/a
CMB	1,245.3	16,447.8	7.57	152.1	12.21	8,721	13	17.08
CEB	855.8	16,789.3	5.1	67.7	7.92	n/a	30	n/a
SPDB	777.6	10,321.0	7.53	117.7	15.14	4,150	165	18.25
CITICIB	727.5	15,733.4	4.62	113.9	15.66	6,664	237	n/a
FIB	324.1	4,918.3	6.59	43.8	13.51	n/a	12	n/a

Source: The Banker, October 2000.
*China Construction Bank.

Table 4.4

Banking-Sector Liabilities (RMB billion)

	1994	1995	1996	1997	1998	1999
A. *State-owned commercial banks* Nonfinancial sectors	250.29	3,308.85	4,240.21	5,190.55	5,947.78	6,976.98
	(65.5)	(71.4)	(72.0)	(75.1)	(75.4)	(78.8)
Central bank	1,018.22	1,109.62	1,408.85	1,388.51	1,186.72	755.98
	(26.7)	(24.0)	(23.9)	(20.1)	(15.0)	(8.5)
Nonmonetary financial institutions	18.11	17.69	14.48	10.11	64.41	124.38
	(0.5)	(0.4)	(0.2)	(1.5)	(0.8)	(1.4)
Bonds	18.89	16.96	28.05	27.76	48.29	47.61
	(0.5)	(0.4)	(0.5)	(0.4)	(0.6)	(0.5)
Owner's equity	184.82	178.85	201.04	202.83	436.87	409.74
	(4.8)	(3.9)	(3.4)	(2.9)	(5.5)	(4.6)
Other (net)	76.73	−38.04	−329.48	−87.92	204.59	540.08
	(2.0)	(−0.8)	(−6.0)	(−1.3)	(2.6)	(6.1)
Total	3,819.67	4,631.97	5,892.63	6,910.75	7,888.66	8,854.77
B. *Other commercial banks* Nonfinancial sectors	242.77	377.98	570.36	637.57	758.34	896.84
	(82.1)	(87.6)	(90.0)	(85.3)	(8.7)	(79.7)
Central bank	9.26	4.37	8.12	5.97	7.78	12.93
	(3.1)	(1.0)	(1.3)	(0.8)	(0.8)	(1.1)
Nonmonetary financial institutions	9.10	149.0	16.67	31.27	35.64	22.62
	(3.1)	(3.5)	(2.7)	(4.2)	(3.8)	(2.0)
Bonds	0.68	0.02	0.69	0.49	1.64	0.44
	(0.2)	(0.0)	(0.1)	(0.1)	(0.2)	(0.0)
Owner's equity	24.24	28.18	42.94	53.07	53.82	66.67
	(8.2)	(6.5)	(6.8)	(7.1)	(5.8)	(5.9)
Other (net)	9.5	6.22	−1,154.0	19.32	71.43	126.47
	(3.2)	(1.4)	(−1.8)	(2.6)	(7.7)	(11.2)
Total	295.55	431.67	627.24	747.90	928.65	1,125.97

Sources: Almanac of Banking and Finance, 1996 and 1999; and PBOC Annual Report, 1999.

Note: The numbers in parentheses are the percentages of total liabilities.

banks. In particular, the figures do not consider inter-enterprise debts, or *sanjiaozhai* (triangular debts), as they are called in the Chinese literature, which occurred also between SOEs and non–state enterprises.[12]

The problem of nonperforming debt stemmed partially from the gradual approach to banking reform. Before 1978, the main task of state banks was to carry out the credit and cash plans formulated by the central government. The financial resources for investment in prioritized projects were generally delivered by the MOF through the banking system in the form of appropriations. Now the new financing policy required state banks to shoulder the policy lending which had been generally considered by SOEs as appropriations. Not surprisingly, SOE managers had no intention of repaying the loans.

A more profound explanation for the nonperformance of loans in the banking system was that this was due to the inefficiency of SOEs, a fact that has not been properly addressed because of the gradualism of reform. SOEs were burdened with "social responsibilities," such as excessive numbers of employees, due to the government policy of full employment, and heavy social-welfare obligations, including accumulated pension liabilities for retired workers. In recent research comparing the performance of SOEs and township and village enterprises (TVEs), Perotti et al. (1999) point out that SOEs are inferior to TVEs in terms of ownership and governance structure. A study of the effects of ownership structure on the performance of public firms in China indicates that firms with ownership with a high concentration of legal persons are generally more profitable than those dominated by the state, and labor productivity is inversely related to the proportion of state shares (Xu and Wang 1999).

Until recently, the government's policy was to subsidize losing SOEs through the banking system to keep them in operation and avoid the possibility of any large-scale unemployment and social unrest. It is estimated that in 1985 only 24 percent of the subsidy came from the banking sector, with the government shouldering the rest through budget appropriation. In 1994, the proportion from the banking sector increased to 43.6 percent. Figures on the size of policy loans are not available, although there are indications that the state banks' nonperforming loans are mostly attributable to policy lending in the 1980s and early 1990s.[13]

With a large proportion of loans deemed nonperforming, state banks as a group are technically insolvent (Lardy 1999). To solve the problem of nonperforming loans, the Chinese government set up four asset-management companies (AMCs) to deal with the debt restructuring of the four state-owned commercial banks, and it followed the Resolution Trust Company model of the United States in handling the savings and loan crisis in the late 1980s. The organizational structure of the AMCs reflected the complexity of the task. For example, the AMCs were led by the State Council, funded by the MOF, and supervised by the PBOC and the State Economic and Trade Commission (SETC). The executive directors of the AMCs have administrative rank equivalent to that of vice minister, which would be helpful in the negotiation of debt restructuring, given China's bureaucratic culture.[14] In debt restructuring, the AMCs issued bonds guaranteed by the government to acquire bad debts from banks at book value.[15] By the middle of 2000, the AMCs completed debt-equity swaps of RMB 1,300 billion with state-owned commercial banks. (See Table 4.5 for the breakdown.) The authorities considered that this basically completed the transfer of nonperforming assets from banks, with 70 percent of bad assets already cleared and the proportion of bad loans in the four banks after the transfer kept below 20 percent.[16]

The completion of the transfer of bad debt from state banks to AMCs only marks the beginning of a long process of debt restructuring. The AMCs' exit strategy is to sell their equity on local stock exchanges or to outsider investors. There are reports that the AMCs are able to generate some income from their acquired assets,[17] but given the poor quality of those assets, it would be unrealistic to think that substantial portions of the debts could be recovered. The AMCs, and ultimately the government, have to absorb the difference in the par value of these assets and their real market value. A more fundamental issue of debt restructuring, however, is the possible moral hazard generated by the government's rescue.[18] The debt-equity swap programs should be considered as measures to make the banking system more market oriented, and they should be a last resort to clear nonperforming loans from state-owned banks. The success of the program depends on the AMCs' ability to identify the right firms for debt-equity swaps and their ability to restructure the target firms for efficiency improvement. SOE managers could view debt-equity swaps as a means of removing the SOEs' financial burden that results from the central government's *bogaidai* policy. Without admitting that the SOEs' insolvency is the consequence of inefficiency, the debt-equity swaps will create this moral-hazard problem and the debt-equity program may end up being considered a free lunch instead of a last supper.[19]

Table 4.5

Debts Restructured by July 2000 (RMB 100 million)

Asset-management company	Bank	Bad assets received
Cinda	PCBC	35.0
Huarong	ICBC	40.8
Great Wall	ABC	28.2
Dongfang	BOC	26.0
Total		130.0

Source: *Zhongguo Zhengquan Bao* (China Securities), July 27, 2000.

Conclusion

China has adopted a gradualist approach to banking reform. This approach served to minimize its impact on existing market order and hence preserved a high savings rate for economic development. By the late 1990s, China completed the construction of a modern banking sector with compatible banking regulations in place. Yet the problems and challenges facing the banking sector today also stem from the gradualism of reform. The problem of nonperforming loans is a consequence of the partial reform that left a burden of policy lending on state-owned commercial banks. More important, the banking reform so far has preserved state ownership of the four major commercial banks and has not addressed the issue of corporate governance.

The lesson learned from the Japanese banking crisis in the 1990s should be illuminating. The long-lasting crisis was not only a consequence of speculation in real estate, but was mainly a result of the system of "collusive regulation" in which both the regulators and regulatees were uninterested in disclosure and enforcement of rules.[20] The lax disclosure rules allowed banks to hide losses or phony deals, and regulator apathy about bringing problems to the surface may well have intensified the crisis. Had the Japanese banks had a more effective corporate-governance structure, the intensity of the crisis might have been diminished and its duration shortened.

Notes

1. Xu 1998, 11.
2. The Chinese authorities recognized that nonbank financial institutions are

important complements to banks in raising funds. In the 1980s, as many as one hundred international trusts and investment companies were established, predominantly in the coastal Special Economic Zones. These banks served mostly to finance foreign investment from foreign funds.

3. To preserve the dominance of public ownership, state and local governments are the majority holders of shareholding banks.

4. Yi 1994, 34.

5. TICs were initially established by the specialized banks to go around credit quotas. By the end of the 1980s, there were more than three hundred TICs. However, TICs themselves began to embark on the banking business, making the PBOC's supervision almost impossible. The number of TICs was later reduced to around one hundred.

6. "Nationwide commercial banks" were formerly called "universal banks."

7. China Minsheng Bank was listed in 2000. The other two banks listed were Shenzhen Development Bank in 1991 and Pudong Development Bank in 1999.

8. This point is further elaborated in Article 59 of the PBOC General Rules on Loans (Trial Implementation) promulgated by the PBOC in July 1995. The regulation stipulates that no work unit or individual may forcibly demand a lender to grant a loan. The General Rules on Loans also stipulate that borrowers who fail to repay the loans are liable for breach of contract.

9. Annual Report of the People's Bank of China, 1999.

10. Dai Xianglong, the governor of the PBOC, explained in a press conference on March 17, 1999, that the concept of nonperforming loans was defined in three categories: loans in arrears, loans in arrears by two years or more, and unrecoverable loans. According to this definition, nonperforming loans amount to 25 percent.

11. *Almanac of Finance and Banking of China*, 1999.

12. Lardy 1998, 41.

13. As stated in the 1999 Annual Report of the PCBC, "Most of these assets [the nonperforming loans] were problem commercial assets we originated prior to the introduction of the new commercial banking law; these assets were primarily policy loans to state-owned enterprises, provided in accordance with the government's policy lending plan."

14. Zhu and Huang 1999.

15. For example, by the end of 1999, the PCBC had transferred RMB 250 billion in nonperforming loans to Cinda AMC. The transfer was funded at book value through a bond issuance from Cinda backed by the MOF.

16. *Zhongguo zhengquan bao* (China Security), July 27, 2000.

17. A newspaper story reported that Great Wall AMC successfully signed asset-leasing accords with fifteen lessees, including twelve private investors, involving leased assets worth RMB 76.44 million. *Jingji ribao* (Economic Daily), June 16, 2000.

18. Chinese economists are well aware of the moral-hazard problem. For example, the problem is discussed in depth in the article cited in note 13.

19. Steinfeld 2000.

20. Ulrike Schaede, "The 1995 Financial Crisis in Japan." BRIE (Berkeley Roundtable on the International Economy) working paper 85, University of California, Berkeley (February 1996).

References

Lardy, N.R. 1998. *China's Unfinished Economic Revolution.* Washington, DC: Brookings Institution.

———. 1999. "When Will China's Financial System Meet China's Needs?" Conference on Policy Reform in China, Center for Research on Economic and Policy Reform, Stanford University, Stanford, November 18–20.

Lin Y.; F. Cai; and Z. Li. 1997. *The Chinese Miracle: Development Strategy and Economic Reform.* Hong Kong: Chinese University Press.

Mehran, H., et al. 1996. *Monetary and Exchange System Reforms in China: An Experiment in Gradualism.* Washington, DC: IMF.

Naughton, B. 1998. "China's Financial Reform: Achievements and Challenges." BRIE (Berkeley Roundtable on the International Economy) working paper 112, University of California, Berkeley.

Perotti, E.C.; L. Sun; and L. Zou. 1999. "State-Owned Versus Township and Village Enterprises in China." *Comparative Economic Studies* 41, nos. 2–3: 151–79.

Steinfeld, E.S. 2000. "Free Lunch or Last Supper? China's Debt-Equity Swaps in Context." *China Business Review,* July–August. Also available at www.chinabusinessreview/007/steinfeld.html.

Yang, H. 1996. *Banking and Financial Control in Reforming Planned Economies.* New York: St. Martin's.

Xu, X. 1998. *China's Financial System Under Transition.* New York: St. Martin's.

Xu, X., and Y. Wang. 1999. "Ownership Structure and Corporate Governance in Chinese Stock Companies." *China Economic Review* 10, no. 1 (spring): 75–98.

Yi, G. 1994. *Money, Banking, and Financial Markets in China.* Oxford: Westview.

Zhu, M., and J. Huang. 1999. "Lun Zhongguo de zichan guanli gongsi" (On asset-management companies in China). *Jingji yanjiu* (Economic Studies), no. 12: 3–13.

5

The Development of Nonbank Financial Institutions in China

Martin Hovey

Introduction

As China moves steadily ahead with reforms, prepares for entry into the World Trade Organization (WTO), and steps cautiously toward a free-market economy, it has an immense responsibility to contend with. At this juncture of its development, the most significant concerns facing China derive from economic and social issues. While social issues are not addressed in this paper, they should not be overlooked in the broader context. We shall, however, address an economic issue within the context of the financial reforms—the development of nonbank financial institutions in China.

In China, as in other countries, nonbank financial institutions (NBFIs) are heterogeneous, multifaceted, and numerous. Generally speaking, and for the purposes of this paper, we refer to NBFIs as being any financial institution that is not a bank. To the extent that NBFIs are depository institutions—that is, they obtain funds by issuing financial claims against themselves and make direct or other investments with the funds thus derived—they may be denoted as quasi-banks. Typically, the funds obtained will be indirect investments or deposits, and the direct investments will be loans or other financial assets. These depository nonbank

I would like to acknowledge with appreciation the encouragement and support of Tony Naughton and Mike Dempsey in the preparation of this paper. I also wish to acknowledge the unwavering support and encouragement of my wife, Delia.

institutions do not hold a license to conduct banking but conduct business in financial intermediation, albeit often with severe restrictions. In a general sense, these institutions include savings and loan societies, credit unions, credit cooperatives, finance companies, and various forms of merchant banks. Thus, herein we will distinguish between NBFIs that conduct business as financial intermediaries and those that do not. This second grouping of NBFIs that are not direct financial intermediaries consists of those institutions that pull together a pool of common funds that they administer on behalf of clients or investors. A variety of retirement pension funds, managed investment funds, and life insurers are principally included.

Benchmarking and comparing of NBFIs is somewhat difficult. There is a diverse range of institutions and instruments and a wide scope of players in the marketplace, plus the assortment of regulatory regimes that vary from country to country. In addition, the diversity makes the task of comprehensive coverage problematical, as information is often scant and difficult to come by. Notwithstanding these limitations, the objective of the chapter is to review the role and potential of the major types of NBFIs as they relate to the financial reform framework in China.

Overview of Financial Development Theory

Financial development theory came to be recognized as a distinct branch of economic theory in the late 1960s. The relationships connecting economic and financial development are now well ingrained in the literature, which attempts to account for the wide-ranging structural and institutional determinants of financial development. For instance, in the early 1990s economic development was considered to take place through the process of physical and human capital, policy and institutional reform, and social development (Kenny and Williams 2001). Economic development generally takes place side by side with gradual financial deepening, which is recognized by a steady increase in the ratio of various financial assets to GDP. Goldsmith (1969) proposed that the degree of a country's financial development can be measured by a ratio of the combined market value of all financial instruments to the value of national wealth and that financial institutional development may be measured by the proportion of financial assets held by the institutions to the total of financial assets in the economy. Accordingly, attention was paid to the build-up of financial assets by financial institutions and the expansion of holdings of these assets.

The finance and development literature emphasizes that one of the principal factors through which the financial sector influences the real economy is the productivity of the capital stock. Theory holds that financial development occurs when the financial framework—encompassing institutions, instruments, and markets—becomes progressively more sophisticated and expands over time (Drake 1980). Financial efficiency is gained when bank intermediation and capital markets function efficiently. The goal is to attain financial efficiencies so that the cost of capital and economic rents can be clearly ascertained. This can be modeled as a Tobin's Q ratio—the ratio of net market value of productive assets to the cost of replacement of the underlying physical assets. In theory, the ratio identifies the juxtaposition of the marginal efficiency of capital and the financial cost of capital (Tobin 1969, 1978).

Financial repression constrains economic growth due to its impedance on financial sector development (McKinnon 1973; Shaw 1973; and others, see for instance, Fry 1995; Kapur 1976; Mathieson 1980; Roubini and Sala-i-Martin 1992). Financial repression refers to interest rate controls and other restrictions on the volume of bank assets and liabilities, implicit taxation on savings, or other government interventions in the financial sector. An obvious example is interest rate ceilings set below equilibrium market rates. The theory holds that interest rate ceilings induce an excess demand for loanable funds, consequently, they are allocated by non-price methods that reduce the average product of the capital and distort financial prices. They are often set based on government priorities. Developing countries are frequently financially repressed, normally due to interest rate ceilings. This causes unsound and inefficient financial markets. Repression, in conjunction with directed lending, gives rise to a misallocation of resources—credit subsidies for preferred creditors and investment in inferior projects. The situation generally leads to unsatisfactory returns for the risk borne by the holders of financial assets and a dearth of funds for prospective premium investment projects.

A strategy for liberalizing both the real and financial sectors of the economy is prescribed in the McKinnon-Shaw hypothesis. The authors hypothesize that a program of liberalization cultivates an environment in which financial development occurs (McKinnon 1973; Shaw 1973), though many caution against rushing into liberalization without due consideration and careful planning (Arestis and Demetriades 1999; Stiglitz 2000). After liberalization, countries that are free of financial repression tend to have improved financial development (Demirguc and Detragiache 1998).

Significant links between financial development and economic growth have been established by empirical studies. Gupta (1984) attributes financial development and liberalization to economic development with increased savings and enhanced capital creation. Fry (1988) also argues that sound prudential supervision of the financial system, a robust legal framework, and macroeconomic stability are the fundamental requisites for development in the financial sector—a view that is now largely accepted as being the case. When financial intermediaries are efficient, it enhances the mobilization of domestic resources and the productivity of capital by channeling available funds to the most productive users. An efficient, robust, and competitive financial system is vital to financial development (Greenwood and Jovanovic 1990).

An integral and consequential part of economic development in China is thus financial sector reform. Taking into account both economic and social considerations (Hovey 2000), many factors should be considered in the reform of the financial system in China, not the least of which is the discontinuation of any form of directed lending, sound prudential supervision and regulation, a strong legal structure, and macroeconomic stability. A financial system that is competitive, efficient, and sound is able to increase savings and enhance capital creation in China.

China's Financial Sector Reform

China is both a developing economy and a transitional market economy. Financial development in China reflects the influence of both these contexts. It is opening its economy, approaching WTO entry, and proceeding tentatively along the path toward a free market economy (Unsworth 2000). Conceivably, in the process an extensive tide of hitherto protected industries will be opened for the first time to international competition, eventually including the financial sector. This will no doubt give added impetus to China's pursuit of financial sector reforms that began in 1979, along with other economic reforms. In 1998, Chinese officials announced major new initiatives to reform money-losing state-owned enterprises and China's banking system. However, the slowdown in the Chinese economy in 1998 and 1999 appears to have delayed the implementation of some of these reforms (Morrison 1999).

A dominant institutional feature of China is that the financial sector faces tight governmental control. Thus far, reform of the sector has been gradual and pragmatic and has been somewhat ad hoc and experimental. The authorities have favored a gradual approach concurrently across sectors, though it has not been driven by a predetermined, unyielding, or all-embracing master plan (Henning and Lu 2000). China was well positioned and had ample financial resources to initiate radical financial development during the initial stages of reform, yet policymakers held the position that, in the long run, measured reform maintains stability. However, the inferior productivity of China's financial resources has largely been a hindrance and, for the most part, presently still is (Fung, Ho, and Zhu 2000).

Notwithstanding the above misgiving, the measured, gradual approach has helped China steer clear of many of the predicaments of the shock therapy stratagems embraced in other former socialist countries (Benziger 1998).[1] Rather China followed the models adopted in Asian emerging economies (Mehran, Quintyn, Nordman, and Laurens 1996). In several Asian economies, the financial sector has continued to be tightly controlled, while measured steps to remove market controls are taken. For instance, highly regulated financial sectors have been retained in Korea and Japan while their economies developed. The apparent successes of their strategies, at the time, encouraged China to follow suit.

The transition of a centrally planned economy to a market economy has been analyzed from the broadened McKinnon-Shaw framework of financial repression hypothesis. Attempts to substantiate financial repression in the case of China have generated some diverse responses. On the one hand, W. Byrd (1983) and O.K.Tam (1986) contend that China was not a classic case of repression. Nonetheless, K.W. Li (1994) and C.E. Bai, D. Li, Y. Qian, and Y. Wang (1999) propose that financial repression has occurred. Li (1994) argues that repression has been in existence since the early 1950s and that it is the most appropriate framework for the reform of China's financial sector. He presents a case that other price ceilings can be an expansion of interest rate ceilings. He contends further that typical predicaments resulting from repression were unmistakably evident—for example, low marginal productivity of loans. Supporting the case of repression are factors such as vague policy making and financial inflexibility during the early years of reform (see also Li 1992). Bai and others (1999) contend that the government has ben-

Figure 5.1 **Savings Deposits per Capita in China Urban and Rural in Comparison to Population**

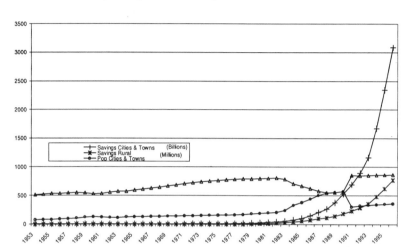

Source: China Economic Information (CEI), 1999.

efited by collecting quasi-fiscal revenues from the state banking system through controls on interest rates and restrictions of international capital flows. They show that the major features of the economy of China can be understood better by means of a financial repression analytical framework.

China has not taken the bumpy road of rapid liberalization but approached it gradually over a longer time frame, up to thirty years (Arestis and Demetriades 1999; Fry 1988; Stiglitz 2000). The policies adopted by China were aimed at attaining a high savings ratio and macroeconomic stability. Generally, both objectives have been achieved. For example, China has historically maintained a high rate of savings. When reforms began in 1979, domestic savings as a percentage of GDP stood at 32 percent (nearly as high as Japan's at the time). Since 1985, savings deposits per capita have increased substantially, especially in the urban centers, providing a low-cost source of funds (see Figure 5.1). However, most of the savings during this period were generated by the profits of SOEs, which were used by the central government for domestic investment. Economic reforms, which included the decentralization of economic production, led to substantial growth in Chinese household savings

Table 5.1

China's Average Annual Real GDP Growth: 1960–1998

Time Period	Average Annual Percent Growth
1960–1979 (pre-reform)	5.3
1979–1998 (post-reform)	9.8
1990	3.8
1991	9.3
1992	14.2
1993	13.5
1994	12.7
1995	10.5
1996	9.7
1997	8.8
1998	7.8

Sources: Official Chinese government data reported by the World Bank, *World Development Report* (various issues), IMF (various issues), Morrison (1999).

(which now account for half of China's domestic savings). As a result, savings as a percentage of GDP have steadily risen; from 6 percent of GDP in 1979 to 42.7 percent in 1998, among the highest savings rates in the world (Morrison 1999; Naughton 1998). The increase in household saving rates cannot be explained simply by the more rapid growth in household income during those years. Instead, savings behavior shifted upward in response to the changed environment.

On the economic front, average real growth of 7 to 9 percent per annum has been achieved since 1979, amid fewer and less painful vicissitudes. Indeed, the economic growth ran at more than 13 percent in a few topmost years (see Table 5.1). Furthermore, income per capita has almost quadrupled. M2 (currency in circulation, demand deposits, and some savings) increased from 32 percent of GDP in 1979 to 112 percent in 1996. This illustrates that China has had a "deeper" financial system than any other major transition economy since 1992 (Naughton 1998). The greatest part of financial deepening was due to increases in household savings deposits. It has proved to be a solid foundation for reform in the pragmatism that has ensued since 1979 in the political environment.

A salient illustration of the gradual and experimental nature of the reform approach taken by China is the establishment of special economic zones (SEZs). These have been the birthplace of many of the foremost developments that have evolved from modest trials conducted in them. Foreign firms are allowed to enter China's banking and life insurance markets in SEZs, for example, but entry to other areas is restricted. Furthermore, greater flexibility as to credit quotas and interest rates are permitted to domestic banks operating in the zones. The success of decentralized decision making and increased flexibility in the SEZs is demonstrated by the impressive economic growth attained in the regions.

Many more challenges will doubtless arise as the financial system steps out of the statism of its past toward a market-driven system in the future. Even though financial-sector reform has been impressive to date, essential moves are yet to be made. For instance, thus far, because the focus has been on institutional development, the liberalization of financial institutions and operation and development of markets have received secondary consideration. To a reasonable extent, this approach is linked to the past statism in that the centrally planned economy relied on the monetary sector to provide macroeconomic control. Fundamentally, the emergence of market-driven financial pursuits was considered complementary to this core charter. Financial allocation continues in line with government priorities through pricing controls and the apportionment of credit. Effectively, Beijing's strategy is to preserve the reformed financial sector as a crucial component in the enduring interventionist model of economic development. Here again we have an example of the resemblance of China's approach to financial sector reform to that of other Asian economies.

Financial Sector Reform in China

The genesis of financial sector reform in the late 1970s has become an intriguing part of China's history. Characteristics and practices of capital and financial markets, such as commercial-based financial institutions and stock and derivative markets, are now being implemented. However, it was not until 1993 that the financial sector was afforded considered deliberation at the Third Plenum of the Chinese Communist Party (CCP) Fourteenth Central Committee. At this time it was acknowledged by the authorities that a financial system that facilitated the efficient utilization of capital resources without impedance was a precondition if China was to attain a flourishing semimarket, or as referred to by authorities in China, a "socialist market economy." Accordingly, a system of market forces was adopted that would enhance resource allocation while yet remaining constrained by a regime that was, and to a degree still is, subject to state-controlled macroeconomic policy.

Within the area of financial development theory, a widely accepted view is that banks are the principal providers of capital during the formative stages of economic development. Nonbank instruments and institutions take on a more important role as an economy becomes more highly developed, and middle- and high-income status improves (Drake 1980; Fry 1988). At this stage, dedicated intermediaries, such as NBFIs, play an increasing role. For example, specialized institutions including credit societies and cooperatives, finance companies, and fund managers such as life insurers and pension funds, develop a greater share of the financial system.[2] Thus, financial development theory holds that the share of the financial system commanded by NBFIs expands and that which is controlled by the banks wanes. While in China there is a substantial number of nonbank institutions, such as rural and urban credit cooperatives, their overall market share is relatively insignificant. Thus, it is reasonable to propose that China's financial system has a considerable way to go before it can be regarded as fully developed.

If Chinese enterprises are to remain competitive within a deregulating economy post-WTO membership, the issue of financial sector reform should be addressed urgently. The development of NBFIs is of strategic consequence to the economic development of China. First, as dedicated intermediaries, they are a central part of the process by which monetization occurs, particularly in the rural sectors. Second, they play a significant social role in economic development. We shall turn to the NBFIs' role as dedicated intermediaries in a later section.

Nonbanking Financial Institutions and Their Development

Virtually all of the financial deepening that has occurred in recent years has been channeled into the banking system. Despite the reforms, essentially China's financial system remains bank-dominated, and the growth of competition to the state-owned banking system has been real, but much too slow. NBFIs compose only 10 percent of financial intermediation in China. Thus, with 90 percent of financial intermediation being channeled through banks, China's NBFI sector accounts for a much smaller share of intermediation than elsewhere in Asia (Lardy 1998; Park and Ren 2001). The five primary types of NBFIs in China are trust and investment corporations (TICS), and tens of thousands of both rural credit cooperatives (RCC) and urban credit cooperatives (UCC) that

Figure 5.2 **Structure of Nonbank Financial Institutions**

The Central Bank	
The People's Bank of China	

Non-bank Financial Institutions	Trust and Investment Corporations
	Rural Credit Cooperatives
	Urban Credit Cooperatives
	Finance Companies
	Leasing Companies

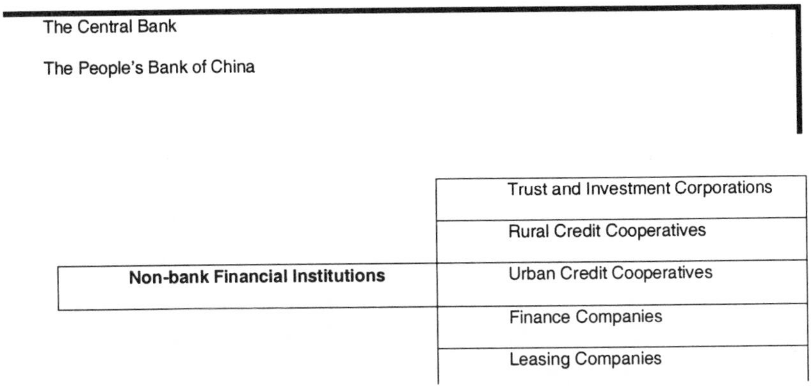

Note: Life insurance firms are under the China Insurance Regulatory Commission.

often, in reality, operate like banks. Finance, leasing, and life insurance companies have also emerged convincingly.

It should be noted that in addition there are less formal yet significant financial markets that are quite large. Organizations such as informal rural credit mechanisms include rural financial associations, credit clubs, moneylenders, and unregistered private banks. These are informal and important, yet they have not been studied as information is scant. They have held a considerable slice of the market pie, as estimates indicate that the rural informal financial markets surpassed formal rural institutional lending in size in 1986 (Park and Ren 2001). Thus a large amount of financial intermediation is occurring that is often not captured or is captured inadequately by officially reported statistics (Naughton 1998).

As illustrated by Figure 5.2, NBFIs are generally under the supervision of the People's Bank of China (PBOC), which is the central bank. Life insurance companies operate under the oversight of the China Insurance Regulatory Commission (Girardin 1997b; Kennedy 1995; Lake, Ming, and Cossette 1994).

The proliferation of informal financial intermediaries such as NBFIs in China is an outcome of the controls and credit quotas imposed by statism. Especially during the 1980s, there was a surge in the formation of nonbank and nonstate financial institutions. During the 1990s, there has also been considerable growth in their intermediation. For example, intermediation by credit cooperatives more than tripled from 1993 to

Figure 5.3 **Credit Cooperatives Liabilities**

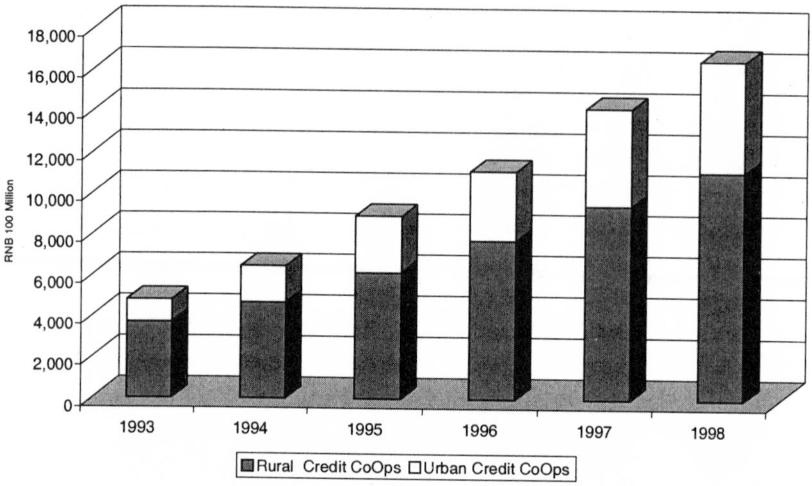

Sources: CEI 1999; *Almanac of China's Finance and Banking.*

1998, with deposits rising from RMB 467.8 (US$56.5) billion[3] in 1993 to RMB 1722.6 (US$208.1) billion in September 1998 (see Figure 5.3).

NBFIs play an important role in China since they provide services otherwise not available to local communities, individuals, and businesses. Largely, they developed in response to controls, inflexibilities, and inadequacies in the state-banking sector. NBFIs have the added advantage of being supported by local authorities and provincial governments that draw funds from them; such transactions are easier than accessing loan facilities from specialized banks. Since the mid 1980s, NBFIs have gained an increasing share of financial assets with striking growth which has helped satisfy the growth in the demand for investment loans by state and nonstate enterprises. Yet, despite the rapid growth of NBFIs, their market share is quite small in comparison to that of the immense state banks. One reason is that they suffer from a deficiency of backing from the government in attracting deposits (Girardin 1997a; Girardin and Bazen 1998). NBFIs have received little scrutiny, in part because they are new players in the financial system. Furthermore, they operated simply as "deposit-taking stations" for the Agricultural Bank of China until a few years ago. As such, they played a passive role, simply extending passbook savings account services to farmers and depositing the resulting funds with the Agricultural Bank. However, the 1990s saw cooperatives spun off and empowered to issue loans themselves.

Initially, because NBFIs primarily financed the nonstate sector, they did not compete directly with banks. However, in a survey, Caprio (1995) identified that one of the most significant characteristics of nonbank financial institutions is that now they compete with state banks. The main area in which they compete is the loans market. Thus, to some extent, they have broken the monopoly of the state banks. In addition, the centrally controlled credit plan does not extend to NBFIs. This is an important loophole, as it has allowed state banks and regional authorities to establish NBFIs and sidestep the credit plan. By this means, many NBFIs are controlled by banks and often make use of the same personnel, information, and funds. Consequently, NBFIs face considerable moral hazard, especially as they are frequently utilized by the controlling organizations to evade regulation and supervision.

In effect, there are few laws and regulations pertaining to NBFIs. Moreover, those that do exist are not enforced effectively, certainly not as effectively as regulation concerning state-owned banks (SOBs) (Girardin and Bazen 1998). As a result, NBFIs have greater autonomy and independence than banks. Consequently they tend to be more entrepreneurial. This can lead to mismanagement or undue risk taking. Conversely, it may be argued that it increases motivation to maximize returns.

As noted previously with regard to financial development theory, Fry (1988) argues that sound prudential supervision of the financial system is a basic prerequisite for financial sector development. However, central bank regulation and supervision of the banking and financial sectors remains weak in China, and some NBFIs manage to elude supervision and regulation by their very structure (Hovey and Naughton 2000). Be that as it may, regulation and supervision of NBFIs in China is difficult and challenging for the following reasons: their considerable numbers and diversity, their frequently isolated locations, the physical vastness of China, and the limited resources and competence of supervisors. It follows then, that for reform to be successful, the PBOC must be resolute in its quest to build a financial system that has adequate prudential regulation, is adeptly supervised, and has appropriate accounting standards and systems.

Further development of the financial system is anticipated through major reforms. It is expected that some trust and investment corporations, security companies, and other NBFIs will be restructured as investment banks. This will generate funds that can be applied to institutional investment. It is also expected that they will provide listing, merger, and acquisition consulting services. The strategy is that these institutions will assist in reorganizing assets of enterprises and businesses and assist with or facilitate their public listing and the raising of funds from markets overseas.

However, given the current lack of prudential supervision and regulation, two points should be highlighted. First, the finding of Carlos Diaz-Alejandro (1985) that liberalization in some developing countries has led to acute financial distress or even failures; second, the subsequent argument of Fry (1988) that adequate prudential supervision is a prerequisite for effective financial liberalization. We can conclude, then, that the current lack of prudential supervision and regulation of the NBFI sector in China should be setting off danger signals. There is a strong possibility of further financial distress, insolvency, or crashes. For example, in 1997 at the beginning of a purge of NBFIs, more than 400 smaller institutions were closed (*Sichuan China Business*). It will be necessary to maintain the fine balance between having sufficient prudential regulation to avoid undue risk and allowing the autonomy needed to encourage sound management and maximum returns.

Microfinance and Cooperatives

For the purpose of clarity, microfinance denotes the financial activities of the smaller institutions of the financial market; characteristically these consist of cooperatives, nongovernment organizations, village banks, development projects, informal intermediaries, and other institutions that fulfil an intermediation role. Even though China has a bank-dominated financial sector, as do most economies in Asia, microfinance institutions fulfil a significant role. This is especially so in the emerging economies. Microfinance organizations do not face the same restrictions and regulations as larger organizations and are able to service a wider community base than do banks that tend to be concentrated in the primary business centers. Thus, the institutions, which are typically localized and communal in nature, are able to meet the needs of rural and urban communities that are not met to any great extent by banks. Frequently, cooperative types of intermediaries have taken on the role of community banks in rural areas and have developed extensive networks that provide rudimentary banking services. This explains why in China a plethora of microfinance organizations, such as credit cooperatives, provided the urban and rural, mainly poor, population with access to structured savings and credit facilities. In so doing, the extensive networks of cooperatives have a vital role to play in the economic empowering of these sectors. Thus, microfinance involvement at the rural level continues to grow and to develop in diversity, mainly at the local grass-roots level. Larger institutions like banks find it difficult to enter the sector. They face difficulty in penetrating the regions, regulations, and other constraints.

Cooperatives by their very nature tend to be price driven. The notion is carried over to credit cooperatives where the expectation of members is that the credit needs of the community will be served well below market rates while reasonable returns to depositors are maintained. If the market moves adversely, the institution is exposed to liquidity risk. While loans offered by microfinance institutions may be insignificant in absolute terms, in proportion to the borrower's assets and income, they are often as large as more formal loans. These aspects, along with supervision and limited regulation, such as prudential ratio constraints, allow very little room for error. Further contributing factors are isolation, lack of infrastructure such as communications, and the relative lack of management sophistication.

A considerable hazard in the growth of microfinance intermediation lies in the deficiencies of personnel in applicable knowledge, skills, and training. This lack is accentuated when the institutions expand and begin to encroach into urban areas. The attraction of being drawn into speculative pursuits exposes the institutions to risk-taking beyond the competence of personnel and management. In recognition of these factors, most emerging countries have introduced standard management practices and have endeavored to provide some level of supervision, regulation, and training.

As microfinance is generally characterized by smaller firms, we will briefly consider some of the difficulties that they typically face. To begin with, regional institutions such as cooperatives face risk through a general lack of diversification or by being trapped by the economic business cycles of the region. A concentration of loan assets in a region or economic sector, or a limited spread of agricultural or industrial involvement, could cause prohibitive credit risk. This is especially so as the limitations may also result in insufficient net interest margins. Furthermore, economies of scale sufficient to satisfy operating efficiency can be difficult to attain. It is generally considered that processing efficiencies are not met until institutions attain an operationally efficient size, which might be of the order of RMB 400 (US$48) million.

Microfinance organizations make a significant contribution to the pooling of savings. Such aspects as personalized service, informal dealing, better-than-market interest rate returns, agents who solicit deposits, and innovative saving plans all contribute to their success. These savings deposits in turn can be utilized by the formal banking sector. However, the small-time borrowers of microfinance organizations frequently use credit more productively, thus producing higher social marginal returns. Consequently, efficiency and equity ends are better served, benefiting the economy as a whole.

Microfinance in China is very much driven by the rural financial environment. Essentially the reforms have not increased formal intermediation in rural areas to any extent. Informal sources continue to provide most rural loans. The main financial institutions in rural China are the Agricultural Bank of China (ABC), the Agricultural Development Bank of China (ADBC), and the Rural Credit Cooperatives (RCCs, which will be discussed in detail in the next section). The ABC is one of four specialized banks in China and has the largest branch network, which extends to nearly all townships. The ADBC is one of three policy banks established in 1994. It separated from the ABC and has branches at primarily county level. Most of its loans were for agricultural purchases, predominantly grain. RCCs have a vast network with branch outlets in most villages. They are the principal source of formal credit in rural areas. Rural cooperative foundations (RCF) were an important part of many townships in China until 1999, when they were dissolved. They were under the administrative supervision of the Ministry of Agriculture. RCFs were quasi-governmental organizations and often had considerable engagement with township officials. They did not have actual legal status as financial institutions, and they frequently charged interest rates above regulated rates. RCF deposits were calculated to be about 10 percent of total RCCs deposits in 1996 (Park, Brandt, and Giles 1997).

China's Credit Cooperatives

There is an extensive network of credit cooperatives in China. The rural credit cooperatives collect deposits from, and extend credit to, rural households and enterprises. Urban credit cooperatives perform similar functions in urban areas. The phenomenon of cooperatives, peasant associations, and credit unions that offer mutual financial assistance is not new in the financial system of China. Credit cooperatives have been in existence at least since 1919, when the first recorded European-style agricultural credit cooperative was established in association with Fudan University in Shanghai (Lai 1988). Since that time they have had their ups and downs, but have continued to play a role in the economy of China (Trescott 1993). Their importance has been increasing in the last two decades in particular. They have played a significant role in invigorating local economic development, enhancing the daily lives of communities, and meeting the financial needs of local businesses and private enterprise, and have acted as catalysts in the revitalization of the financial sector.

Credit cooperatives in China are titular cooperatives, that is they are cooperatives in name only. They are not cooperatives in governance (Naughton 1998). Typically, credit cooperatives are financial institutions that are collectively and cooperatively owned, have independent accounting and operational self-determination, and are entirely accountable to their mutual owners for their performance. However, while they were originally mutually owned in China, most are currently owned by various levels of government and have little autonomy. Typically, they have close ties with rural state banks. In many cases, it is difficult to hand them back, as the identities of the original mutual owners are now somewhat clouded.

In China, credit cooperatives operate under the oversight of the People's Bank of China (PBOC). The two primary credit cooperatives are rural credit cooperatives (RCCs) and urban credit cooperatives (UCCs). Currently, cooperatives' principal business revolves around receiving deposits, giving credit, executing settlement, and remitting of transactions for private industry, commerce, and collective enterprises. They strive to meet the needs of small or medium enterprises that are generally declined credit by the bank.[4] Under the strategy to consolidate cooperatives three Urban Credit Cooperative Banks were established in Shanghai, Beijing, and Shenzhen in 1995. The plan is to consolidate all cooperatives into a Rural Cooperative Bank and an Urban Cooperative Bank.

By and large, credit cooperatives have a decided comparative advantage over the huge impersonal state banks. They are relatively small and flexible, and there are hundreds of thousands of offices; virtually every community has a representative or office. Thus, they are able to communicate directly with their customers and monitor them more closely. They play a significant role in the collection of deposits, which in turn provides them with a low-cost and expanding source of funds (see Figure 5.1). Their relative autonomy leads to a desire to maximize returns and seek overall to better performance. For example, Girardin and Bazen (1998) conducted a survey of fifty-seven UCCs in eight cities from three regions and concluded that their financial performance was a great deal healthier than that of SOBs. For example, UCCs' ratio of earnings over assets was ten times higher, and nonperforming loans were a quarter of SOBs.' Nonperforming loans are a serious problem for SOBs; official figures suggest 20 percent of loans are nonperforming, but the real figure could be much higher than this (Hovey and Naughton 2000). The high relative profitability of UCCs can be explained in part by their lower administrative costs compared to those of SOBs, because UCCs do not share the burden of granting direct "cradle to the grave" welfare benefits to their employees.

Cooperatives also have an advantage in that they have local information through individual employees who have a variety of social or community interactions in nonmarket contexts. Thus, they tend to be on familiar terms with each other and have local information, which in turn gives a comparative advantage to the cooperative institutions. This information can be used in credit and project-feasibility checks, in assessing loan applicants' ability and willingness to make and maintain loan payments, and in appraising the quality of relevant collateral offered. This aspect has been studied and is known by the term *peer monitoring view* (Arnott and Stiglitz 1990; Stiglitz 1990). In contexts where formal institutions are unsuccessful, informal institutions may still be able to succeed, partly due to the local information available to them. For instance, in low-income settings where formal banks often fail, the cause of failure is frequently recognized as poor information resulting in unfavorable selection and moral hazard (Binswanger 1986; Braverman and Guasch 1986). Furthermore, the knowledge can be used in the monitoring and oversight of sanctions imposed on borrowers. These combine to reduce loan collection costs and decrease the incidence of nonperforming loans. Thus, overall they have the advantage of being able to retail credit more efficiently; whereas, the SOBs tend to be poor at assessing the viability of credit lines and at monitoring borrowers' performance, and most of their credit goes to loss-making state-owned enterprises (SOEs).

On the other hand, in general, the two chief problematic issues that credit cooperatives in low-income countries face are free riding and collusion (Besley 1995). Cooperative "members" may very well be nonborrowers, yet may play a monitoring role. If they are not willing to put in the effort required to perform the task successfully and attain an optimal level of monitoring, the possibility of free riders arises. In addition, there is the hazard of collusion between borrowers and nonborrowers. Borrowers may collude with nonborrower cooperative "members" and not maintain loan repayments or simply not settle the loan at all. This is the negative side of individuals being known to each other. Thus, there are positive and negative effects of local information. Given that cooperatives generally have loan portfolios of superior quality and performance, it could be contended that the positives outweigh the negatives.

A negative aspect from the monetary authorities' perspective may relate to government planning objectives. Credit cooperatives, though generally supervised by the PBOC, are not under direct credit control and do not necessarily adhere to controls. Thus, problems arise for monetary authorities with stabilization policies to consider, especially when attempting to limit inflationary pressures. For example, credit cooperatives frustrate selective credit controls by fueling demand pressures in particular markets. Nevertheless, it can be argued that informal finance, such as credit cooperatives, actually augment productivity and allocative efficiency by limiting efforts to control credit too closely.

As stated previously, prudential regulation is of primary importance to stability and economic development. Credit cooperatives do not offer the same level of prudential protection as large banks. In China, the state-owned banks have the added security of being backed by the state, and the depositor insurance that this implies to the populace. The government has tried repeatedly to highlight and enforce existing regulations with less than satisfactory results so far, though a new round began in 1998. However, it is almost impossible for the PBOC to carry out the level of regular supervision required or that they feel necessary. Thus, it can be expected that a lack of compliance may be widespread. Contributing factors are the large numbers of credit cooperatives, their diversity and, at times, isolation; and the lack of expertise and needed resources. As an alternative form of management to credit ceilings, asset/liability ratios have been introduced and recently reinforced.

Credit cooperatives have played a significant role in the economy of China by contributing greatly to the development of local economies

Table 5.2

RCCs Staff and Institutions (thousands)

	1987	1989	1991	1993	1998
Staff	434	488	539	594	650
Institution	61	58	58	51	50

Source: Girardin 1997a; *Finance Express* 1998.

and improving the lot and daily lives of the people; they have also augmented the financial needs of private enterprise and local business. Moreover, they have been significant catalysts in the reforms of the financial industry. In the following sections, we will highlight the activities of the two primary cooperative institutions: rural and urban credit cooperatives.

Rural Credit Cooperatives

Since their small beginnings fifty years ago in their present form rural credit cooperatives (RCCs, or *xinyongshe*) have grown in popularity and market share in rural communities. They have played a significant role in the monetization in these communities. Essentially, there is credit cooperative representation in every rural township and village in China. By September 1998, the number of RCCs had grown to more than 50,000; in addition, there were roughly a quarter of a million village credit stations and another 50,000 or so branches and savings offices. In total there are over 650,000 full-time and part-time officers at village credit stations. They conduct savings and credit business in over 350,000 institutions in China (CEI 1999; Ling, Zhongyi, and von Braun 1997).

As rural credit cooperatives receive about 80 percent of deposits in rural areas and 25 percent of savings deposits in urban areas, they also play a quantitatively significant role in deposit collection. Since the reforms started in 1979, RCC deposits have increased 72–fold and loans 208 times (see Figure 5.4 on page 75 for recent indications). For example, since 1993, deposits grew 3.1–fold from RMB 371.7 (US$44.9) billion[5] to RMB 1,166.5 (US$140.9) billion by September 1998. Outstanding credit grew 3.3 times from RMB 275.0 (US$33.2) billion to reach RMB 900.8 (US$108.8) billion (CEI 1999; Ling *et al.* 1997). By September 1998, they provided about 80 percent of the agricultural loans with about 52 percent going to township and village enterprises (TVEs) and 24 percent to agriculture (including households). Their role in townships is significant as they provide 70 percent of the loans for township enterprises. Numerically there are fifteen times more RCCs than urban credit cooperatives (UCC). Yet, despite these impressive numbers, they are only twice as large economically. They have considerably less market share than the banking sector, holding about one-tenth of the total of the entire financial and banking sector. Then again, a consideration in their favor is that the quality of their loan portfolios in the main is better than that of state-owned commercial banks that have an enormous nonperforming loan problem—their share of nonperforming loans is at least four times greater (Girardin and Bazen 1998; Hovey and Naughton 2000).

The People's Bank of China (PBOC), the nation's central bank, has announced that it wishes to work with institutions that are linked closely to significant economic development. Thus, they are taking measures to ensure the healthy development of the regional financial sector. They are also working at improving the legal environment, and in some provinces they have launched pilot initiatives to restructure rural credit cooperatives in an endeavor to protect against financial risk (CEI 1999). In a bid to open up market opportunities, reduce risk, and improve the quality of the assets of smaller financial institutions, state-owned commercial banks will primarily concentrate their business in large and medium cities and will focus on medium and large SOEs.

An examination of the consolidated balance sheet of RCCs in Table 5.3, and as diagrammatically represented in Figure 5.4, reveals that households' share of deposits continued to rise strongly. Savings are by far the dominant deposits—more than doubling during the years 1994 to 1998 from RMB481.6 (US$58.2) billion to RMB1014.6 (US$122.6) billion. Demand deposits, or checking accounts, grew by around 60 percent in the same period, up from RMB80.5 (US$9.7) billion to RMB128.4 (US$15.5) billion, while time deposits, or certificates of deposit, just got a look in, although they tripled from RMB6 (US$0.7) billion to RMB20 (US$2.4) billion. Thus, there is little diversity, compared to UCCs that have significantly increased their mix over savings, demand, and time deposits. This demonstrates the relative lack of sophistication of the RCC market place and institutions, and also that the community as a whole is essentially cash and barter based. Generally loans more than doubled during the period 1994 to 1998. The claims on "other sectors" grew from RMB416.9 (US$50.36) billion to RMB867.8 (US$104.8) billion.

Table 5.3

Consolidated Balance Sheet of Rural Credit Cooperatives
(unit: RMB 1 billion)

	1994	1995	1996	1997	1998
Foreign assets	0	0	0	0	0
Reserve assets	88.5	121.8	193.6	224.3	187.8
Claims on central government	0	33.9	40.6	18.64	29.32
Claims on other sectors	416.9	523.4	636.5	766.2	867.8
Claims on non-monetary financial institutions	0	0	0	3.14	3.61
Total	505.3	679.1	870.7	1,012.2	1,088.5
Liabilities to non-financial sectors	568.1	717.3	879.4	1,060.9	1,166.5
Liabilities to the central bank	0	1.6	2.9	1.6	2.9
Liabilities to non-monetary financial institutions	0	0.3	0.3	0.3	0.3
Bonds	0	0	0	0	0
Owner's equity	61.7	63.2	54.8	31.0	9.4
Paid-in capital	69.4	37.8	40.1	63.1	63.7
Others (net)	−124.5	−101.4	−63.5	−81.6	−90.6
Total	505.3	679.1	870.7	1,012.3	1,088.5

Source: CEI 1999; *Almanac of China's Finance and Banking.*

Urban Credit Cooperatives

Urban credit cooperatives (UCC) have gained acceptance in urban communities particularly in the 1990s, with phenomenal growth of more than sixfold since 1993. For instance, deposits grew from RMB96.1 (US$11.6) billion[6] in 1993, to RMB556.0 (US$67.2) billion by September 1998—which is now about half of that of the RCCs. Outstanding credit grew an incredible sevenfold from RMB 61.5 (US$7.4) billion to RMB439.1 (US$53.1) which is the sum of the three claims (see Table 5.4 on page 76). Despite the presence of rural credit cooperatives, 80 percent of UCC savings deposits arise from rural areas and 25 percent from urban areas (Girardin 1997b). Loans to individual proprietors are twice those of the state banks. Loans to urban and township collective enterprises are about 50 percent of the same market. Thus, rapidly developing urban collectively owned and private enterprises have been a catalyst for UCC expansion.

Whilst UCCs are still small compared to the massive state banks, there were 3,200 at the end of 1998 (CEI 1999). In recent times there has been a number of mergers, and some UCCs have gained banking licenses; also some UCCs have closed down, contributing to a decline

Figure 5.4 **Rural Credit Cooperatives Assets**

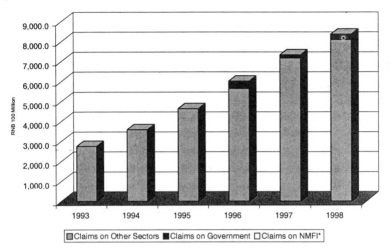

Rural Credit Cooperatives Liabilities

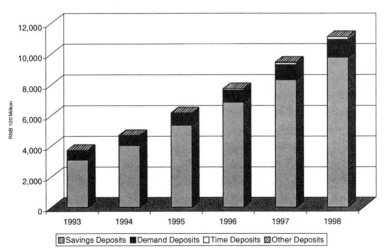

in numbers from a peak of 5,230 in 1994 (TEJ 2000) (see Table 5.5). In general, the UCCs are located in middle-to-large cities and do not have branches. For example, there are about 60 UCCs in Beijing.

A second kind of UCC is an affiliate (urban credit cooperative affiliate), which is a financial institution that is owned by a UCC. Affiliates are completely independent and separate legal entities. Transactions between both organizations are meant to be on an equal footing. Never-

Table 5.4

Consolidated Balance Sheet of Urban Credit Cooperatives
(unit: RMB 1 billion)

	1994	1995	1996	1997	1998
Foreign assets	0	0	0	0	0
Reserve assets	49.8	68.3	77.9	100.28	75.68
Claims on central government	6.8	9.8	9.9	24.58	36.79
Claims on other sectors	144.3	206.8	263.1	351.68	381.61
Claims on non-monetary financial institutions	14.0	19.0	23.8	22.07	20.73
Total	214.9	303.9	374.8	498.6	514.8
Liabilities to non-financial sectors	235.4	335.7	399.8	538.3	556.0
Liabilities to the central bank	3.5	3.0	3.4	3.8	3.7
Liabilities to non-monetary financial institutions	4.4	5.8	17.8	14.0	11.4
Bonds	0.0	0.0	0.0	0.3	0.1
Owner's equity	16.2	20.1	21.2	28.1	22.9
Paid-in capital	11.1	13.6	15.8	25.3	26.8
Others (net)	−44.5	−60.7	−67.4	−85.4	−79.0
Total	214.9	303.9	374.8	498.9	515.1

Source: CEI 1999; *Almanac of China's Finance and Banking.*

Table 5.5

UCCs Staff and Institutions (thousands)

	1987	1989	1991	1993	1998
Staff	26.5	60.3	77.3	122.9	145.0
Institutions	1.6	3.4	3.5	4.8	3.2

Source: Girardin 1997a; *Finance Express* 1998; TEJ 2000.

theless, the affiliate is likely to be "subsidiary" to the UCC. Affiliates are located in an area where the UCC would not otherwise be represented (Girardin and Bazen 1998).

UCCs have played an essential role in the development of private enterprises and small-to-medium–sized firms. About 80 percent of the credit of UCCs is directed into these enterprises. It is desirable that the support of these enterprises continue. The PBOC is undertaking a series of actions to assist in the viability and development of UCCs. For example, measures are being taken to develop urban cooperatives to better serve the private and urban economies of a region. The PBOC has applied the strategies of merging UCCs into new urban cooperative banks and of standardizing UCCs.

On reviewing the consolidated balance sheet of UCCs (see Table 5.4), it is worth noting that total deposits exceeded aggregate credit—the deposits collected exceed the loans granted. Households' share of deposits continued to rise strongly, chiefly in savings deposits that tripled from RMB73.4 (US$8.87) billion in 1994 to RMB257.3 (US$31.08) billion in 1998. Demand deposits, or checking accounts, held the dominant position in 1994 with RMB99.9 (US$12.1) billion; however they doubled to RMB224.5 (US$27.1) billion in 1998. Time deposits, or certificates of deposit, have around 14 percent of the market but grew strongly, more than tripling from RMB 20.4 (US$2.5) billion in 1994 to RMB66 (US$7.9) billion in 1998.

Thus, the deposit diversity has widened considerably, particularly since 1993–1994 (see Figure 5.5). During that period, the demand deposits were predominant, with savings and other deposits taking an even share of the balance. This is in contrast to RCCs where savings deposits remain dominant with little growth in other deposit sectors. This highlights the added sophistication of the urban institutions, the services offered, and the markets they pursue.

A high proportion of UCC equity is taken by individuals and collective enterprises, more than existing regulations actually allow. About 20 to 30 percent of credit is granted to SOEs, although the granting of loans to SOEs is actually against regulations. The attraction is that these loans are less risky and hence the practice remains. The continuation of the arrangement may well be desirable. The overall earnings/asset ratio and performance of UCCs are better than, and the share of nonperforming loans is four times less than that of state banks (Girardin and Bazen 1998).

In a study conducted by Girardin and Ping (1997), it was found that UCCs are profitable and have a low ratio of nonperforming loans in the eastern and middle parts of China—regions with mild to high development. In these areas, to some degree, they attract deposits from collectives and make loans to SOEs. In less developed regions, such as the western parts of China, UCCs perform poorly where the reverse intermediation situation is predominant. Interestingly, in both situations, intermediation between collective enterprises increases performance. As previously mentioned, Girardin and Bazen (1998) found that the pecuniary performance of UCCs' was a great deal healthier than that of SOBs—UCCs ratio of earnings over assets

Figure 5.5 **Urban Credit Cooperatives Assets**

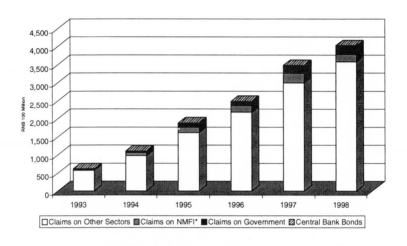

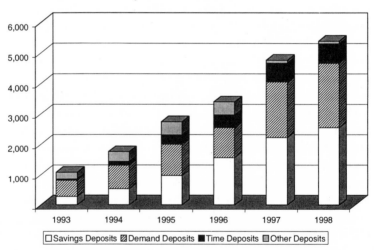

was tenfold that of SOBs, and nonperforming loans were a quarter of those held by SOBs.

In conclusion, credit cooperatives facilitate services that satisfy the financial needs of rural and urban households and enterprises. Credit cooperatives overall have played a major role in the development of China's financial system and in its economic growth. Through their intermediation they have been a major catalyst in pooling the savings of the populace and, in so doing, are a principal source of capital stock that is in turn put to use to drive reforms.

Trust and Investment Corporations of China

Trust and investment corporations (TICs) and international trust and investment corporations (ITICs) first came into existence during the 1980s in China. They are a hybrid of a trust company and a development bank. Like trust companies, they accept deposits with a maturity greater than one year. These are the main source of funding—about 60 percent—and usually from SOEs and SOBs. Not unlike a development bank, they invest the funds in approved projects. They have no credit ceiling as they are not part of the credit plan. Their primary activity is lending, however they also get involved in leasing, project management, issuing securities, and consulting (Kumar et al. 1997).

There were around 244 TICs and ITICs in existence at the end of 1998, the largest being the People's Construction Bank of China. It is the biggest nonbanking securities house in China. TICs total assets were valued in 1998 at RMB 434.2 (US$52.5) billion and they held slightly less than 10 percent of the financial sector assets (CEI 1999). Several years ago there were as many as 700, but recently there were moves to separate them from specialized banks, which has reduced the total considerably. Announcements made in December 1998, through the China Economic Information network, point toward the merger of the current 244 into 40 TICs. The move heralds changes in the "ways and means of overseas financing" (CEI 1999). However, it is likely that in the future, support offered by local government may decline as changes take place in local government powers and finance.

TICs are sponsored by local governments and are permitted to raise foreign capital and invest in long-term projects such as infrastructure, for instance, power stations, roads, bridges, telecommunications, and so forth. For example, recent projects announced include a continuous casting and rolling project in Shanghai—RMB1285 (US$155) million, financed from Germany; Jitong Golden Bridge project—RMB500 (US$60) million, funded out of Israel; Sichuan post and telecommunications project—RMB415 (US$50) million, financed from Spain; and the third phase of the Dezhou Power Plant project—RMB612 (US$74) million, funded from Germany (CEI 1999). In this role, TICs have become an important part of China's finance sector, offering financing and services not offered by the SOBs (Girardin 1997b).

A serious problem that TICs and ITICs face has been that, in the quest for quick returns, they have engaged in risk-taking ventures such as speculative investments in property and equities. In addition, over the years TICs have had poor supervision and have generally failed to operate on sound commercial terms; consequently, many have asset-quality and liquidity dilemmas. The situation was highlighted in October 1998 when the second largest, Guangdong International Trust and Investment Corporation, was forced into bankruptcy by the PBOC, with RMB 21.5 (US$ 2.6) billion in total assets and debts amounting to RMB 36.2 billion (US$4.4) billion. The Bank of China was instructed to take over its liabilities. Earlier in the year, one of the largest TICs, China Agribusiness Development Trust and Investment Corporation (CATIC) was placed under administration due to an incapacity to repay debts and mismanagement problems. It was originally formed to direct loans and aid to China's agricultural sector from the World Bank and other development agencies. In June 1998, the closure of China Venturetech Investment Corporation (CVIC) was also ordered (*Sichuan China Business* January 9, 1997; *Economist* 10 October 1998:80–84; *Wall Street Journal* 11 October 1998:A18; CEI 1999).

By insisting that the TICs close down, the government is demonstrating that it is unwilling to continue to guarantee the obligations of state borrowers in their risky investments. The moral hazard is that with the knowledge of continued backing, TICs would continue to make risky investment decisions. However, the closure does pose a dilemma as the signals are not only received by the TICs in China, but around the world, and China relies heavily on foreign finance. Though there is some initial pain, it is a move in the right direction.

The figures and tables presented (Figure 5.6 and Table 5.6), provide consolidated figures of "specific deposit institutions," which include trust and investment corporations and leasing companies, as well as the State Development Bank of China and the Export-Import Bank of China. Of particular note on the assets side is that domestic credit more than doubled from RMB240.3 (US$29.0) billion to RMB534.0 (US$64.5) billion from 1994 to 1996 and continued to grow strongly through to 1998 to a total of RMB726.1 (US$87.7) billion. Moreover, "other loans" quadrupled, whereas trust loans and designated loans weakened by around 1.5 percent in the year 1995–96.

On the liabilities side of Figure 5.6 and Table 5.6, deposits rose by 19

Figure 5.6 **Consolidated Balance Sheet of Specific Deposit Institutions***

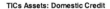

TICs Assets: Domestic Credit

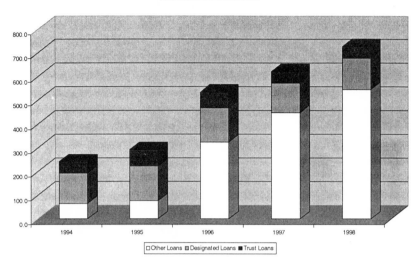

Liabilities: Trust and Investment Corporations

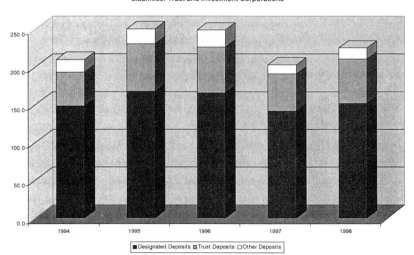

percent in the year 1994–95, but the trend reversed to record around a 20 percent decrease in 1996–97, but increased 11 percent in 1998. In particular, designated deposits declined by 8.5 percent, while trust deposits, which are surplus funds that are not directed to a particular project, were reduced by 2.3 percent from 1995 to 1998.

Table 5.6

Consolidated Balance Sheet of Specific Deposit Institutions
(unit: RMB 1 billion)

	1994	1995	1996	1997	1998
Foreign assets	0	0	−30.9	7.0	4.4
Reserve assets	16.9	16.6	17.5	18.2	10.8
Domestic credit	240.3	290.1	534.0	620.2	726.1
Claims on central government	1.8	1.6	1.9	2.4	1.7
Claims on deposit money					
banks	21.2	17.9	23.7	33.4	38.6
Total	280.0	326.0	546.0	681.0	782.0
Liabilities to non-financial					
sectors	209.6	249.9	248.2	202.5	224.7
Bonds	1.7	1.9	1.2	325.5	406.4
Liabilities to the central bank	2.8	2.4	2.3	3.6	3.4
Liabilities to deposit money					
banks	31.7	34.4	30.6	20.3	19.7
Owner's equity	51.4	54.5	81.6	97.5	103.8
Paid-in capital	42.5	44.9	69.5	88.9	97.4
Foreign liabilities				63.0	58.9
Others (net)	−17.1	−16.9	182.3	−31.1	−35.3
Total	280.0	326.0	546.0	681.0	782.0

Source: CEI 1999; *Almanac of China's Finance and Banking.*
Note: The deposit institutions include financial trust and investment corporations and financial leasing companies, as well as the State Development Bank of China and the Export-Import Bank of China in 1996.

The growth of various TICs can be seen as an endeavor to evade the punitive taxation on the banking system. State banks have established many of the TICs. In September 1995, over 60 percent were associated with the specialized (commercial) banks and many of the rest were connected to local governments. They are a means of avoiding the regulatory framework. TICs afford opportune outlets for bank money to attract superior returns over that which regulated lending brings in.

Life Insurance

The insurance industry in China is in its initial development stages, but is emerging rapidly. The China Insurance Regulatory Commission was introduced in late 1998 to supervise the insurance sector. It has taken a stand against illegal operations and undertaken to improve the legal

Table 5.7

Premium Income of Domestic Companies (unit: RMB 1 billion)

Year	Property premium	Life premium	Annual premium
1994	34	16	50
1995	42	19	62
1996	45	31	76
1997	48	60	108

Source: CEI, 1999: China's Insurance Market.

framework of the industry. The supervision and regulation of the industry was previously undertaken by the PBOC.

For most of the last two decades it has been completely dominated by the monopolistic, state-owned, People's Insurance (Group) Company of China (PICC). Competitors are now beginning to make inroads into the market as it opens up. At the end of 1998, there were twenty-four insurers in total operating in China. This was made up of thirteen domestic insurance companies, nine foreign-funded insurers, and two joint venture firms. The number has now increased, as a few joint ventures and foreign-funded insurers have been or are in the process of being established; currently there are sixteen foreign insurers operating in China. At the end of 1997 there were close to 170,000 staff involved in the insurance industry and 8,745 insurance company offices (TEJ 2000).

Overall, insurance premium income more than doubled from 1994 to 1997 and increased by 40 percent in 1997 to RMB108 (US$13.5) billion for life and property casualty insurance (see Table 5.7). The assets totaled RMB164.6 (US$19.9) billion. The bulk of insurance business is conducted by three insurance companies, which lay claim to a combined premium income of 96.6 percent of the premium aggregate. The largest by far is still PICC, which has 71.1 percent of the market, based on premium income in 1997. Next is the Ping An Insurance Company of China at 14.2 percent, and the China Pacific Insurance Company Ltd., with 11.8 percent of the market.

Life insurance companies are of particular interest in the study of NBFIs, for as nonintermediating financial institutions they contribute to capital stock. Presently cooperatives and banks hold the bulk of household savings; but as financial development occurs, other institutions will evolve and they will conceivably take a share of the market, thus leading to a decline in the dominance of banks. In China, the life insurance sector has seen remarkable growth in the last few years. In just one year, 1997, the premium income increase was not far from doubling—it grew by 94 percent. Overall from 1994 to 1997, the premium income nearly quadrupled from RMB16 (US$1.9) billion to RMB60 (US$7.3) billion (see Table 5.7).

Authorities in China have begun the process of cautiously liberalizing the insurance market. The special economic zone of Shanghai was chosen as the experimental region to try out the impact of competition on the insurance industry. The local insurers were concerned that, with the added competition of the liberalized market and the entrance of foreign firms, they would lose a substantial slice of the insurance pie and associated earnings. As expected, domestic insurers lost significant market share to the new competitors. Nonetheless, their earnings have increased dramatically as the pie has expanded considerably. The PICC's premium income multiplied to RMB8.7 (US$1) billion in 1997, which represented an 800 percent increase in the six years from 1991 (*Reactions* 1998). Actually, the foreign competitors stimulated the market, because the increased competition brought superior products and service, and the market responded accordingly.

The above figures indicate that there is considerable market potential in relation to insurance density and insurance market penetration in China. In general, the higher the GDP, the greater the premium income. For instance, the growth rate of gross premiums written grew at an average annual rate of 32.2 percent during the years from 1987 to 1997. This exceeded the annual average growth of nominal GDP of 20.7 percent by 11.5 percent. In thirteen years (1981–1994) life and property casualty insurance premiums increased at a compound rate of 39 percent per annum, from RMB1.7 (US $0.2) billion to RMB49.7 (US $6) billion. If the premiums for life and property casualty insurance premiums were to rise at a compound rate of 30 percent, by 2003 they could total RMB526.5 (US$63.6) billion (*China Economic Review* 1998). The World Bank calculates that the approximate insurance premium income in the year 2000 will increase to RMB 200–250 (US$24.2–30.2) billion.

Life insurance premiums have experienced significant growth of 92 percent per annum from 1994 to 1997. Assuming the rate of growth drops to 50 percent of that, by 2003 life insurance premiums would stand at RMB683 (US$82.6) billion. At 75 percent growth, the market would be worth RMB1,723 (US$208.2) billion.

Notwithstanding the great prospects, there are many frustrations, including the slow and sometimes tedious path of reform. For example, a considerable frustration is that insurers in China are restricted to placing premiums in the fixed income market, in either fixed rate bank deposits or government bonds. The bond market of China is quite small, only 5 percent of the overall money supply. In addition, the market is illiquid, with very little trading and that occurs mainly between banks and insurance companies. These constraints tend to reduce profitability, as insurers need to set the returns for policyholders above prevailing interest rates to attract their custom. Because of the reliance on the fixed rate market and interest rate decreases during 1996 to 1997, returns were adversely effected. The industry was keen for restrictions to be lifted and opened up to include the stock market, mutual funds, and real estate (Hovey and Naughton 2000). In 1999 insurance companies finally received permission to invest some of their assets in the domestic stock markets. By the end of June, twenty insurance companies had invested RMB9.2 billion (US$1.1 billion), or 0.04 percent of China's total stock market value. However, authorities were disappointed that they invested less than allowed by current regulations. The CSRC is presently looking to a trial run of open securities funds for the insurance industry (ChinaBiz 2000).

Foreign insurers' operations are still severely restricted. Non–life insurance licenses currently allow insurers to write business related only to foreign-partnered joint ventures. Furthermore, they are allowed to sell policies only in SEZs, namely four cities—Shanghai, Beijing, Guangzhou, and Foshan. Pilot programs have been set up on a trial basis in Chongqing. Authorities have committed to open more cities after WTO entry and allow foreign insurers to sell most services within three years. Recently foreign enterprises have entered the market by buying equity in Chinese insurance firms. This is allowed on the condition that they provide advanced technology and management know-how as set out in transfer of technology agreements (Unsworth 2000).

As nonintermediary financial institutions, the development of life insurance offices is of specific interest to the study of NBFIs and the financial development of China. As financial development deepens, other institutions emerge reducing the dominance of banks. In the last few years, the life insurance industry has experienced outstanding expansion in China. Yet it is still in its infancy and is not open to full market competition.

The reform of SOEs will potentially be the catalyst to a privatization program of unmatched proportions. Entry into the WTO will no doubt be a driving force in the reform of SOEs as they prepare to meet the challenge of global competitive forces (Hovey 2000). A privatization program of this magnitude will require a deep capital market to offset the possibility of a liquidity squeeze. Within this context, as with other similar financial institutions, the growth of life insurance pooled savings will be an important source of capital to fund future privatization.

China's first insurance company to sell shares to foreign enterprises was the New China Life Insurance Co Ltd. In August 2000, it sold shares to firms that include the Zurich Insurance Company, the International Finance Corporation, and Japan-based Meiji Life Insurance Company. The insurance market in China potentially has considerable development opportunities that the foreign partners can expect to tap into (ChinaBiz 2000).

Pension Funds

Recent developments in China have resulted in the planned introduction of compulsory pension programs for at least part of the population. China has instituted a multi-tier social security pension system through the Unified Pension System Reform Law introduced in 1997. It is designed to establish funded pensions on a staged basis, commencing with the urban population. It includes established individual pension accounts for active workers in SOEs and a defined benefit pay-as-you-go and investment-based contribution portion (CEI 1999). The new system is expanding coverage to the urban workforce outside the state sector and protecting benefits against inflation. Both workers and employers are to contribute to it monthly (Li 2000).

This program will be managed by 800 municipalities, which have strict guidelines on investment strategies. For example, pension funds are restricted in investment choices as authorities in China consider it premature to allow pension funds to be invested in the securities market. The sustainability of the system will demand close attention to fund management regulations. It will also have to be mindful of the rapidly aging population in China (West 1999).

China is the only country in the East Asian region that does not offer any private sector pension coverage, or comparable forms of life insurance, in at least some sectors of the economy (Hovey and Naughton 2000). Foreign companies see the huge potential in the pension pool of China and are keen to enter the market.

However, a significant problem is that the pension funds cover neither workers hired before 1997 nor those who retired before that date. China will also need to expand coverage to rural wage earners. They all expect equal treatment, but the present system does not cover them. At least RMB1.8 trillion (about US$ 217 billion) is required to meet the shortfall (Xinhua News 2000). Furthermore, China may need to consider reducing benefits if it is to adequately manage the funds (West 1999). In addition, China is currently experiencing the longest period of deflation in recent history, a slower than expected growth in consumer spending, falling retail prices, and decreasing foreign direct investment and commitment to investment (Lawrence 2000; Leggett 2000). Furthermore, China's capacity to cope financially with the social burdens has been diminishing since the mid-1980s (Hu 2000).

As it moves toward entry into the WTO, there is no doubt that pension funds are seriously needed to ease the "cradle to grave" social obligations of SOEs to their workers and families, which has been a heavy burden for many enterprises (Hovey and Naughton 2000; Naughton and Hovey 1999). The authorities are wrestling to revitalize unproductive, unprofitable, debt-ridden SOEs. The social obligations will continue to be a heavy burden for SOEs until an all-encompassing pension plan is fully instituted.

Another aspect of the evolvement of pension funds is that as financial development intensifies, these other institutions emerge, reducing the dominance of banks. As they grow, pension funds will contribute significantly to financial development in that household savings lodged with them will play a primary role in financial deepening. In that case, the development of pension funds will provide a substantial source of capital in China as the various reforms progress.

China's Managed Funds

The professional fund and fund management industry in China is in its infancy, and private pension plans do not exist. Under current regulations domestic fund-management companies are presently required to invest 80 percent of their assets in stocks and 20 percent in treasury bonds. There are presently ten domestic fund-management firms in China. They manage thirty closed-end securities investment funds that have almost RMB80 (US$9.64) billion in domestic bonds and stocks (Saywell 2000b).

Investment choices are typically domestic bonds and publicly issued stocks. Funds must be closed-end funds, although open-ended fund are expected to be introduced by the end of 2000, and most fund companies are setting them up (Asiainfo 2000). In order to enrich the investment variety, the vision is to try to make open funds the mainstream of the fund market within five years. Certainly the introduction of professional funds and fund management in China, as well as unit trusts and mutual funds, has the potential of moderating the volatility of the markets. In China, the huge number of small investors who trade frequently, often with a "herd mentality," destabilize the market. Thus, professionally managed funds should be a greatly needed stabilizing factor. Encouraging stock market participation through funds typically reduces volatility. The added benefit is that these large funds have the potential to enhance economic development through their investments.

It is expected that China's fund management sector will grow very quickly. Currently, there are about 50 million investors in the stock market and it had a combined market capitalization of RMB4,650 (US$562) billion as of November 2000 (TEJ 2000). Combined, China's Shanghai and Shenzhen stock exchanges make up the third-largest stock markets in Asia, behind Japan and Hong Kong. As previously mentioned, China also has one of the world's highest savings rates. All in all, it projects all the signs of eventually having a very large fund-management market. At present however, there are no stock index futures, which would allow institutional investors to manage risks. If the sector is to flourish, financial instruments such as index derivatives should be introduced so that risks can be adequately hedged.

Foreign firms presently are not allowed to enter the fund-management market in China. However, many foreign firms are looking to enter the market as soon as it is opened. They will be able to take stakes of up to 33 percent in Chinese fund-management companies when China joins the WTO. It will then rise to 49 percent three years later (Saywell 2000b). Numerous foreign firms are courting Chinese companies in preparation for entry into the market.

The reform of SOEs will potentially be the catalyst to a privatization program of unmatched proportions. Entry into the WTO will no doubt be a driving force in the reform of SOEs as they prepare to meet the challenge of global competitive forces (Hovey 2000). A privatization program of this magnitude will require a deep capital market to offset the possibility of a liquidity squeeze. Within this context, financial development, and especially the development of responsible and professional funds and a well-established fund market, will be essential.

As financial development deepens, the emergence of other institutions will reduce the dominance of banks. In the last few years, the life insurance industry has experienced outstanding expansion in China. Yet it is still in its infancy and is not open to full market competition. As with other similar financial institutions, the growth of life insurance pooled savings will be an important source of capital to fund future privatization.

China's Investment Industry

There are over 150 investment companies in China. A quasi-governmental investment organization, the China National Investment Association (CNIA), includes sixty-three of these companies. Over the past decade, the investment companies have invested over RMB 400 (US$48.3) billion in China's economic construction. Recently the primary focus of most companies has been the infrastructure and high-technology industries. These involve sizable investments and considerable risk.

In recent years, as with many financial institutions, the industry has been restructured to improve performance. In the process, around 300 small state-owned firms have been transferred, merged, leased, or declared bankrupt. The CNIA has aided in recirculating stock assets to the tune of RMB 5 (US$0.6) billion. This also heralds a shift of investment focus from the power industry to the previously mentioned infrastructure and high-tech industries (CEI 1999).

Finance Companies

There were sixty-nine finance companies in China at the end of 1996. The aggregate of the finance companies' assets in 1998, as shown in Table 5.8, was RMB110.9 (US$13.4) billion, which is a fourfold increase from RMB27.6 (US$3.3) billion in 1994. Lending also increased

Table 5.8

Consolidated Balance Sheet of Finance Companies (unit: RMB 1 billion)

	1994	1995	1996	1997	1998
Foreign assets	0	0	0	0	0
Reserve assets	1.4	4.5	6.9	10.43	8.38
Claims on central					
government	0.1	0.4	3	4.95	5.71
Claims on other sectors	24.5	40.6	66.9	83.38	95.35
Claims on nonmonetary					
financial institutions	1.6	3.4	5.2	1.66	1.47
Total	27.6	48.9	82.0	100.4	110.9
Liabilities to					
nonfinancial sectors	18.3	45.1	81.8	103.71	123.8
Liabilities to the central bank	0.7	0.5	0.7	0.4	0.36
Liabilities to nonmonetary					
financial institutions	3.8	5.4	9	3.48	1.97
Bonds	0	0.01	0.03	0.1	0.06
Owner's equity	5	6.7	9.8	16.15	16.26
Others (net)	−0.03	−8.8	−19.4	−28.08	−2.47
Total	8.9	81.9	95.8	110.0	

Source: CEI 1999; *Almanac of China's Finance and Banking.*
Note: There are some discrepancies in the figures gathered—in particular, the 1997 figures do not balance.

dramatically, nearly quadrupling during the same period from RMB 24.5 (US$3.0) billion to RMB95.4 (US$11.5) billion.

Finance companies tend to be established by commercial conglomerates or "groups." Thus, most are affiliates of sizable industrial groups and control at least a quarter of the fixed assets of SOEs. As in most countries, they take deposits only from firms that are affiliated—they do not hold banking licenses. They are also extremely restricted in their operations, as they do not have branches.

Summary and Conclusions

Financial reforms began in 1979 in China, but have been gradual and unhurried. Up to this time, China has been in the early stages of financial deepening—positive real interest rates have helped achieve this. However, the financial sector is still bank-dominated and subject to heavy state regulation. The ensuing credit allocation has not been adequately effective in channeling the surplus units from savers to borrowers. Nonetheless, some economic decisions have been delegated to the microeconomic level, which has served to bolster the development of financial intermediaries, in particular NBFIs. In a bid to finance growth in the non-state financial sector and the economy as a whole, the development of various types of NBFIs has been encouraged, particularly since the mid-1980s. They have expanded quickly and have gained an ever-increasing share of the financial asset pie. Numerous high-quality institutions have spawned, yet, unfortunately, among the successes, many poor-quality institutions emerged and major failures occurred.

As demonstrated in this chapter, an indispensable part of the financial development process in China has been the advancement and expansion of NBFIs. This niche is primarily filled by the cooperative-type intermediaries, which have expanded rapidly, particularly as the rural residents enjoy greater direct economic participation. Though NBFIs are vulnerable to many hazards, they play an important social role and provide significant economic input—by making major contributions to savings, which in turn is utilized by the formal financial sector.

As well-functioning NBFIs perform an important role in the development of China, balanced policies are required—on the one hand to screen poorly managed institutions and, on the other, to provide sufficient freedom for innovative management. The objective is that well-run organizations can exercise their competitive advantage and in so doing maximize returns, with minimal risk to depositors. NBFIs provide additional competition to the formal financial system. To this end, the development of the nonbank financial sector has been only marginally successful and requires greater impetus. However, the very restrained and restricted role allowed to foreign financial institutions has reduced the opportunities for innovation that they would cultivate.

Recent pressures faced in the financial sector and the subsequent reforms have highlighted a series of social and economic concerns that China has no option but to tackle if the potential expansion is to be managed equitably and efficiently. Taking all this into account, China must extend assiduous consideration and extensive resources to the guidance, regulation, and supervision of NBFIs to maximize their benefit to the community and to foster the sector as a sound element of the financial system. This is particularly important as China opens its market and as it moves toward WTO accession in the too distant future.

Notes

1. China's GDP has almost doubled since 1989, whereas Russia's has nearly halved. Nevertheless, Poland, the Czech Republic, and Hungary initiated decisive reforms and have experienced much better outcomes (Kenny and Williams 2001).

2. Interestingly, the allocative role played by stock markets is limited throughout the various stages of development (*Development Report* 1998).

3. Taken as RMB1 = US$0.1208.

4. The banks are only just starting to offer loans to these clients and households (Saywell 2000a).

5. Taken as RMB1 = US$0.1208.

6. Taken as RMB1 = US$0.1208.

References

Almanac of China's Finance and Banking (Zhongguo Jinrong Nianjian). Various issues. (Annual ed.). Beijing: Zhongguo Jinrong.

Arestis, P., and P. Demetriades. 1999. "Financial Liberalization: The Experience of Developing Countries." *Eastern Economic Journal* 25, no. 4: 441–457.

Arnott, R., and J. Stiglitz. 1990. "Moral Hazard and Nonmarket Institutions: Dysfunctional Crowding Out or Peer Monitoring." *American Economic Review* 81, no. 1.

Asiainfo. October 24, 2000. "New Fund Ordinance Unveiled." *Asiainfo Daily China News*.

Bai, C., D. Li, Y. Qian, and Y. Wang. 1999. "Anonymous Banking and Financial Repression: How Does China's Reform Limit the Government Predation without Reducing Its Revenue?" Paper presented at the 4th Annual International Conference on Transition Economics, Beijing (July).

Benziger, V. 1998. "Can China's Gradualist Reform Strategy Be Applied in Eastern Europe?" *Journal of Asia Pacific Economy* 3, no. 1.

Besley, T. 1995. "Nonmarket Institutions for Credit and Risk Sharing in Low-Income Countries." *Journal of Economic Perspectives* 9, no. 3 (summer).

Binswanger, H. 1986. "Risk Aversion, Collateral Requirements, and the Markets for Credit and Insurance in Rural Areas." In P. Hazell, C. Pomerada, and A. Valdes (eds.), *Crop Insurance for Agricultural Development*. Baltimore: Johns Hopkins University Press.

Braverman, A., and J. L. Guasch. 1986. "Rural Credit Markets and Institutions in Developing Countries: Lessons for Policy Analysis from Practice and Modern Theory." *World Development* 14: 1253–1267.

Byrd, W. 1983. "Enterprise-Level Reforms in Chinese State-Owned Industry." *American Economic Review* 73, no. 2: 329–332.

Caprio, G. 1995. "The Role of Financial Intermediaries in Transitional Economies." *Carnegie-Rochester Conference Series on Public Policy* 42: 257–302.

ChinaBiz. 2000. "Insurers Wait for Further Opening up Securities Market." (www.ChinaBiz.org); October 8, 2000.

CEI (China Economic Information). 1999. "China Economy Home" (various Web pages). China State Information Center. (Home Index: http://www.cei.gov.cn/sicnet/siccew/index.htm); July 1999.

China Economic Review. 1998. "Life under a New Body: Chinese Insurance Industry under the Insurance Regulatory Commission." *China Economic Review* (December): 25.

Demirguc, K.A., and E. Detragiache. 1998. "Financial Liberalization and Financial Fragility." International Monetary Fund Working Paper. Washington, DC: World Bank, IMF.

Diaz-Alejandro, C. 1985. "Goodbye Financial Repression. Hello Financial Crash." *Journal of Development Economics* 19, no. 1 (February): 1–24.

Drake, P. J. 1980. *Money, Finance and Development*. London: Wiley.

Economist. (Various issues): The Economist Newspaper Ltd.

Fry, M. J. 1988. *Interest and Banking in Economic Development*. Baltimore: Johns Hopkins University Press.

———. 1995. *Money, Interest, and Banking in Economic Development* (2d ed.). Studies in Development. Baltimore and London: Johns Hopkins University Press.

Fung, M.K.Y., W.M. Ho, and L.J. Zhu. 2000. "The Impact of Credit Control and Interest Rate Regulation on the Transforming Chinese Economy: An Analysis of Long-Run Effects." *Journal of Comparative Economics* 28, no. 2: 293–320.

Girardin, E. 1997a. *The Dilemmas of Banking Sector Reform and Credit Control in China*. Paris: Development Centre, Organisation for Economic Co-operation and Development.

———. 1997b. *Banking Sector Reform and Credit Control in China*. Paris: Development Centre, Organisation for Economic Co-operation and Development.

Girardin, E., and S. Bazen. 1998. "An Empirical Study of Urban Credit Cooperatives in China." *International Review of Applied Economics* 12, no. 1: 141–155.

Girardin, E., and X. Ping. 1997. *Urban Credit Co-Operatives in China*. Paris: Organisation for Economic Co-operation and Development.

Goldsmith, R.W. 1969. *Finance Structure and Development*. New Haven: Yale University Press.

Greenwood, J., and B. Jovanovic. 1990. "Financial Development, Growth, and the Distribution of Income." *Journal of Political Economy* 98, no. 5: 1076–1107.

Gupta, K. L. 1984. *Finance and Economic Growth in Developing Countries*. London: Croom-Helm.

Henning, C.H.C.A., and X. Lu. 2000. "The Political Foundation of Chinese Style Gradualism: A Paradox of Too Strong Private Interests?" *Journal of Institutional and Theoretical Economics* 156, no. 1: 35–59.

Hovey, M. 2000. *Alternative Corporate Governance Models as They Prevail in China and Are Applicable to China*. Gold Coast, Queensland, Australia: Griffith University.

Hovey, M., and T. Naughton. 2000. "Financial Market Reform." In C. Harvie (ed.), *Contemporary Developments and Issues in China's Economic Transition*. London: Macmillan/St.Martin's Press, 101–136.

Hu, X. 2000. "The State, Enterprises, and Society in Post-Deng China: Impact of the New Round of SOE Reform." *Asian Survey* 40, no. 4: 641–657.

Kapur, B. K. 1976. "Alternative Stabilization Policies for Less-Developed Economies." *Journal of Political Economy* 84, no. 4: 777–795.

Kennedy, S. 1995. "Beijing Sheds Some Weight." *Banker* 145: 829.

Kenny, C., and D. Williams. 2001. "What Do We Know About Economic Growth? Or, Why Don't We Know Very Much?" *World Development* (January 2001) 29, no. 1: 1–22.

Kumar, A., N. Lardy, W. Albrecht, T. Chuppe, S. Selwyn, P. Perttunen, and T. Zhang. 1997. *China's Non-Bank Financial Institutions: Trust and Investment Companies*. Washington, DC: World Bank.

Lai, C.C. 1988. "European Cooperativism in Chinese Perspective." *Annals of Public and Co-operative Economy* 59, no. 3: 369–377.

Lake, D., C. Ming, and J. Cossette. 1994. "Profile: State Development Bank." *Euroweek* 381.

Lardy, N.R. 1998. "China and the Asian Contagion." *Foreign Affairs* (July/August): 78–88.

Lawrence, S.V. 2000. "Little New Year Cheer." *Far Eastern Economic Review* 163 (2): 73.

Leggett, K. 2000. "Under Pressure, China Blesses Private Sector." *Wall Street Journal*, March 13.

Li, H. 2000. "Economic Efficiency and Social Insurance Reforms in China." *Contemporary Economic Policy* 18, no. 2: 194–204.

Li, K.W. 1992. "Savings, Foreign Resources and Monetary Aggregates in China 1954–1989." *China Economic Review* 3, no. 2: 125–133.

———. 1994. *Financial Repression and Economic Reform in China*. Westport, CT: Praeger.

Ling, Z., J. Zhongyi, and J. von Braun. 1997. *Credit Systems for the Rural Poor in China*. New York: Nova Science Publishers.

Mathieson, D.J. 1980. "Financial Reform and Stabilization Policy in a Developing Economy." *Journal of Development Economics* 7, no. 3: 359–395.

McKinnon, R.I. 1973. *Money and Capital in Economic Development*. Washington, DC: Brookings Institute.

Mehran, H., M. Quintyn, T. Nordman, and B. Laurens. 1996. *Monetary and Exchange Reforms in China: An Experiment in Gradualism*. Washington, DC: International Monetary Fund.

Morrison, W.M. 1999. "China's Economic Conditions." *Congressional Research Service Issue Brief for Congress*: 98014.

Naughton, B. 1998. "China's Financial Reform : Achievements and Challenges." Paper presented at Berkeley Roundtable on the International Economy, University of California, Berkeley.

Naughton, T., and M. Hovey. 1999. "Non-Bank Financial Institutions." In East Asia Analytical Unit (ed.), *Asia's Financial Markets: Capitalising on Reform*. Canberra: EAAU, Department of Foreign Affairs and Trade, 139–157.

Park, A., L. Brandt, and J. Giles. 1997. "Giving Credit Where Credit Is Due: The Changing Role of Rural Financial Institutions in China." Paper presented at the annual meeting of the Association for Asian Studies.

Park, A., and C. Ren. 2001. "Microfinance with Chinese Characteristics." *World Development*, (January 2001) 29, no. 1: 39–62.

Reactions. 1998. "Cautious Giants." *Reactions* 18: 31.

Roubini, N., and X. Sala-i-Martin. 1992. "Financial Repression and Economic Growth." *Journal of Development Economics* 39, no. 1: 5–30.

Saywell, T. 2000a. "Mrs. Wang Gets a Taste for Credit." *Far Eastern Economic Review* 163: 56–58.

———. 2000b. "The Rush Is On." *Far Eastern Economic Review* 163: 71–72.

Shaw, E.S. 1973. *Financial Deepening in Economic Development.* New York: Oxford University Press.

Sichuan China Business. (Various issues). Dow Jones and Company Inc.

Stiglitz, J.E. 1990. "Peer Monitoring and Credit Markets." *World Bank Economic Review* 4, no. 3.

———. 2000. "Capital Market Liberalization, Economic Growth, and Instability." *World Development* 28, no. 6: 1075–1086.

Tam, O.K. 1986. "Reform of China's Banking System." *World Economy* 9, no. 4: 427–440.

TEJ (*Taiwan Economic Journal*). 2000. "Greater China Database." *Taiwan Economic Journal,* November.

Tobin, J. 1969. "A General Equilibrium Approach to Monetary Theory." *Journal of Money Credit and Banking* 7, no. 1: 15–29.

———. 1978. "Monetary Policies and the Economy: The Transmission Mechanism." *Southern Economic Journal* 44, no. 3: 421–431.

Trescott, P.B. 1993. "John Bernard Tayler and the Development of Cooperatives in China, 1917–1945." *Annals of Public and Cooperative Economics* 64, no. 2: 209–226.

Unsworth, B.E. 2000. "China's Push to Join WTO Opening Market." *Business Insurance* 34: 21.

Wall Street Journal. (Various issues).

West, L.A. 1999. "Pension Reform in China: Preparing for the Future." *Journal of Development Studies* 35, no. 3: 153–183.

World Development Report. (Various issues). Oxford and New York: Oxford University Press.

World Economic Outlook. (Various issues). Washington, DC: International Monetary Fund.

Xinhua News. 2000. "China to Liquidate State Assets for Pension Funds." April 17, Xinhua News Agency.

Part II

Recent Developments in Stock Markets

6

The A- and B-Share Chinese Equity Market: Segmentation or Integration

Wai Kin Leung and Hung-Gay Fung

1. Introduction

Between the open-door policy of economic reforms in 1978 and the Asian financial crisis, China experienced a remarkable annual economic growth of up to 8 percent per year. The Chinese stock market has attracted extensive research interest in recent years for two reasons. First, more and more Chinese companies have listed on stock exchanges to raise capital for financing their growth (Mok and Hui 1998; Su and Fleisher 1999). Stock market capitalization was about 22 percent of GDP in 1997 and 26 percent in 1998 (Fung and Leung 2001), and market capitalization as of April 2000 was more than 4 percent of the 1999 GDP (see Table 6.1). Such tremendous growth in the Chinese equity market is impressive; its stock market has achieved a size comparable to that of some industrialized countries.

Second, Chinese companies, after satisfying certain requirements, can issue two types of shares, A and B: A shares are issued for domestic residents and B shares for foreign investors. A share prices are, in general, higher than B share prices of the same company, although in most countries domestic shares are sold at a discount to foreign shares (Bailey 1994; Bailey and Jagtiani 1994; Domowitz, Glen, and Madhavan 1997). Market segmentation and market liquidity are possible explanations for the price differential between the A and B shares (Wo 1997; Poon, Firth, and Fung 1998; Fernald and Rogers 1998; Chui and Kwok 1998; Bailey, Chung, and Kang 1999). A recent study by Fung, Lee, and

Table 6.1

General Chinese Stock Market Summary for Two Exchanges

	Shanghai		Shenzhen	
	1994/5	2000/4	1994/5	2000/4
Composite index	556.257	1,836.321	1,299.386	4,683.17
Number of listed companies	164	494	105	477
A-share market capitalization (billion in RMB)	215.1	2009.5	94.38	1730.5
B-share market capitalization (US$ for Shanghai and HK$ for Shenzhen in billions)*	1.26	1.95	6.3	16.32
Stock market capitalization/GDP	4.83%	24.35%	2.17%	21.01%

*The exchange rate for RMB/US$ was 8.6597 and 8.2799 in 1994 and 2000, respectively; the exchange rate of HK$/US$ about 7.8. Source of composite index is *Taiwan Economic Journal.* 1994 GDP is from http://www.stats.gov.cn/yearbook/indexC.htm. 1999 GDP is estimated from http://cninfo.com.cn/tjfx/scztzb.htm.

Leung (2000) demonstrates that the return-generating process for the A- and B-share markets appears to be different, confirming the market segmentation hypothesis.

Although there is strong evidence indicating the segmentation of A and B shares in China, there are also forces that can potentially mitigate the market segmentation. In the process of Chinese financial liberalization, many policies have been implemented to improve the liquidity and transparency of its stock markets. The policies include the recent establishment of security laws (enacted in July 1997) and enforcement of accounting regulations governing the availability of company information to investors. Accounting regulations have undergone several phases of change in establishing a more objective procedure for companies to follow. Investors have also become familiar with the workings of the Chinese stock market in a market-oriented economy.

As a result, it is conceivable that the A- and B-share markets will tend to move closer together over time as regulations continue to make the stock market more transparent and as investors look more and more at a similar information set in evaluating Chinese companies.

There have also been rumors and speculation that the two markets will merge. To a great extent, it is investors' expectations of a merger that have helped move prices of the two markets closer in recent years.

Another reason the A- and B-share markets have moved closer together actually has to do with Chinese citizen investment. Although

Chinese citizens cannot invest in B shares, which are denominated either in U.S. dollars for Shanghai B shares or in Hong Kong dollars for Shenzhen B shares, many Chinese citizens have been able to invest in B shares by setting up nominal brokerage accounts in Hong Kong. The number and size of these accounts are believed to be large.

It is also possible that Chinese companies in Hong Kong and other offshore markets that can trade B shares have a role in mitigating the price differentials between the A- and B-share markets. Chinese companies following a government policy that intends to mitigate the gap between the two markets have the resources to achieve that objective. Such interventions by Chinese companies are not easily noticeable.

It is conceivable that Chinese companies holding A shares could set up offshore subsidiaries selling equity derivatives (financial assets derived from underlying assets), such as puts and calls to foreign investors. Foreign investors could thus affect the market value of A shares through trading in these over-the-counter derivatives. The extent of offshore, over-the-counter equity derivatives trading is believed to be minimal because there are considerable default risks involved in these transactions, given the restricted free flow of capital in the Chinese balance of payments account.

Foreign insurance companies can do business in China in two ways. They can join with Chinese insurance companies in joint ventures or form a wholly owned insurance company. Joint-venture insurance companies or foreign-owned insurers can invest in the Chinese A-share stock market in amounts up to 10 percent of their assets; traditionally these amounts were up to 5 percent. While insurance companies are conservative and not necessarily ready to engage fully in stock market investment, the fact that they are entitled to invest may to some extent in the future mitigate the difference between A and B shares in general.

Our focus is the segmentation or integration of the A- and B-share Chinese stock markets over time. Using a microstructure approach that relates the volatility of a security to its bid–ask spread and trading volume for the A- and B-share markets, we first compare these relationships in the two markets and then test the difference in these relationships across the two markets to shed light on whether the two markets are moving closer together.

In the finance literature, it is well established that market frictions may potentially increase price volatility. Kyle (1985) suggests that market depth changes with trading activity and is related to market frictions or liquidity. Using the bid–ask spread to proxy for market frictions such as transaction costs or information asymmetry, we examine whether price volatility is positively related to the bid–ask spread. A study by Fung, Hwang, and Leung (1998) has indicated a positive relationship of volatility with the bid–ask spread and volume in the Hong Kong stock market.

The relationship between return volatility and volume is the subject of extensive examination (see, for example, Lamoureux and Lastrapes 1990; Jones, Kaul, and Lipson 1994; Andersen 1996). The positive relationship between volatility and volume can be broadly explained by two hypotheses. The first one relates to the idea that trading volume can be regarded as a conduit for information, which affects the movement of stock prices (Grundy and McNichols 1990; Campbell, Grossman, and Wang 1993). The other relates to the mixture of distribution hypothesis (MDH), which suggests that price changes are drawn from a mixture of normal distributions. The MDH postulates that price changes and volume are jointly distributed so that the change in volume is positively related to volatility (see, for example, Tauchen and Pitts 1983; Andersen 1996).

An interesting element of our study is that it focuses on the relationship of volatility with the bid–ask spread and volume during trading days. We thereby avoid the compounding effect of offshore information released during the nontrading hours of the Chinese stock market that can affect these relationships. Also, because B shares are issued to foreign investors, it is conceivable that their prices may be affected by foreign information. Our response is to compute the volatility measure based on the open-close prices to be compatible with the bid–ask prices and volume information released during trading hours of the stock market.

The rest of the paper is organized as follows. Section 2 briefly describes the methodology and data. Section 3 discusses and explains the empirical results. We extend the empirical analysis for robustness. The final section contains the conclusion.

2. Methodology and Data

2.1 Methodology

We compute daily return volatility using a procedure following Schwert (1990) and Bessembinder and Seguin (1992). We estimate the return volatility measure using an iterating procedure between a pair of equations as follows:

$$R_{i,t} = a + \sum_{j=1,4} \alpha_{i}, {}_i d_{t-j} + \sum_{j=1,n} \beta_{i,j} R_{i,t-j} + \sum_{j=1,n} \beta_{i,j} \sigma_{i,t-j} + U_{i,t} \quad (1a)$$

$$\sigma_{i,t} = b + \sum_{j=1,4} \rho_{i,j} dum_{i,t-j} + \sum_{j=1,n} \tau_j \sigma_{i,t-j} + \sum_{j=1,n} \delta_j U_{i,t-j} + e_{i,t} \quad (1b)$$

where $R_{i,t}$ is the daily return based on open-close price quotes at time t for the security i of a company listed on both the A- and B-share market. $s_t = |U_t| \, (\sqrt{\pi}/2)$ is the estimated conditional standard deviation on time t, U_t is the residual from equation (1a), and four day-of-the-week dummy variables (dum) represent Monday, Tuesday, Wednesday, and Thursday.

In the second pass, we examine the relationship of volatility with volume (Vol) and the bid-ask spread (BA). The equation for these three variables is specified as follows:

$$\sigma_{i,t} = s_{i,0} + s_{i,1} Vol_{i,t} + s_{i,2} BA_{i,t} + \sum_{j=1,4} \rho_{i,j} dum_{i,t-j} +$$
$$\sum_{j=1,n} \tau_{i,j} \sigma_{i,t-j} + \sum_{j=1,n} \delta_{i,j} U_{i,t-j} + \varepsilon_{i,t} \quad (2)$$

for i = 1, . . ., n securities in both A-and B-share markets.

Our focus in this regression is on the behavior of the coefficients of volume and the bid–ask spread over time for A shares and B shares of the same company. If A- and B-share markets do move closer together, we expect that the difference in the s_1 (volume coefficient) for the A- and B-share market will tend to be smaller over time. Similarly, the difference of s_2 (the bid–ask spread coefficient) between the A-share and B-share market will be expected to be zero if the A- and B-share markets become more and more integrated.

2.2. Procedure for Comparing A- and B-Share Markets

After obtaining the coefficients from estimating equation (2), we save the results for each firm for the respective A- and B-share market. Given that firm has two sets of results, each firm is compared individually. For example, for any security i (i = 1, . . . , n) in both the A-share and B-share markets, we have a pair of estimated parameters for the Vol in equation (2) as $\{(s^A_{1,1}, s^B_{1,1}) , . . . , (s^A_{n,1}, s^B_{n,1})\}$. Other parameters are obtained in the same fashion.

After all parameters are stored, the difference in the coefficients of the volume variable for the security i (i.e., $d_i = s^A_{i,1} - s^B_{i,1}$) is computed. The null hypothesis is that the difference in the pair coefficients (d_i) of the same company is, on average, equal to zero for all securities in the A- and B-share market. Similarly, we can test for other parameters such as the bid-ask spread.

2.3 Data and Measurement of Variables

Daily data for the listed Chinese companies on exchanges are obtained from the *Taiwan Economic Journal* data base. Our sample includes Chinese companies that issue both A and B shares. Companies that issue A shares only or B shares only are excluded. The sample data in this study cover the May 1994 through December 2000 period. Our analysis requires companies with bid–ask prices, open–close prices, and volume data. Companies with significant missing observations are dropped from the analysis.

We form a stationary time series of trading volume by incorporating the procedure in Campbell, Grossman, and Wang (1993), which uses a twenty–day backward moving average:

$$Vol_t = \frac{VT_t}{(1/20)\sum_{i=1}^{20} VT_{t-i}} \tag{3}$$

where VT is the trading volume at time t. The volume metric produces a stable time series that captures the change in trading volumes after adjusting for the past trending effect.

For the return computations, we use the open–close prices to derive the return time-series. The return series based on the open-close prices is intended to capture the information flows related to the trading volume and the bid–ask spread during the day.

Table 6.1 displays the general stock market information. The market value of the A- and B-share companies grew over the 1994–2000 period. The market composite index more than doubled its value during the six years. In Shenzhen, there were about 27 million stock account holders as of September 8, 2000. It seems likely that such a level of active trading in the stock market forced the A- and B-share markets to reduce their differences over time.

3. Empirical Analysis

3.1 Results

Table 6.2 displays a year-by-year comparison between the A- and B-share markets. The results for the bid–ask spread variable indicate that coefficients for 1994 and 1997 are significant at the 5 percent level. From 1998 onward, the difference in bid–ask spreads between the two markets is not significant. These results imply that the two markets have become more integrated.

The difference in the volume coefficient between A and B shares is significant at 5 percent in four of the earlier years (1994, 1995, 1997, and 1998). For the two most recent years (1999 and 2000), the volume variable is not significant. This result is consistent with results for the bid–ask variable, implying that the A- and B-share markets are becoming more integrated.

The lagged volatility and day-of-the-week dummy variables and lagged residual errors appear also to be generally less significant in recent periods, a result confirming integration.

3.2 Extension of Results

Results for lags other than five days are similar to those reported here. We also use thirty- and forty-day detrended volume besides the past twenty-day average. The results are similar to the twenty-day average, and they are not reported here.

An implied volatility measure is a procedure widely used in the literature, but we investigate other measures of volatility as well. Table 6.3 reports the results of the analysis using squared return based on the open-close quotes as a proxy for volatility. The model specification is similar in spirit to equation (2). The independent variables include the bid-ask spread, volume, five lags of volatility, and day-of-the-week dummy variables.

The results for the bid–ask spread and volume using the squared returns are similar to those using the implied volatility in equation (2). Again it appears that the significance of the difference in parameters is diminished in later as compared to earlier periods. The results basically confirm the notion that the Chinese A- and B-share markets are coming closer together. Other parameters such as lagged volatility and day-of-

Table 6.2

Differences in Coefficients For A and B Shares—The Implied Volatility as Dependent Variable

$$\sigma_{i,t} = s_{i,0} + s_{i,1}BA_t + s_{i,2}\,Vol_{i,t} + \sum_{j=1,n}\tau_{i,j}\sigma_{i,t-j} + \sum_{j=1,n}\delta_{i,j}U_{i,t-j} + \sum_{j=1,4}\rho_{i,j}dum_{i,t-j} + \in_{i,t}$$

where σ is the implied volatility at time t, BA is the bid-ask spread, Vol is the volume, d is the day-of-the-week dummy, and U_t is the residual error from the first pass regression. $\in_t$ is the random error time.

Coefficient	1994	1995	1996	1997	1998	1999	2000
Intercept	-0.0054 (-1.27)	0.0011 (0.56)	-0.0031 (-1.18)	-0.0035 (-2.90)*	-0.0061 (-2.85)*	-0.0111 (-5.44)*	0.0314 (0.99)
BA	1.1009 (3.87)*	0.3348 (2.13)*	0.1125 (0.57)	0.4842 (4.97)*	-0.0472 (-0.47)	-0.0766 (-0.85)	0.1094 (0.34)
Vol	0.0060 (5.40)*	0.0033 (3.31)*	0.0018 (1.76)	0.0040 (7.24)*	0.0017 (3.59)*	0.0013 (1.90)	0.0005 (0.33)
σ_{t-1}	0.0585 (1.19)	-0.0385 (-0.88)	-0.1497 (-5.31)*	0.0251 (1.44)	-0.0712 (-4.11)*	-0.0484 (-2.60)*	-0.2061 (-1.22)
σ_{t-2}	0.0934 (1.90)	0.0583 (1.65)	0.0459 (1.74)	-0.0477 (-2.73)*	0.0203 (1.07)	0.0041 (0.25)	-0.1935 (-0.98)
σ_{t-3}	-0.0888 (-1.26)	0.0030 (0.10)	0.02257 (0.98)	0.0140 (0.94)	0.0391 (2.30)*	0.0325 (1.87)	0.0141 (0.48)
σ_{t-4}	0.1111 (2.86)*	-0.0263 (-0.82)	-0.0700 (-2.11)*	0.0328 (2.55)*	-0.0086 (-0.49)	0.0240 (1.64)	0.0119 (0.44)
σ_{t-5}	0.1020 (2.30)*	0.0822 (1.86)	0.0165 (0.55)	0.0356 (3.13)*	0.0266 (1.59)	0.0180 (0.99)	-0.0122 (-0.33)

U_{t-1}	-0.2080 (-6.16)*	-0.0210 (-0.70)	-0.0584 (-2.01)*	-0.0984 (-6.55)*	-0.1017 (-7.26)*	-0.0181 (-1.30)	-0.526 (-0.72)
U_{t-2}	0.0554 (1.50)	0.0351 (0.91)	0.0498 (2.31)*	-0.0067 (-0.47)	-0.0335 (-1.80)	0.0005 (0.04)	0.0130 (0.63)
U_{t-3}	0.0735 (1.11)	-0.0298 (-0.92)	0.0057 (0.29)	-0.0028 (-0.25)	-0.0081 (-0.55)	-0.0081 (-0.64)	0.0887 (1.08)
U_{t-4}	0.0533 (1.60)	-0.0246 (-0.78)	-0.0345 (-1.15)	-0.0190 (-1.65)	-0.0220 (-1.56)	0.0043 (0.31)	0.0370 (0.52)
U_{t-5}	-0.0894 (-3.00)*	-0.0150 (-0.58)	-0.0836 (-4.10)*	0.0212 (1.81)	0.0180 (1.19)	-0.0247 (-2.04)*	-0.0714 (-0.83)
DumMON	-0.0025 (-0.80)	0.0025 (1.10)	0.0016 (0.38)	0.0007 (0.68)	0.0064 (4.72)*	0.0020 (1.44)	-0.0099 (-0.95)
DumTUE	-0.0063 (-2.13)*	-0.0009 (-0.33)	0.0122 (3.29)*	0.0009 (0.90)	0.0019 (1.31)	-0.0007 (-0.52)	-0.0150 (-1.07)
DumWED	0.0106 (4.57)*	0.0013 (0.63)	0.0114 (3.09)*	-0.0018 (-1.62)	0.0033 (2.31)*	0.0025 (1.93)	-0.0068 (-0.94)
DumTHU	0.0068 (2.55)*	-0.0025 (-0.91)	0.0085 (2.31)*	-0.0039 (-3.31)*	0.0010 (0.56)	0.0014 (1.25)	-0.0166 (-1.34)
No. of Firms	17	18	48	71	66	74	76

T-test is the test for the difference in the coefficients between the A- and B-share markets.
* Significant at the 5% level.

Table 6.3

Differences in Coefficients for A and B Shares—Return Squared as Dependent Variable

$$R^2_{i,t} = s_{i,0} + s_{i,1}BA_t + s_{i,2}Vol_{i,t} + \sum_{j=1,n}\tau_{ij}R^2_{i,t-j} + \sum_{j=1,4}\rho_{ij}dum_{i,t-j} + \in_{i,t}$$

where R^2_t is the squared return at time t, a proxy for volatility, BA is the bid-ask spread, Vol is the volume, d is the day-of-the-week dummy, and $\in_t$ is the random error term.

Coefficient	1994	1995	1996	1997	1998	1999	2000
Intercept	-0.0010 (-1.51)	0.0002 (0.85)	-0.0020 (-1.45)	0.0000 (0.51)	-0.0002 (-1.49)	-0.0006 (-4.11)*	-0.0001 (-1.03)
BA	0.2282 (3.61)*	0.0280 (1.67)	0.0331 (0.93)	0.0267 (3.63)*	-0.0129 (-2.12)*	-0.0012 (-0.21)	0.0059 (0.33)
Vol	0.0013 (4.92)*	0.0004 (4.67)*	0.0003 (2.11)*	0.0002 (4.35)*	0.0001 (1.41)	0.0001 (2.38)*	0.0001 (1.34)
R^2_{t-1}	-0.1082 (-1.95)	-0.1213 (-2.30)*	-0.1589 (-3.94)*	0.0244 (1.49)	-0.0828 (-4.78)*	-0.0273 (-1.59)	-0.0047 (-0.19)
R^2_{t-2}	0.1399 (2.85)*	0.0350 (0.93)	0.0824 (3.36)*	-0.0235 (-1.83)	0.0322 (1.89)	0.0038 (0.24)	-0.0179 (-0.97)
R^2_{t-3}	-0.1100 (-2.30)*	0.0480 (1.52)	-0.0165 (-0.80)	0.0069 (0.60)	0.0046 (0.24)	-0.0125 (-1.10)	0.0364 (1.98)
R^2_{t-4}	0.1298 (4.25)*	0.0046 (0.16)	-0.0385 (-1.46)	0.0118 (1.01)	-0.0140 (-0.93)	0.0233 (1.72)	-0.0250 (-1.49)

R^2_{t-5}	0.1626 (3.54)*	0.0519 (2.01)*	-0.0397 (-1.56)	0.0339 (2.74)*	-0.0048 (-0.42)	-0.0035 (-0.25)	-0.0043 (-0.22)
DumMON	-0.0002 (-0.48)	-0.0004 (-2.43)*	0.0010 (0.59)	-0.0002 (-2.59)*	0.0004 (3.72)*	-0.0000 (-0.03)	0.0002 (1.29)
DumTUE	-0.0013 (-2.97)*	-0.0003 (-2.87)*	0.0026 (1.48)	-0.0002 (-2.59)*	0.0002 (2.49)*	-0.0000 (-0.39)	0.0000 (0.03)
DumWED	0.0014 (3.40)*	-0.0002 (-2.13)*	-0.0003 (-0.09)	-0.0003 (-4.37)*	0.0003 (2.41)*	0.0000 (0.32)	0.0001 (1.21)
DumTHU	0.0006 (1.68)	-0.0004 (-2.28)*	0.0021 (1.32)	-0.0005 (-5.70)*	0.0001 (0.62)	-0.0001 (-0.62)	-0.0003 (-2.82)*
No. of Firms	17	18	48	71	66	74	76

T-test is the test for the difference in the coefficients between the A- and B-share markets.
*Significant at the 5% level.

the-week dummy variables are not significant at the later periods.

We also experiment with another measure of volatility, the log of the ratio of the high and low prices, and a moving standard deviation of daily return that is based on the past twenty and thirty days. Results are similar to those of the squared returns; thus they are not reported here for space consideration.

3.3 Beta Risk Analysis

We also analyze the difference in risk behavior of A- and B-share companies by comparing their beta risk with a market model. Two different market indexes are used. First, we use a market index that corresponds to the company A or B shares. This market index is called the single index. We then use a second market index that combines all A and B shares to form the composite index.

Table 6.4 reports results of the market model estimates. Panel A shows the average beta difference between A and B shares for the same company. The size of the differences and their t-values appear to drop over time. Panel B, using the ratio of the betas from the A and B shares, indicates a similar pattern of beta differences. These results suggest that the risk characteristics of the two markets appear to have become more similar over time.

3.4 Correlation of Return and Volatility

Our microstructure analysis indicates that volatility is similarly related to the bid–ask spread and volume in both A- and B-share markets. We also want to know whether the returns and volatility of the A and B shares show a closer relationship over time. For each year, we compute the correlation of returns and volatility between A and B shares for the same company. The averages of these correlations are reported in Table 6.5.

Table 6.5, Panel A, reports returns based on both open–close and close–close prices. In the earlier years, the correlations of returns are very low, confirming a definite segmentation of the A- and B-share markets. In the later periods, results using both open–close and close–close returns indicate an increased correlation of returns over time, implying a closer relationship between the two markets.

Table 6.5, Panel B, displays the correlations of volatility based on

Table 6.4

Estimation of the Market Models

$R_{i,j,,t} = a_i + b_{i,j} R_{jm} + e_{i,j,t}$

where $R_{i,j,,t}$ is the daily return for stock i for the j share (A or B) at time t. Daily return is computed based on open-close (OC) or close-close (CC) quotes. R_{jm} is the market return based either on a single market index based on the j share (A or B shares) or a composite index of all A and B shares together. $b_{i,j}$ is the beta risk of either A or B shares for the same company. The residual term is $e_{i,j,t}$.

Panel A: Difference in beta (i.e., beta of A share less beta of B share for the same company)

	OC Single Index	CC Single Index	OC Comp. Index	CC Comp. Index
1994	0.1800	0.2874	1.0244	1.0439
	(2.90)*	(9.03)*	(35.95)*	(34.65)*
1995	0.8543	1.0504	0.9695	0.9725
	(38.91)*	(36.18)*	(31.15)*	(50.30)*
1996	0.1222	0.0278	0.5597	0.5555
	(3.26)*	(0.72)*	(17.89)*	(20.86)*
1997	0.3054	0.0808	0.5518	0.4534
	(13.12)*	(4.73)*	(23.37)*	(24.86)*
1998	0.3800	0.1486	0.7784	0.6283
	(10.53)*	(4.55)*	(19.38)*	(19.54)*
1999	0.2172	0.0289	0.0139	-0.1500
	(10.64)*	(1.49)	(0.51)	(-6.49)*
2000	0.1678	0.0393	0.2380	0.1480
	(4.89)*	(1.31)	(6.92)*	(5.23)*

Panel B: Average ratio of beta (i.e., b_A/b_B -1) of the same company

	OC Index	CC Comp. Index	OC Index	CC Comp. Index
1994	-1.1276	-5.3037	26.9505	66.8552
	(-3.54)*	(-0.56)	(2.91)*	(1.97)*
1995	41.3208	2.2280	-2.7455	16.4073
	(1.05)	(0.45)	(-0.18)	(1.83)
1996	0.6395	0.2888	2.3958	1.5925
	(4.63)*	(3.80)*	(5.98)*	(9.99)*
1997	0.8572	0.1422	2.8693	0.9299
	(4.67)*	(4.18)*	(2.00)*	(14.57)*
1998	1.0316	0.2580	4.7999	1.5752
	(6.26)*	(5.02)*	(0.46)	(3.87)*
1999	0.3884	0.0508	0.0831	-0.1268
	(9.30)*	(2.05)*	(2.13)*	(-5.73)*
2000	0.4124	0.0840	0.2267	0.3555
	(4.45)*	(1.97)*	(-0.28)	(4.41)*

T-values are in parentheses.* Significant at the 5% level.

Table 6.5

Results of Correlation of Return and Volatility Measures Based on Daily Open-Close (OC) and Close-Close (CC) Prices between A Shares and B Shares

Panel A: Correlation of Returns

	Return (OC)	Return (CC)
1994	0.111	0.118
1995	0.041	0.125
1996	0.141	0.233
1997	0.232	0.331
1998	0.058	0.125
1999	0.246	0.332
2000	0.344	0.470

Panel B: Correlation of Volatility

	σ (CC)	Return squared (OC)	σ (CC)	Return squared (CC)
1994	0.050	0.008	0.030	0.015
1995	0.018	0.004	0.093	0.026
1996	0.158	0.001	0.203	0.047
1997	0.173	0.146	0.237	0.176
1998	0.022	0.030	0.070	0.081
1999	0.184	0.185	0.275	0.037
2000	0.225	0.173	0.305	0.346

Note: σ is the volatility generated from equation (2).

implied volatility and return squared. As expected, these results confirm the notion that correlations of volatility for different measures are on a rising trend, implying a closer relationship between the A- and B-share markets.

4. Conclusion

Using daily return volatility based on open–close quotes, we investigate the relationship of volatility with the bid–ask spread and trading volume for the A- and B-share Chinese equity markets for the period 1994–2000. Various measures of volatility are used in our study, including an implied volatility and the return squared. The results appear to be robust.

We find that the relationship of volatility with the bid-ask spread and trading volume is becoming more similar for A- and B-share markets in the more recent periods as compared to the earlier periods. This indicates that the two markets show a trend toward integration. Risk analysis based on a market model indicates that the beta risk of A- and B-share stocks is tending to become more similar. The correlations of returns for A and B shares across companies are also higher in later periods rather than earlier periods. Analysis using the correlations of volatility confirms a similar pattern of increasing linkage. These results imply that A- and B-share markets are moving closer together.

We do not examine specific policies that might mitigate the segmentation of the A- and B-share markets. Future research on the effect of specific policies on price behavior and market segmentation would be worthwhile. The results will help market participants and policy makers better understand the influences on stock prices.

References

Andersen, T.G. 1996. "Return Volatility and Trading Volume: An Information Flow Interpretation of Stochastic Volatility." *Journal of Finance* 51: 169–204.

Bailey, W. 1994. "Risk and Return in China's New Stock Markets: Some Preliminary Evidence." *Pacific Basin Finance Journal* 2: 243–260.

Bailey, W., Y.P. Chung, and J.K. Kang. 1999. "Foreign Ownership Restrictions and Equity Price Premiums: What Drives the Demand for Cross-Border Investments?" *Journal of Financial and Quantitative Analysis* 34: 489–511.

Bailey, W., and J. Jagtiani. 1994. "Foreign Ownership Restrictions and Stock Prices in the Thai Capital Market." *Journal of Financial Economics* 36: 57–87.

Bessembinder, H., and P.J. Seguin. 1992. "Futures-Trading Activity and Stock Price Volatility." *Journal of Finance* 47: 2015–2034.

Campbell, J.Y., S.J. Grossman, and J. Wang. 1993. "Trading Volume and Serial Correlations in Stock Returns." *Quarterly Journal of Economics* 49: 153–181.

Chui, A.C., and C.Y. Kwok. 1998. "Cross-Autocorrelation Between A Shares and B Shares in the Chinese Stock Market." *Journal of Financial Research* 21: 333–353.

Domowitz, I., J. Glen, and A. Madhavan. 1997. "Market Segmentation and Stock Prices: Evidences from an Emerging Market." *Journal of Finance* 52: 1059–1085.

Fernald, J., and J.H. Rogers. 1988. "Puzzles in the Chinese Stock Market." International Finance Discussion Paper, No. 619. Washington, DC: Board of Governors of the Federal Reserve System.

Fung, H.G., C.Y. Hwang, and W.K. Leung. 1998. "The Relationship Among Volatility, Volume, Bid-Ask Spread and Number of Brokers: Evidence from Intra-Day Data on the Hong Kong Stock Market." *Review of Pacific Basin Financial Markets and Policies* 1: 303–320.

Fung, H.G., W. Lee, and W.K. Leung. 2000, "Segmentation of the A- and B-Share Chinese Equity Markets." *Journal of Financial Research* 23: 179–195.

Fung, H.G., and W.K. Leung. 2001. "Financial Liberalization and Corporate Governance in China." *International Journal of Business* 6: 3-31.

Grundy, B. and M. McNichols. 1990. "Trade and the Revelation of Information Through Prices and Direct Disclosure." *Review of Financial Studies* 2: 495–526.

Jones, C.M., G. Kaul, and M.L. Lipson. 1994. "Information, Trading and Volatility." *Journal of Financial Economics* 36: 127–154.

Kyle, A.S. 1985. "Continuous Auctions and Insider Trading." *Econometrica* 53: 1315–1335.

Lamoureux, C.G., and W.D. Lastrapes. 1990. "Heteroskedasticity in Stock Return Data: Volume versus GARCH Effects." *Journal of Finance* 45: 221–229.

Mok, H., and Y.V. Hui. 1998. "Underpricing and Aftermarket Performance of IPOs in Shanghai, China." *Pacific Basin Finance Journal* 6: 453–474.

Poon, W.P.H., M. Firth, and H.G. Fung. 1998. "Asset Pricing in Segmented Capital Markets: Preliminary Evidence from China Domiciled Companies." *Pacific Basin Finance Journal* 6: 307–319.

Schwert, G.W. 1990. "Stock Volatility and the Crash of '87." *Review of Financial Studies* 3: 77–102.

Su, D., and B. Fleisher. 1999. "An Empirical Investigation of Underpricing in Chinese IPOs." *Pacific Basin Finance Journal* 7: 173–202.

Tauchen, G.E., and M. Pitts. 1983. "Price Variability–Volume Relationship in Speculative Markets." *Econometrica* 51: 483–505.

Wo, C.S. 1997. "Chinese Dual-Class Equity: Price Differentials and Information Flows." *Emerging Markets Quarterly* 1: 47–62.

7

Ownership Restrictions and Stock-Price Behavior in China

Kam C. Chan, Louis T.W. Cheng, and Joseph K.W. Fung

I. Introduction

Many stock markets in the world are subject to some form of restrictions or barriers. These include voting rights, taxes, capital flows, investment-profit repatriation, and ownership restrictions. It is understandable that any form of limitation creates a barrier of capital flow. Hence, the price behavior of a restricted stock may be different from that of an unrestricted one. An extreme type of barrier is ownership restriction. Ownership restrictions are usually used to prevent foreigners from owning a controlling interest of a country's companies.

Many stock markets have or used to have such restrictions. According to Eun and Janakiramanan (1986), foreign investors were only allowed to purchase a limited number of shares of a firm in Finland, France, India, Indonesia, South Korea, Mexico, Spain, and Sweden. In Australia, Canada, Japan, Malaysia, and Norway, limited foreign ownership was employed in selective industries. In addition, Bergström, Rydqvist, and Sellin (1993) reported that a capital-outflow constraint limiting the amount of capital that domestic investors could export was enforced in the United Kingdom until 1979, and in Sweden until 1989. In Ireland, the capital-outflow constraint was still in effect in 1993.

Ownership restrictions may induce different stock-price behaviors among different classes of stocks. Recently, Booth, Chowdhury, and Martikainen (1994) studied the Finnish ownership-restricted stock market from 1984 to 1989 and found that: (1) unrestricted stocks were more volatile than restricted ones; and (2) the two types of stocks were cointegrated. The cointegrated results suggest that there is an equilibrium relationship between the ownership-restricted and unrestricted stocks. In a similar study of the Finnish ownership-restricted stock market, Hietala (1989) showed that unrestricted shares had a positive price differential relative to restricted shares. Errunza and Losq (1985) suggested that, due to capital-flow restrictions, many international capital markets are "mildly segmented." However, the majority of the literature mainly focused on established markets such as Finland, and the analysis was conducted primarily on highly aggregated stock-market indices. Exceptions in the literature are Bailey (1994), Bailey and Jagtiani (1994), and Ma (1996). Bailey and Jagtiani studied the price difference between domestic and foreign-owned shares and found that ownership restrictions, liquidity, information availability, and foreign-investor "familiarity" explain the price premium of foreign-owned shares. Using weekly stock prices from newly launched Chinese stock markets, Bailey and Ma provided preliminary results on the ownership-restricted Chinese stock markets. Essentially, they found that stock prices in the segmented Chinese stock markets were different. Foreign-owned shares traded at a premium over domestic-owned shares.

The objective of this chapter is to examine the stock-price behavior in the ownership-restricted stock markets in China. This investigation is important for three different but related reasons. First, we examine the long-term price dynamics of two ownership-restricted share classes (called A and B shares) of the socialist economic system in China by using firm-level daily data over a reasonable period of time. Because of limited data availability, the literature (e.g., Bailey 1994 and Ma 1996) used only weekly data and studied a limited number of companies. For instance, Bailey had eight companies' B shares in his analysis, while Ma's study had only 20 to 104 observations. While the studies by Bailey and Ma are interesting, the results are more preliminary in nature. In this study, we expand our data to fifty-one companies with 252 to 967 daily observations. Thus, our findings should add a new dimension to the literature. Second, the ownership restrictions in Chinese stock markets are different from other ownership-restricted markets such as Finland and Switzerland. For instance, in the Finnish market during the period 1984–89, both foreign and domestic investors were able to invest in the unrestricted-share market while only domestic investors were allowed to invest in the restricted-share market. In Switzerland, a firm can issue bearer shares and registered shares. Domestic investors can invest in both shares, but foreign investors are allowed to trade bearer shares only. However, the two-tier trading system with A and B shares on the China stock exchanges is more restrictive. Local investors are allowed to own and trade A shares only, while foreign investors are allowed to invest in B shares. These A shares are denominated in local currency, and B shares are denominated in foreign currencies (in U.S. or Hong Kong dollars). Chinese ownership restrictions do not allow domestic investors to participate in B-share trading or vice versa. To our knowledge, China's two-tier trading system is unique among the capital markets in the world. This study of the Chinese stock markets will add new insight into the impact of ownership restrictions on stock-price behavior, beyond the preliminary analysis of Bailey and Ma. Third, unlike the studies of Bailey and Ma that did research on the price differences between restricted vis-à-vis unrestricted shares, we use cointegration tests to allow for random errors of A- and B-share prices. If an empirical test is done on the price difference, the statistical test is too restrictive. With cointegration, we examine the price dynamics between A- and B-share prices. In the process, the cointegration model allows random errors in the price movements of A- and B-share prices. In addition, we provide an ad hoc, empirical logit model to relate the results of cointegration (i.e., whether A- and B-share prices move closely in the long run) to the ownership distribution, liquidity, and financial characteristics of the firm. The logit model helps us to understand the factors determining the price dynamics of A and B shares.

Our results show that in more than two-thirds of the firms, A- and B-share prices do not move together (or the A- and B-share prices are not cointegrated), with or without an adjustment for the impact of the currency component. It seems that A- and B-share prices are driven by their own underlying economic forces, and the two markets are segmented by the Chinese government's restricted-ownership policy. Moreover, the total number of shares (TOTAL), B shares' average daily volume to number of outstanding B shares ratio (VB/NB), and earnings per share (EPS) are found to be positively related to the probability of cointegration of the A and B shares of a firm. In contrast, the total number of non-negotiable shares (NONNEG) tends to reduce the probability of cointegration between A- and B-share prices. The ownership-distribution factor (TOTAL and NONNEG), the liquidity factor (VB/NB), and the financial factor (EPS) explain the price dynamics of ownership-restricted stocks in China.

The chapter is organized as follows: section II discusses the data and market structure; hypotheses and methodology are presented in section III; empirical results are discussed in section IV; and a brief summary is presented in section V.

II. Data and Market Structure

Under the aggressive economic-reform programs in China, liberal reformers favor stock markets over the traditional monopolized bank-loans market as a viable alternative for companies to raise capital. However, cautious reformers fear the loss of central control in the ownership of the originally state-owned enterprises. Hence, a middle route has developed. The Chinese government uses non-negotiable shares (called C shares) and A shares to secure local ownership of companies through domestic investors (both individuals and institutions), while it uses B shares to attract foreign capital and enhance the flexibility of companies raising capital. The non-negotiable or C shares are owned by state-owned enterprises and are not tradable on stock exchanges. A shares are owned by local individual investors and these are tradable on stock exchanges. Accordingly, tradable shares are A and B shares, and the stock markets in China are traded in two tiers.

The first tier, A shares, is designed for domestic investors. The second tier, B shares, is targeted exclusively for international investors. On the Shanghai Stock Exchange (SHSE) in eastern China, A shares are denominated in Chinese currency (RMB) and B shares are denominated in U.S. dollars. On the Shenzhen Stock Exchange (SZSE) in southern China, A shares are denominated in Chinese currency and B shares are denominated in Hong Kong dollars. Shanghai is one of the major designated coastal cities open to international trade and investments, while Shenzhen is a special economic zone. Both cities enjoy a large degree of autonomy in terms of capital flows and governmental regulations. The city administrations, which are usually headed by prominent political figures, are not subject to provincial control, and they report directly to the central government in Beijing.

Our stock data are provided by the Center for Financial Research on China at the Chinese University of Hong Kong. The longest covered period of the daily market price of both tiers (A and B shares) of both exchanges is January 1993 to December 1995. However, some stocks began trading at a later date. Thus, the number of observations varies from 252 to 967. Data were available for thirty-two and nineteen stocks on the SHSE and SZSE, respectively. The stock data were dividend-adjusted. In 1995, the total market value of Shanghai A shares was RMB 243 billion, while Shanghai B shares had a total market value of RMB 9.2 billion. Average daily volume was 197 million and 7.8 million for A and B shares respectively. On the SHSE, the total market value of A and B shares was RMB 88 billion and RMB 7.2 billion, respectively, with an average daily volume of 76 million A shares and 2 million B shares.

In order to control for a possible foreign-exchange bias in the B shares, the analyses are repeated with the currency component of B-share prices separated from the returns. For the currency adjustment, the B-share prices are multiplied by the corresponding daily exchange rate of RMB/US$ or RMB/HK$. The exchange-rate data are obtained from the Research Center at the Chinese University of Hong Kong and Data Stream.

III. Hypotheses and Methodology

Hypothesis

A study of stock-price dynamics has implications for the degree of segmentation of the A- and B-share markets. We may expect that a company's fundamentals should drive both A- and B-share prices, because the shares represent the same claim on a firm's underlying assets. We would then expect A- and B-share prices to move together. On the other hand, if A- and B-share markets are segmented markets due to strict ownership restrictions or because such ownership restrictions distort the impact of companies' fundamentals on stock prices, we would expect that A- and B-share prices have their own price dynamics. By examining the stock-price dynamics between A and B shares, we are able to make inferences about the degree of market segmentation due to ownership restrictions and hence draw implications about the "success" of China's two-tier trading system in limiting foreign ownership. Thus we have the following null hypothesis:

> The Chinese government's ownership-restriction policy is successful, A- and B-share markets are segmented, hence A- and B-share prices are not cointegrated.

Cointegration

Engle and Granger's cointegration test (1987) provides a natural vehicle to investigate whether two variables move together (i.e., they have the same underlying equilibrium relationship). In this study, the two variables are A- and B-share prices. A necessary condition for cointegration is the existence of unit roots in the variables (i.e., the order of integration). We use the Pantula, Gonzalez-Farias, and Fuller unit-root test (1994) to examine if the stock-price series are order one (i.e., if the first difference of the variable is stationary). They show that their unit-root test has a better power than the Dickey-Fuller and Phillips-Perron unit-root tests. Three different models of unit-root tests are performed to capture possible nonstationarity of the stock-returns series due to intercept and trend terms. They are:

Model 1: $S_t = \mu' + \alpha' S_{t-1} + e_t'$ (with intercept)

Model 2: $S_t = \mu^* + \beta^*(t-T/2) + \alpha^* S_{t-1} + e_t^*$ (with intercept and trend)

Model 3: $S_t = \alpha S_{t-1} + e_t$ (no intercept and no trend)

where S_t = any stock-price series;

α, α^*, α' and β^* = coefficients of the regression models;

μ^* and μ' = the intercept terms;

T = total number of observations;

e_t, e_t^* and e_t' = error terms that could be ARMA processes with time-dependent variances.

The testing hypotheses are:

$H_0 : \alpha' = 1$ vs $H_A : \alpha' < 1$;

$H_0 : \alpha^* = 1$ vs $H_A : \alpha^* < 1$;

$H_0 : \alpha = 1$ vs $H_A : \alpha < 1$;

The data used in all models are transformed to natural logarithms.

To look into the possibility of cointegration of A- and B-share prices, we use the cointegration tests of Johansen (1988 and 1991) and Johansen and Juselius (1990). Engle and Granger (1987) prove that if two variables are cointegrated, they can be written as an error-correction model. Johansen (1988) and Johansen and Juselius (1990) extend Engle and Granger's cointegration to a multivariate framework. Johansen and Juselius consider a fairly general unrestricted error-correction model of the form:

$$\Delta S_t = \Gamma_1 \Delta S_{t-1} + \ldots + \Gamma_{k-1} \Delta S_{t-k+1} + r S_{t-k} + \mu + e_t \qquad (1)$$

where S_t = (p x 1) vector of stock prices at time t;

r = (p x p) parameter matrix;

m = (p x 1) intercept term.

p is the number of stock-price series.

In our study, the value of p is 2. The parameter matrix, r, indicates whether the (p x 1) vector of stock prices has a long-run dynamic relationship or not. The rank of r equals the number of cointegrating vectors. If the rank of r is zero, equation (1) reduces to a standard vector autoregression model. If r has full rank, then all the stock-price series are stationary in levels. Cointegration is suggested if the rank of r is between zero and the number of stock series. Since we have a bivariate setup in A- and B-share prices, we are examining if the rank of r is 1. We use the trace statistics proposed by Johansen to test the null hypothesis of no cointegration between the A- and B-share prices. Specifically, we test:

$H_0 : r = 0$

$H_0 : r \leq 1$

If the trace statistics suggest that $H_0 : r = 0$ is rejected while $H_0 : r \leq 1$ is not rejected, then r is 1 (i.e., the A- and B-share prices are cointegrated). Diebold, Gardeazabal, and Yilmaz (1994) suggested the inclusion of intercept and trend might change the conclusion of cointegration tests. Therefore, we conducted cointegration tests with different assumptions of intercept and trend (intercept/no trend, intercept/trend, and no intercept/no trend).

Logit Equation

After the cointegration study, we then move to examine the factors that contribute to the results of cointegrated/noncointegrated A- and B-share prices. We hypothesize that ownership-distribution factors, liquidity factors, and financial factors may determine whether A- and B-share prices are cointegrated or not. Then the model becomes:

$$C = X\beta + Y\gamma + Z\delta + \varepsilon \qquad (2)$$

where

C = is a matrix that contains the binary variable of cointegration results. C is 1 if a firm's A and B shares are cointegrated; otherwise C = 0;

X = ownership variable matrix that contains variables including total number of nonnegotiable shares, total number of A shares, total number of B shares, total number of negotiable shares, total number of shares, the ratio of A shares to total shares, the ratio of B shares to total shares, and the ratio of negotiable shares to total shares;

Y= liquidity variable matrix that contains variables including average daily volume of A shares, average daily volume of B shares, the ratio of average daily A-share volume to number of A shares outstanding, the ratio of average B-share volume to number of B shares outstanding, end of 1994 market capitalization of A shares, and end of 1994 market capitalization of B shares;

Z = financial characteristic variable matrix that contains variables including earnings per share, total assets, return on equity, and equity-to-total-asset ratio;

β, γ, and δ = coefficients to be estimated;

ε = random error term.

All variables are calculated with data from 1994 financial statements. The dependent variable is a binary variable. A consistent estimate of the coefficients can be obtained by a logit procedure. To obtain the best explanatory power among all potential independent variables, we use a stepwise logit procedure to select the best possible subset among the ownership distribution, liquidity, and financial variables. The stepwise selection procedure also preserves the power of the estimated equation as we have only fifty-one observations. The estimated coefficients are interpreted as the probabilities of cointegration.

IV. Empirical Results

Summary Statistics

The summary statistics for thirty-two Shanghai A-, B-, and currency-adjusted B-share returns[1] are presented in Table 7.1, panel A. There are several interesting results. First, in all except one company, the standard deviations of B shares and currency-adjusted B shares are smaller than those of the A shares. Second, the daily mean returns of A, B, and currency-adjusted B shares are mostly negative. Third, there is not much difference in mean and standard deviation of returns between B and currency-adjusted B shares.

Table 7.1, panel B, displays the summary statistics of Shenzhen stocks. Unlike the Shanghai Stock Exchange results, it is not clear that the standard deviations of B shares and currency-adjusted B shares are smaller or bigger than those of the A shares. Nevertheless, most of the stocks exhibit negative daily mean returns.

Cointegration

To conserve space, detailed unit-root test results are not reported.[2] There were some stock prices on both the Shanghai and the Shenzhen Stock Exchanges that did not have unit root at price levels for some of the unit-test models. Accordingly, for the stock price in these specific models, we did not conduct cointegration analysis. For the stocks that did have unit root in the stock-price levels, we also performed unit-root tests on the changes in the price levels. Unit roots in price-level changes were rejected at a level of 1 percent. Hence, A-, B-, and currency-adjusted B-share price series are I(1) and may be cointegrated since the existence of a unit root in price levels is a necessary (but not sufficient) condition for cointegration.

The cointegration results of Shanghai stocks are displayed in Table 7.2. The lags, namely, the order of k in equation (1), were determined by AIC criteria. Nevertheless, the results were qualitatively unchanged from lag 1 to lag 8. The null hypotheses of r £ 1 are not rejected in all cointegration tests. Hence, we only reported the trace statistics of the null hypotheses of r is zero in Table 7.2. Given that r is 1, a trace statistic rejects the null hypothesis of r = 0, and the result suggests cointegration.

There was no single stock indicating cointegration in all three cointegration models. To provide a conservative conclusion in hypothesis 1 (about the relationship between ownership restriction and stock-price-dynamic behavior) and the logit-model estimate, we consider A and B prices are cointegrated if at least two cointegration relationships are found among all six possible cointegrating equations from the three models. The status of cointegration is presented in the third column of Table 7.2. We found nine stocks that have cointegration between A- and B-share prices as well as A- and currency-adjusted B-share prices. There were twenty-three stocks that did not show evidence of cointegration for the Shanghai data.

Table 7.1

Summary Statistics of Shanghai and Shenzhen Stocks

Panel A: Shanghai stocks

Code	Name	A share		B share		B share (adj.)		Listing date
		mean (%)	s.d. (%)	mean (%)	s.d. (%)	mean (%)	s.d. (%)	
602	Vacuum & Electron Devices	-0.01	4.82	-0.10	3.43	-0.06	3.58	Feb. 21, 1992
604	Shanghai Erfangii Co.	-0.14	4.78	-0.12	3.24	-0.01	3.38	July 1, 1992
610	China Textile Machinery Stock	-0.08	5.17	-0.11	3.75	-0.10	3.90	July 28, 1992
611	Dazhong Taxi	0.11	4.93	0.06	3.33	0.07	3.41	July 22, 1992
612	China First Pencil	0.01	4.99	-0.28	8.70	-0.27	8.76	July 28, 1992
613	Wing Song Stationery	-0.11	4.19	-0.16	4.05	-0.14	4.17	July 22, 1992
614	Rubber Belt	-0.05	5.11	-0.10	3.73	-0.08	3.83	July 28, 1992
617	Lianhua Fibre Corporation	-0.12	4.77	-0.16	2.68	-0.17	2.69	Sep. 28, 1993
618	Chlor Alkai Chemical	0.10	5.02	-0.09	3.03	-0.07	3.27	Aug. 20, 1992
619	Refrigerator Compressor	-0.07	4.59	-0.03	3.52	-0.02	3.62	Jan. 18, 1993
623	Tyre & Rubber	-0.10	4.54	-0.13	3.11	-0.11	3.26	Aug. 28, 1992
639	Jingqiao Export Proc. Zone	0.05	4.14	0.02	2.82	0.03	3.05	May 31, 1993
648	Outer Gao Qiao F. T. Zone	0.20	4.45	0.08	2.63	0.07	2.64	July 26, 1993
950	Jinjiang Tower	-0.01	4.95	-0.07	3.34	-0.08	3.34	Oct. 18, 1993
679	Phoenix Bicycle	-0.13	4.71	-0.27	3.58	-0.28	3.57	Nov. 19, 1993
689	Sanmao Textile	-0.05	4.69	-0.15	2.25	-0.15	2.26	Dec. 31, 1993

Code	Company							Date
695	Dajiang (Group)	−0.02	4.78	0.02	2.60	0.01	2.60	Dec. 15, 1993
818	Forever Bicycle	−0.09	4.77	−0.28	3.43	−0.29	3.43	Nov. 15, 1993
819	Yaohua Pilkington Glass	−0.07	4.64	−0.06	3.06	−0.07	3.07	Dec. 10, 1993
827	Friendship Overseas Chinese Co., Ltd.	−0.03	5.35	−0.04	2.82	−0.05	2.82	Jan. 5, 1994
835	Shangling Electric Appliances Co., Ltd.	0.02	4.88	0.01	2.70	0.00	2.70	Jan. 31, 1994
822	Goods & Materials Trade Centre Co., Ltd.	−0.15	4.85	−0.11	2.88	−0.12	2.87	Mar. 30, 1994
841	Diesel Engine	−0.09	4.79	−0.20	2.43	−0.21	2.43	Dec. 28, 1993
843	Industrial Sewing Machine	0.01	5.18	−0.27	3.32	−0.28	3.32	Jan. 12, 1994
844	Hero	−0.06	5.02	−0.04	2.88	−0.05	2.88	Dec. 28, 1993
845	Steel Tube Co., Ltd.	−0.20	5.40	−0.21	3.27	−0.22	3.27	Mar. 15, 1994
848	Automation Instrumentation	−0.04	5.22	−0.06	2.73	−0.07	2.73	Apr. 29, 1994
851	Haixin Co., Ltd.	−0.09	3.99	−0.06	3.50	−0.07	3.50	Dec. 8, 1993
680	Posts & Telecommunication Equipment Co., Ltd.	−0.09	3.40	−0.07	2.59	−0.09	2.59	Oct. 20, 1994
625	Narcissus Electric Appliances Co., Ltd.	−0.18	3.49	−0.15	2.14	−0.17	2.14	Nov. 10, 1994
663	Lujiazui Finance & Trade Zone Development Co., Ltd.	−0.11	3.26	−0.12	1.85	−0.13	1.85	Nov. 22, 1994
801	Huaxin Cement Co., Ltd.	0.04	4.01	0.15	2.21	0.15	2.21	Dec. 9, 1994

Table 7.1 (continued)

Summary Statistics of Shanghai and Shenzhen Stocks

Panel B: Shenzhen Stocks

A share		B share		B share (adj.)			
Code	Name	mean (%)	s.d. (%)	mean (%)	s.d. (%)	mean (%)	s.d. (%)	Listing date
2003	Gintian Industry	-0.19	3.52	0.01	4.16	-0.04	4.26	June 30, 1993
2011	Shenzhen Prop. & Res. Dev.	-0.07	3.74	-0.11	3.44	-0.09	3.54	Mar. 31, 1992
2012	China Southern Glass	0.02	3.97	-0.00	3.27	0.02	3.38	Mar. 2, 1992
2013	Shenzhen Petrochemical	-0.12	4.02	-0.14	4.00	-0.12	4.14	May 7, 1992
2015	Zhonghao (Group)	-0.13	4.12	-0.21	4.09	-0.19	4.16	June 26, 1992
2016	Konka (Group) Co.	-0.01	3.52	-0.02	3.69	-0.00	3.85	Mar. 30, 1992
2017	China Bicycles	-0.10	4.00	-0.15	3.59	-0.13	3.67	Apr. 1, 1992
2018	Victor Onward Textile	-0.12	4.32	-0.25	5.22	-0.23	5.30	June 17, 1992
2019	Shenbao Industrial	-0.15	4.40	-0.19	4.52	-0.17	4.63	Oct. 13, 1992
2020	Huafa Electronics	-0.16	4.09	-0.20	7.14	-0.18	7.20	Apr. 29, 1992
2022	Chiwan Wharf Holdings	-0.18	4.16	0.05	3.87	0.04	4.06	May 7, 1993
2024	China Merch. Shekou Port	-0.08	4.21	0.10	3.65	0.09	3.85	June 8, 1993
2025	Shenzhen Tellus Holding Co.	-0.17	4.46	-0.15	3.64	-0.19	3.76	June 22, 1993
2026	Fiyta Holdings	-0.02	3.77	0.05	3.68	0.01	3.80	June 9, 1993
2028	Yili Waters	-0.06	4.50	-0.08	2.53	-0.09	2.56	Aug. 11, 1993
2029	Shenzhen Health Min. Water	-0.12	4.11	-0.14	3.67	-0.16	3.69	Jan. 11, 1994
2030	Lionda Holdings	-0.20	4.41	-0.16	6.12	-0.17	6.15	Oct. 6, 1993
2037	NanShan Power Station	-0.22	3.71	-0.34	3.42	-0.36	3.44	Nov. 29, 1994
2039	China Intl. Marine Container	0.06	3.85	0.01	2.04	-0.01	2.08	Apr. 11, 1994

Table 7.2

Johansen Cointegration Tests of Shanghai Stocks

Code	Name of company	Coinegration	Intercept; no trend		Intercept; trend		No intercept; no trend	
			A/B shares	A/ adj. B shares	A/B shares	A/adj. B shares	A/B shares	A/adj. B shares
602	Vacuum & Electron Devices	Yes	19.04* (0.035)	20.07* (0.025)	16.03 (0.101)	19.62* (0.030)	6.37 (0.393)	8.68 (0.186)
604	Shanghai Erfangii Co.	No	11.27 (0.336)	12.04 (0.277)	14.47 (0.157)	14.88 (0.140)	3.30 (0.803)	4.05 (0.711)
610	China Textile Machinery Stock	Yes	19.25* (0.033)	20.42* (0.023)	N.A.	N.A.	4.51 (0.647)	4.08 (0.708)
611	Dazhong Taxi	No	7.19 (0.690)	7.42 (0.671)	11.60 (0.335)	10.77 (0.404)	4.86 (0.592)	2.70 (0.884)
612	China First Pencil	No	N.A.	N.A.	N.A.	N.A.	13.53* (0.035)	N.A.
613	Wing Song Stationery	No	N.A.	N.A.	N.A.	N.A.	3.17 (0.824)	3.04 (0.843)
614	Rubber Belt	No	N.A.	N.A.	N.A.	N.A.	4.39 (0.664)	2.18 (0.936)
617	Lianhua Fibre Corporation	No	8.47 (0.583)	8.53 (0.578)	11.36 (0.351)	11.46 (0.346)	4.78 (0.604)	3.38 (0.793)
618	Chlor Alkai Chemical	Yes	27.20* (0.004)	23.16* (0.011)	30.27* (0.001)	27.97* (0.003)	4.71 (0.616)	9.85 (0.125)
619	Refrigerator Compressor	No	14.05 (0.159)	14.61 (0.136)	14.90 (0.139)	14.61 (0.151)	3.85 (0.738)	7.02 (0.325)
923	Tyre & Rubber	No	4.94	4.63	16.42	18.11	1.43	1.74

Table 7.2 (continued)

Johansen Cointegration Tests of Shanghai Stocks

Code	Name of company	Coinegration	Intercept; no trend A/B shares	Intercept; no trend A/B shares (adj.)	Intercept; trend A/B shares	Intercept; trend A/B shares (adj.)	No intercept; no trend A/B shares	No intercept; no trend A/B shares (adj.)
639	Jingqiao Export Proc. Zone	No	11.97 (0.834)	10.38 (0.849)	12.92 (0.089)	12.92 (0.051)	5.40 (0.985)	2.93 (0.969)
948	Outer Gao Qiao F. T. Zone	Yes	16.24 (0.282)	15.82 (0.411)	15.23 (0.239)	15.05 (0.239)	15.22* (0.017)	13.75* (0.032)
650	Jinjiang Tower	Yes	7.34 (0.084)	7.26 (0.095)	23.04* (0.011)	22.70* (0.013)	1.54 (0.980)	1.36 (0.988)
679	Phoenix Bicycle	Yes	13.57 (0.678)	13.31 (0.684)	21.06* (0.019)	20.85* (0.021)	3.67 (0.761)	3.50 (0.781)
689	Sanmao Textile	No	N.A.	N.A.	12.72 (0.253)	12.51 (0.267)	3.75 (0.238)	3.48 (0.783)
695	Dajiang (Group)	No	N.A.	N.A.	13.19 (0.222)	13.15 (0.224)	3.51 (0.779)	4.62 (0.629)
818	Forever Bicycle	No	N.A.	N.A.	N.A.	N.A.	5.62 (0.477)	N.A.
819	Yaohua Pilkington Glass	No	N.A.	N.A.	17.27 (0.068)	17.20 (0.069)	N.A.	9.70 (0.131)
827	Friendship Overseas Chinese	No	N.A.	N.A.	9.70 (0.498)	9.59 (0.507)	3.58 (0.771)	3.08 (0.837)
835	Shangling Electric Appliances	No	13.98 (0.162)	14.66 (0.134)	15.25 (0.126)	15.64 (0.113)	3.66 (0.762)	8.89 (0.173)
822	Goods & Materials Trade Ctr.	Yes	13.29 (0.196)	12.98 (0.214)	20.22* (0.024)	19.60* (0.030)	2.52 (0.903)	2.14 (0.938)
841	Diesel Engine	No	8.95 (0.539)	9.03 (0.523)	15.90 (0.105)	16.30 (0.093)	4.43 (0.658)	8.99 (0.167)

Code	Company							
843	Industrial Sewing Machine	Yes	8.86 (0.548)	8.83 (0.550)	18.50* (0.045)	18.62* (0.043)	10.80 (0.090)	9.21 (0.156)
844	Hero	No	N.A.	11.60 (0.310)	17.40 (0.065)	17.04 (0.073)	6.78 (0.350)	4.84 (0.595)
845	Steel Tube Co., Ltd.	Yes	13.29 (0.200)	13.33 (0.194)	19.83* (0.028)	19.65* (0.030)	3.77 (0.748)	2.25 (0.929)
848	Automation Instrumentation	No	N.A.	N.A.	N.A.	N.A.	7.24 (0.303)	7.64 (0.266)
851	Haixin Co., Ltd.	No	N.A.	12.28 (0.260)	15.24 (0.127)	15.14 (0.130)	2.44 (0.911)	3.47 (0.784)
680	Posts & Telecom. Equipment	No	11.97 (0.281)	12.28 (0.260)	13.78 (0.189)	13.70 (0.193)	2.04 (0.946)	8.66 (0.187)
625	Narcissus Electric Appliances	No	5.74 (0.790)	5.72 (0.791)	12.77 (0.249)	12.38 (0.276)	3.77 (0.749)	2.51 (0.903)
663	Lujiazui Fin. & Tr. Zone Dvpt.	No	8.98 (0.537)	8.56 (0.575)	14.78 (0.144)	14.78 (0.144)	3.45 (0.786)	5.21 (0.535)
801	Huaxin Cement Co., Ltd.	No	12.81 (0.224)	12.28 (0.260)	14.81 (0.143)	14.40 (0.160)	4.48 (0.651)	9.55 (0.139)

Notes: (1) N.A. = unit-root tests were rejected for the stock-price level; (2) the trace statistics are reported with p-value in parentheses; and (3) * = the trace statistics are either 5% or 1% statistically significant.

Table 7.3 (pages 132-33) presents the cointegration results of stocks that are listed on the Shenzhen Stock Exchange. The reporting format and the results are similar to those of Table 7.2. Among the nineteen firms in the analysis, six of them suggest cointegration. On both the Shanghai and Shenzhen Stock Exchanges, in a more than two-to-one ratio, it suggests that A- and B-share prices, with or without currency-component adjustment, have their own price dynamics (not cointegrated). Thus, it seems that the Chinese government is successful in segmenting A- and B-share markets in both exchanges. The results of no cointegration appear to be logical because under a different trading environment (i.e., due to ownership restrictions), the supply and demand for a stock may be very different. For instance, dividends paid on A and B shares of the same stock are not in proportion to the value of the shares. In addition, the amount of capital available for each market is obviously different. The amount of capital of domestic investors (A shares) available for stock investment driven by the risk-and-return characteristics of stocks is relative to other investment channels in China, while international investors (B-share holders) make their investment decisions based upon other investment choices in the global market. These different economic and financial factors cause different long-term price behavior in the two markets.

Logit Equation

The results of the logit equations are shown in Table 7.4. For the stepwise equation, we find that four variables among the ownership-distribution, liquidity, and financial-characteristic factors are statistically significant at a 5 percent level. For ownership distribution, the TOTAL has a positive and statistically significant coefficient. This suggests that the larger the number of outstanding shares, the higher the probability of cointegration. The total number of outstanding shares represents the degree of diverse-ownership spread among investors. A wider ownership enhances trading of both A and B shares and hence, it would be easier for both A and B shares to be cointegrated. On the other hand, the NONNEG shares is negative and statistically significant at the 5 percent level. Non-negotiable shares are not tradable on the stock market and they represent the inside (corporate and state) ownership of the company. A larger non-negotiable-share ownership limits the spread of ownership and thus the effectiveness of the market mechanism. Therefore, the company's A and B shares have a smaller chance of being cointegrated. So, the impact of the total number of nonnegotiable shares would be just the opposite of the total number of outstanding shares.

For the liquidity factor, the ratio of average VB/NB is positive and statistically significant in the logit model. A higher VB/NB ratio represents a higher trading volume (liquidity) for the B shares. This better B-share market for the firm also helps the A-share market, as higher B-share trading will also draw local investors into the A-share market. Thus, A and B shares are more easily cointegrated. Lastly, the financial-characteristic factor is positively related to the probability of cointegration of the A and B shares of a firm. A high EPS definitely draws investors' attention and helps attract more investors and therefore a large investor base for a firm's A and B shares. This results in a stronger cointegration relationship between A- and B-share prices.

To obtain a robust conclusion, we also ran a second logit equation with the ratio of average A-share volume to the number of A shares outstanding and return-on-equity variables in addition to selected variables in the stepwise equation. The results are in the last two columns of Table 7.4. As expected, the results are similar to the stepwise equation. In addition to the four significant coefficients in the stepwise procedure, we also found marginal significance in the variables of the ratio of negotiable shares to total number of shares and the ratio of average A-share volume to number of A shares outstanding. Both of these variables are positive and the results can be interpreted as other ownership and liquidity variables.

V. Summary

Barring the limitation of a short sample period, this research studies the stock-price behavior of China's stock markets under ownership restrictions. We find that foreign-owned B-share price behavior is different from that of domestic-owned A shares. Cointegration tests suggest that A- and B-share prices tend to have their own price dynamics. It appears that the Chinese government has been able to insulate its domestic A-share market from a foreign-owned B-share market.

We further examined the factors that may contribute to the results of cointegration/noncointegration between A- and B-share prices. Essentially, we found the total number of shares, B shares' average daily volume to number of outstanding B shares ratio, and EPS to be positively related to the probability of cointegration of the A and B shares of a

Table 7.3

Johansen Cointegration Tests of Shenzhen Stocks

Code	Name of company	Coinegration	Intercept; no trend		Intercept; trend		No intercept; no trend	
			A/B shares	A/adj. B shares	A/B shares	A/adj. B shares	A/B shares	A/adj. B shares
2003	Gintian Industry	No	8.63 (0.569)	8.99 (0.536)	16.96 (0.075)	16.82 (0.078)	8.10 (0.227)	8.53 (0.195)
2011	Shenzhen Props. & Resources	Yes	10.03 (0.443)	16.62 (0.075)	38.00** (0.000)	43.42** (0.000)	6.59 (0.369)	12.15 (0.057)
2012	China Southern Glass	Yes	12.96 (0.215)	15.58 (0.102)	20.68* (0.021)	20.55* (0.022)	4.01 (0.717)	5.14 (0.547)
2013	Shenzhen Petrochemical	Yes	12.60 (0.238)	11.74 (0.299)	22.71* (0.012)	14.24* (0.027)	N.A.	N.A.
2015	Zhonghao (Group)	No	10.30 (0.418)	11.41 (0.324)	N.A.	N.A.	N.A.	7.21 (0.306)
2016	Konka (Group) Co.	Yes	10.54 (0.397)	N.A.	30.79** (0.001)	34.13** (0.001)	7.99 (0.236)	10.99 (0.084)
2017	China Bicycles	Yes	7.44 (0.670)	7.86 (0.635)	22.50* (0.013)	22.79* (0.012)	6.10 (0.422)	6.88 (0.339)
2018	Victor Onward Textile	No	12.74 (0.229)	11.84 (0.292)	23.11* (0.011)	N.A.	N.A.	N.A.
2019	Shenbao Industrial	No	11.34 (0.330)	11.20 (0.341)	17.42 (0.064)	19.00* (0.037)	4.60 (10.631)	4.07 (0.709)
2020	Huafa Electronics	No	12.30 (0.258)	16.18 (0.086)	N.A.	N.A.	6.22 (0.410)	6.25 (0.406)
2022	Chinwan Wharf Holdings	No	11.41 (0.325)	12.85 (0.222)	13.45 (0.206)	15.21 (0.128)	5.89 (0.447)	6.75 (0.352)
2024	China Merc. Skekou Port Serv.	No	14.52	12.34	12.00	10.77	9.17	6.19

2025	Shenzhen Tellus Holding Co.	No	9.23 (0.139)	8.83 (0.255)	17.67 (0.303)	17.80 (0.404)	6.02 (0.158)	6.88 (0.413)
2026	Fiyta Holdings	No	N.A. (0.515)	N.A. (0.551)	17.74 (0.059) (0.058)	N.A. (0.057)	10.06 (0.432)	6.40 (0.339)
2028	Shenzhen Health Min. Water	No	12.45 (0.248)	12.81 (0.224)	14.43 (0.158)	14.48 (0.156)	2.19 (0.115)	2.31 (0.389)
2029	Shenzhen S. E. Z. Real Estate & Properties (Group)	Yes	11.73 (0.300)	11.35 (0.329)	22.34** (0.014)	22.33** (0.014)	4.39 (0.934)	4.41 (0.924)
2030	Lionda Holdings	No	13.20 (0.201)	11.728 (0.300)	N.A.	N.A.	10.32 (0.664)	8.84 (0.660)
2037	Nanshan Power Station	No	5.31 (0.815)	5.34 (0.813)	12.15 (0.293)	12.16 (0.292)	N.A. (0.105)	N.A. (0.176)
2039	China International Marine Container	No	7.60 (0.658)	6.66 (0.729)	12.24 (0.286)	12.03 (0.301)	4.40 (0.663)	3.43 (0.788)

Notes: (1) N.A.= unit-root tests were rejected for the stock-price level; (2) the trace statistics are reported with p-value in parentheses; and (3) * = the trace statistics are either 5% or 1% statistically significant.

Table 7.4

A Stepwise Logit Equation of Cointegration Results on Ownership Distribution, Liquidity, and Financial Characteristics

Variables		Stepwise equation coefficients (χ^2 statistics)	P-value	Alternative equation coefficients (χ^2 statistics)	P-value
	Intercept	0.0307 (0.0001)	0.9923	-3.6598 (0.6043)	0.4369
Ownership:	Total number of non-negotiable shares	$-6.44*10^{-8}$ (4.3044)	0.0380	$-8.47*10^{-8}$ (5.2089)	0.0225
	Total number of shares	$5.27*10^{-8}$ (5.7071)	0.0169	$6.91*10^{-8}$ (6.6243)	0.0101
	Ratio of negotiable shares to total number of shares	-17.1789 (2.6693)	0.1023	-20.4166 (2.7104)	0.0997
Liquidity:	Ratio of average A-share volume to number of A shares outstanding	—	—	88.7070 (3.8358)	0.0502
	Ratio of average B-share volume to number of B shares outstanding	48.1608 (3.9604)	0.0466	50.7736 (2.8272)	0.0927
	End of 1994 market capitalization of A shares	$-3.34*10^{-9}$ (1.4117)	0.2348	$-9.04*10^{-8}$ (2.1392)	0.1436
	End of 1994 market capitalization of B shares	$-1.12*10^{-7}$ (1.8627)	0.1723	$-1.23*10^{-7}$ (2.4984)	0.1140
Financial:	Return on equity	—	—	0.1293 (2.2507)	0.1336
	Earnings per share	6.4877 (5.6702)	0.0173	6.0826 (3.9145)	0.0479

firm. The total number of nonnegotiable shares tends to reduce the probability of having cointegration between A- and B-share prices. The ownership-distribution factor, the liquidity factor, and the financial-characteristic factor all help to explain the price dynamics of ownership-restricted stocks.

Notes

1. For clarification purposes, when we mention A or B shares we mean share prices that have not been exchange-rate adjusted.
2. Detailed results are available upon request.

References

Bailey, Warren. 1994. "Risk and Return on China's New Stock Markets: Some Preliminary Evidence." *Pacific-Basin Finance Journal* 2: 243–60.

Bailey, Warren, and Julapa Jagtiani. 1994. "Foreign Ownership Restrictions and Stock Prices in the Thai Capital Market." *Journal of Financial Economics* 36: 57–87.

Bergström, Clas; Kristian Rydqvist; and Peter Sellin. 1993. "Asset Pricing with In- and Outflow Constraints: Theory and Empirical Evidence from Sweden." *Journal of Business Finance and Accounting* 20, no. 6 (November): 865–79.

Booth, G.G.; M. Chowdhury; and T. Martikainen. 1994. "The Effect of Foreign Ownership Restrictions on Stock Price Dynamics." *Weltwirtschaft-liches Archiv* 130: 730–46.

Diebold, Francis X.; Javier Gardeazabal; and Kamil Yilmaz. 1994. "On Cointegration and Exchange Rate Dynamics." *Journal of Finance* 49: 727–35.

Engle, R.F., and C.W.J. Granger. 1987. "Co-integration and Error Correction: Representation, Estimation, and Testing." *Econometrica* 55: 251–76.

Errunza, Vihang, and Etienne Losq. 1985. "International Asset Pricing under Mild Segmentation: Theory and Test." *Journal of Finance* 40: 105–24.

Eun, Cheol S., and S. Janakiramanan. 1986. "A Model of International Asset Pricing with a Constraint on the Foreign Equity Ownership." *Journal of Finance* 41: 897–914.

Hietala, Pekka T. 1989. "Asset Pricing in Partially Segmentated Markets: Evidence from the Finnish Market." *Journal of Finance* 44: 697–718.

Johansen, S. 1988. "Statistical Analysis of Cointegrating Vectors." *Journal of Economic Dynamics and Control* 12: 231–45.

———. 1991. "Estimation and Hypothesis Testing of Cointegration Vectors in Gaussian Vector Autoregressive Models." *Econometrica* 59: 1551–80.

Johansen, S., and K. Juselius. 1990. "Maximum Likelihood Estimation and Inference on Cointegration—with Applications to the Demand for Money." *Oxford Bulletin of Economics and Statistics* 52: 169–210.

Ma, Xianghai. 1996. "Capital Controls, Market Segmentation and Stock Prices: Evidence from the Chinese Stock Market." *Pacific-Basin Finance Journal* 4: 219–39.

Pantula, Sastry G.; Graciela Gonzalez-Farias; and Wayne A. Fuller. 1994. "A Comparison of Unit Root Criteria." *Journal of Business and Economics Statistics* 12: 449–59.

Perron, P. 1988. "Trends and Random Walks in Macroeconomic Time Series: Further Evidence from a New Approach." *Journal of Economics Dynamics and Control* 12: 297–332.

Phillips, P. C. B. 1987. "Time Series Regression with a Unit Root." *Econometrica* 55: 277–301.

Woolley, S., and J. Barnathan. 1992. "Bulls in the China Shop." *Business Week*, (September 28): 120.

8

Market Structure, Volatility, and Performance of H Shares

Xiaoqing Eleanor Xu

Introduction

In a decisive effort to lessen the dependence of state-owned enterprises (SOEs) on the government for financial support, reduce the use of debt financing, introduce market discipline, and foster a sound market economy, China opened the Shanghai Stock Exchange (SHSE) in December 1989 and the Shenzhen Stock Exchange (SZSE) in July 1991. There are two types of share classes listed on the domestic exchanges: A shares that are owned and traded by domestic investors; and B shares that are owned and traded by foreign investors in foreign currencies (U.S. dollars on the SHSE or Hong Kong dollars on the SZSE).

China has a short but aggressive history of raising equity capital from foreign investors. Foreign investors were first introduced to Chinese stocks listed on domestic exchanges: B shares. The first B-share issues (stocks available only to non-PRC residents) began trading on the SHSE with the listing of the Shanghai Vacuum Electron Device Corporation in February 1992. Shortly after that, China Southern Glass B shares inaugurated the Shenzhen B-share market. By the end of 1998, there were 825 A shares and 106 B shares listed on the domestic exchanges. However, since B shares are traded on China's domestic exchanges by offshore investors, the market has suffered from a lack of liquidity from the beginning.

Chinese companies were also vigorously looking for other ways to tap into foreign capital markets in order to finance their expansion, reform, and restructuring. In 1993, Chinese companies went beyond traditional domestic equity-financing channels to raise capital by listing in overseas markets such as those in Hong Kong and New York. As the gateway for capital to China, Hong Kong was naturally identified as the primary offshore equity market for Chinese firms to raise capital. In early 1993, the China Securities Regulatory Commission (CSRC) gave nine SOEs authorization to seek direct listings on the Stock Exchange of Hong Kong (SEHK). H shares refer to mainland China–incorporated companies that are listed in Hong Kong. The first batch of chosen listing firms were primarily SOEs that are leaders and model enterprises in heavy industries such as petrochemicals, steel, and infrastructure in mainland China.

The first H-share initial public offering (IPO), a U.S.$115-million issue for Tsingtao Brewery, was more than a hundred times oversubscribed at its July 15, 1993, IPO in Hong Kong. On July 26, 1993, the second H-share IPO, a U.S.$377-million issue for Shanghai Petrochemical, was three times the size of the Tsingtao IPO; it was also marketed internationally and cross-listed on the New York Stock Exchange (called N shares, American depository receipts of the underlying H shares in Hong Kong). Each of the six H-share issues in 1993 (Tsingtao Brewery, Shanghai Petrochemical, Beiren Printing, Guangzhou Shipyard, Maanshan Iron & Steel, and Kunming Machine) met with tremendous demand and considerable interest from both retail investors and fund managers, and a total of U.S.$1.5 billion in capital was raised through the 1993 H-share offerings. Figure 8.1 presents the time-series plots of monthly closing prices for these six H-share issues. With the successful listing of six Chinese companies in 1993, the Hong Kong financial market became a legitimate source of equity capital for mainland China's enterprises and helped raise the global visibility of Chinese domestic enterprises. By the end of 1998, there were forty-one H shares listed on the SEHK, with ten of them cross-listed on the New York Stock Exchange (NYSE) as N shares.

Another type of China-backed securities traded in Hong Kong is called "red chips," shares of Hong Kong–incorporated companies with significant business interests in mainland China or with strong mainland connections. Red chips offer investors liquidity, transparency, and more accessible Hong Kong–based management. They are often highly regarded by foreign investors as the preferred investment vehicle among the various China-backed securities. While H-share firms are generally

Figure 8.1 **Time Series Plots of the Monthly Closing Prices for the First Six H Shares Issued in 1993**

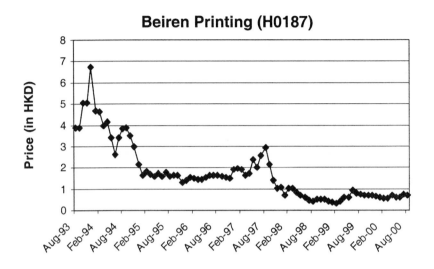

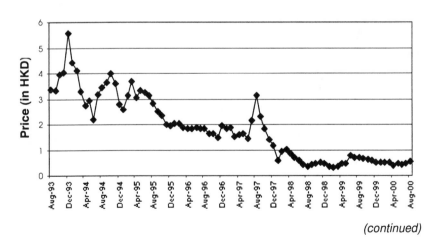

(continued)

leaders and model enterprises in heavy-industry sectors in mainland China, most red chips are highly diversified conglomerates. By the end of 1998, there were forty-seven Hong Kong–incorporated red chips listed on the SEHK.

Table 8.1 summarizes the structure and characteristics of various

Figure 8.1 *(continued)*

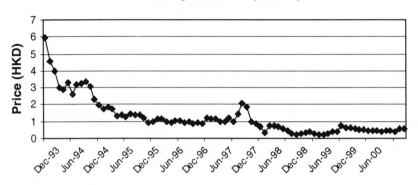

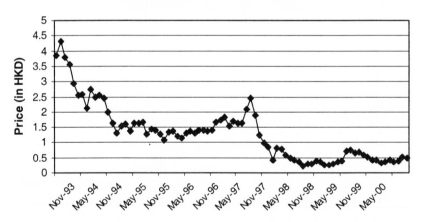

China-backed securities (also called "China plays"), including China-listed A and B shares, Hong Kong–listed H shares and red chips, and New York–listed N shares. This paper will focus on H shares, which are stocks of mainland Chinese enterprises that are listed and traded in Hong Kong.

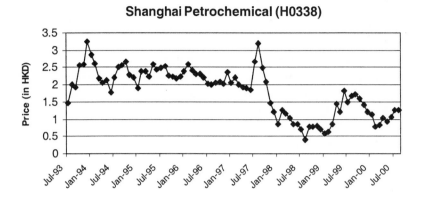

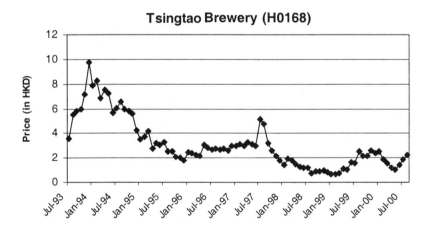

Note: Time period covered: from the H-share listing month to August 2000; frequency: monthly.

Volatility and Performance of the H-Share Market

Since their inception, H shares have been associated with tremendous market volatility. When H shares were first issued in Hong Kong on July

15, 1993, they were greeted with tremendous demand and favorable valuation, given the expectation that they would offer a unique opportunity for investors to cash in on China's rapid economic growth. Enthusiasm for these pure "China plays" reached its peak late that year. However, when Chinese authorities announced an austerity program (effective with the start of 1994) to cool the overheating economy, China-based H shares suddenly lost their investor appeal. Investor sentiment toward Chinese SOEs quickly turned negative and led to a sharp fall of more than 50 percent in the first six months of 1994.

From July 1 to September 2, 1994, H shares rebounded 40 percent due to some positive signs in the economy of mainland China and the publication of the Hang Seng China Enterprises Index (HSCEI) which tracked H shares. However, as the inflation figure in China rose to 27 percent in October 1994, the Chinese government decided to cool down the alarming inflation with even tougher austerity measures. The impact of the central government's two-year austerity program substantially reduced the mainland SOEs' credit availability, expansion capacity, and profitability, and led to a 50 percent decline in the H-share index from early September 1994 to the end of 1995.

The year 1996 marked the rebound of H shares as the Chinese government began to lift its austerity program by cutting interest rates twice—on May 1 and August 23. The H-share index rose by 30 percent that year, the first with a positive annual return since 1994.

After the 1996 financial statements of H shares hit the Hong Kong market in the first half of 1997, share prices rallied. This was despite a large decrease in earnings, as sentiment over the July 1997 Hong Kong handover and the expectation of a strong upswing in China's economy dominated the Hong Kong market. From July 3 to August 25, 1997, the H-share index returned 73 percent following the handover of Hong Kong to Chinese rule.

By the end of August 1997, as several Asian currencies began to devaluate and stock markets in the Asia-Pacific area started to decline sharply, large institutional investors began selling off Chinese stocks in Hong Kong. The Chinese stock prices in Hong Kong came back down to reality amid the Asian financial crisis (Smith 1997). The H-share index tumbled 72 percent between August 26, 1997, and January 22, 1998.

After 1997's astonishing market decline, bargain hunters returned to the H-share market in early 1998. Investor sentiment toward Chinese stocks was by and large upbeat as the market hoped for positive news on

Table 8.1

Structure and Characteristics of Various China-backed Securities (also called "China plays")

China-backed securities	Listing firms	Currency and exchange	Liquidity	Ownership restriction	Statistics as of Dec. 1998
A shares	Mainland China incorporated	Traded in Chinese RMB on SZSE or SHSE	High	Domestic investors	825 A-share issues (425 listed on SHSE and 400 listed on SZSE)
B shares	Mainland China incorporated	Traded in Hong Kong$ on SZSE; US$ on SHSE	Low	Foreign investors	106 B-share issues (52 listed on SHSE and 54 listed on SZSE), 81 with matched A-share issues for domestic investors
H shares	Mainland China incorporated	Traded in Hong Kong$ on SEHK	High	Foreign investors	41 H-share issues (18 issued A shares for domestic investors, 10 are cross-listed in New York as N shares)
Red chips	Hong Kong incorporated and managed, with substantial business interests in mainland China or mainland connections	Traded in Hong Kong$ on SEHK	High	Foreign investors	47 red chips
N Shares	Mainland China incorporated	Traded in US$ on NYSE	Low	Foreign investors	10 N-share issues (all are American depository receipts [ADRs] of the underlying Chinese H shares listed on SEHK)

the restructuring and reform of SOEs from the annual meeting of the National People's Congress in March 1998. Although reform measures were announced, optimism about China did not last long. Bad earnings from H-share firms surprised the market in April 1998 when annual earnings for 1997 were announced. Furthermore, the H-share market was plagued with worries about social unrest triggered by high unemployment in China, and concerns about the overall health of Chinese financial institutions riddled with nonperforming loans.

On October 6, 1998, the Guangdong International Trust and Investment Corporation (GITIC), China's second-largest investment-trust company and the investment arm of the Guangdong provincial government, was shut down by the Chinese authorities for its inability to repay foreign debt. It was the first time that a mainland Chinese company had defaulted on an international bond since 1949. The action by the Chinese authorities, which targeted companies affiliated with local and regional governments and their foreign lenders, symbolized the fact that China was starting to discipline troubled financial institutions, regardless of their connections. However, as the fear of credit risk spilled over to all Chinese enterprises, Hong Kong–listed H-share firms were facing a potential credit squeeze. The H-share index finished 1998 with a disappointing 45 percent negative return amid bad earning surprises, the GITIC default, the possible devaluation of the renminbi, and global financial turbulence.

The beaten H shares failed to recover in the first half of 1999 as the 1998 financial reports surprised the market again, showing falling profits and even losses. To make things even worse, investors discovered that some H-share firms had redirected IPO capital from core-business expansion to finance high-interest loans used to support other enterprises. They later failed to recover these loans (Loong 1998; Keenan 1999). However, the recovery of the Asian financial crisis, compounded with positive sentiment surrounding the landmark trade agreement between China and the United States on November 15, 1999, and expectation of China's entry into the World Trade Organization (WTO), pushed the H-share index 14 percent higher for 1999. In the first eight months of the year 2000, H shares recovered another 14 percent after the listed companies turned in their 1999 annual financial results, which slightly improved over those of 1998. Yet current earnings of most H-share enterprises are still much lower than their pre-IPO earnings, making investors suspicious of their ability to return healthy profits.

In summary, Chinese H shares have had extreme ups and downs since they opened in 1993. In the past seven years, market turbulence has been largely driven by investor sentiment toward the Chinese economy and fundamental concern about the deteriorating profitability of listed Chinese enterprises. The foreign investor has been deterred from H shares due to their lack of financial transparency, poor management, and improper usage of funds in noncore businesses.

Comparison of the H-Share Market with the A- and B-Share Markets

Figure 8.2 and Table 8.2 describe the time-series behavior of the daily H-share index (i.e., the HSCEI), together with China's domestic A- and B-share indices and the Hong Kong Hang Seng Index for the period September 1, 1994, to September 1, 2000. The HSCEI experienced an upward trend for this six-year period, except for the market crash during the Asian financial crisis (between fall 1997 and fall 1998). The Shanghai and Shenzhen A-share indices, which trace the performance of A shares on the Chinese domestic exchanges, show an overwhelming upward trend, despite some short-term ups and downs over the years. China's domestic A-share markets were largely uncorrelated with the listed companies' fundamental financial performance and insulated from global financial-market turbulence. This is primarily due to the following: (1) the Chinese renminbi is not yet fully convertible; (2) foreign investors are not allowed to purchase class A shares; (3) ample domestic savings create high demand for A shares (the only equity-investment opportunity available to Chinese domestic investors); and (4) the market is largely driven by domestic policy and market interventions by the government.

The Shanghai and Shenzhen B-share indices, which trace foreign shares traded on China's domestic exchanges, have a similar pattern to the H-share index. As B and H shares are both traded by foreign investors with many different investment opportunities, there are dramatic ups and downs in both markets that are fueled by changing investor sentiment toward China. They are affected by global market climate and driven by the fundamental profitability of the listed Chinese enterprises. The Hong Kong handover in July 1997 sent B and H shares to historic highs, while the Asian financial crisis brought the B- and H-share markets back down to earth. However, since H shares are traded in Hong Kong, where there is higher liquidity and more institutional-investor

Figure 8.2 **Time Series Plot of Chinese A-, B-, and H-share Indices from September 1, 1994 to September 1, 2000**

**Shanghai Stock Exchange A-Share Index
(September 1994-September 2000)**

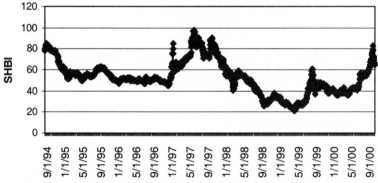

**Shanghai Stock Exchange B-Share Index
(September 1994-September 2000)**

Note: Shanghai Stock Exchange A- and B-share indices.

scrutiny, that market has a higher demand for greater transparency, more disclosure, and better communications with shareholders. While the Shanghai and Shenzhen B-share indices rallied 70 percent and 40 percent between January 1 and September 1, 2000, amid speculation of the near-term merging of A and B shares, H shares remained highly dis-

Figure 8.2 *(continued)*

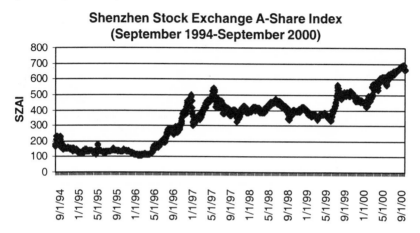

Note: Shenzhen Stock Exchange A- and B-share indices.

counted as the listed firms failed to deliver satisfactory earnings to share-holders.

An examination of the contemporaneous daily returns shows that the H-share index has a 60 percent correlation with the HSCEI, a 32 percent correlation with the Shanghai B-share index, a 24 percent correlation with the Shenzhen B-share index, a 8.5 percent correlation with the

Figure 8.2 *(continued)*

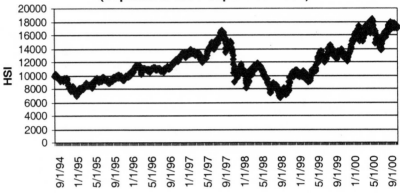

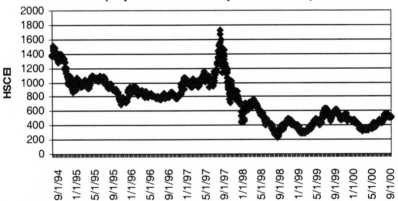

Top: Stock Exchange of Hong Kong Hang Seng index.
Bottom: Hang Seng China Enterprises (H-Share) index.

Shanghai A-share index, and a 10.2 percent correlation with the Shenzhen A-share index. This suggests that there is strong intraday information transmission between B shares, H shares, and Hong Kong stocks, and weak contemporaneous transmission between A and H shares. On the other hand, there is very small correlation between H-share daily returns and the previous day's returns on the A-share, B-share, or Hang Seng indices, indicating that the interday information transmission among these markets is extremely limited.

With regard to stock-market volatility, H shares rate highest. According to the daily return statistics in Table 8.2, the standard deviation of the daily H-share index return is 2.92 percent, which is much higher than that of the HSCEI, and is also higher than that of the domestic exchange–traded A- and B-share indices.

Market Structure of H Shares Versus A Shares
Issued by the Same Companies

Market segmentation on the Chinese domestic A- and B-share stock markets has attracted considerable academic interest in recent years (Chui and Kwok 1998; Bailey, Chung, and Kang 1999; Su 1999; Fung, Lee, and Leung 2000; Xu and Liu 2000). Researchers have generally found segmentation and limited information transmission between A and B shares, with B shares being more sensitive to the listed company's fundamental profitability. In principle, shares issued by the same company should have the same rights, same dividends, and same valuations. Investors should require the same return on these shares and hence price these shares at the same level. However, B shares are generally traded at a deep discount to the same company's A shares (an average 87 percent discount as of December 1998). Ownership restrictions, lower liquidity, different systemic market risk, more rational expectations, and valuation based on economic and financial fundamentals, are cited as reasons for the B-share discount.

Using various market indices, Poon and Fung (2000) examined information flows among various China-backed securities (H shares, red chips, and A and B shares) and found that red chips play a leading role in processing information. However, research has not been conducted to examine the market structure, segmentation, and price dynamics of mainland companies that have issued both A shares on domestic stock exchanges (i.e., the SHSE or SZSE) and H shares on the SEHK. In this article, I examined the above issues using all seventeen mainland China–incorporated companies that had issued both A and H shares by the end of 1997. There are forty China-incorporated companies that had listed H shares in Hong Kong by the end of 1997. Seventeen of those had also listed A shares on China's domestic stock exchanges. The data used in

Table 8.2

Daily Returns of Chinese A-, B-, and H-Share Indices from September 1, 1994, to September 1, 2000

Symbol	Stock Market Index
SHAI	Shanghai Stock Exchange A-Share Index
SHBI	Shanghai Stock Exchange B-Share Index
SZAI	Shenzhen Stock Exchange A-Share Index

Symbol	Stock Market Index
SZBI	Shenzhen Stock Exchange B-Share Index
HSI	Stock Exchange of Hong Kong Hang Seng Index
HSCEI	Hang Seng China Enterprises (H-Share) Index

	Shanghai Stock Exch. (SHSE)				Shenzhen Stock Exch. (SZSE)				Stock Exch. of Hong Kong (SEHK)			
	SHAI		SHBI		SZAI		SZBI		HSI		HSCEI	
Year	Mean	Std Dev	Mean	Std Dev	Mean	Std Dev	Mean	Std Dev	Mean	Std Dev	Mean	Std Dev
1994[1]	-0.029	4.67	-0.316	1.20	-0.025	4.54	-0.336	1.18	-0.221	1.32	-0.276	2.23
1995	0.015	3.28	-0.098	1.05	-0.019	2.96	-0.149	0.94	0.089	1.27	-0.113	1.71
1996	0.223	2.72	0.143	2.21	0.444	3.09	0.420	3.31	0.119	1.07	0.092	1.81
1997	0.153	2.23	-0.064	2.40	0.114	2.52	-0.134	2.46	-0.060	2.59	-0.046	3.84
1998	0.026	1.22	-0.265	2.68	0.000	1.37	-0.232	2.25	-0.065	2.69	-0.315	3.82
1999	0.128	1.71	0.193	3.11	0.124	1.79	0.250	3.29	0.193	1.70	0.108	2.91
2000[2]	0.279	1.57	0.359	2.60	0.312	1.64	0.250	2.60	-0.017	2.00	0.210	2.97
Sep. 1, 1994– Sep. 1, 2000	0.119	2.47	0.005	2.36	0.144	2.54	0.034	2.55	0.032	1.94	-0.039	2.92

Notes: [1] September 1–end. [2] Start September 1.

Table 8.2 *(continued)*

Pearson Correlation Between Daily HSCEI (H share) Index Return and Returns on Other Market Indices

Contemporaneous correlations		Correlations with lag returns	
Correlation $(R_{HSCEI,t}, R_{SHAI,t})$	0.085**	Correlation $(R_{HSCEI,t}, R_{SHAI,t-1})$	0.019
Correlation $(R_{HSCEI,t}, R_{SHBI,t})$	0.317**	Correlation $(R_{HSCEI,t}, R_{SHBI,t-1})$	0.075**
Correlation $(R_{HSCEI,t}, R_{SZAI,t})$	0.102**	Correlation $(R_{HSCEI,t}, R_{SZAI,t-1})$	0.035
Correlation $(R_{HSCEI,t}, R_{SZBI,t})$	0.238**	Correlation $(R_{HSCEI,t}, R_{SZBI,t-1})$	0.064**
Correlation $(R_{HSCEI,t}, R_{HSI,t})$	0.600**	Correlation $(R_{HSCEI,t}, R_{HSI,t-1})$	0.130**

Notes: The daily return of an equity index is computed as the percentage change in the daily closing value of the index. Data of the above six indices from September 1, 1994, to September 1, 2000, are used in the analysis.** indicates that the correlation is significant at 5 percent.

this study were obtained from the China Database and the Hong Kong Database provided by the *Taiwan Economic Journal* (*TEJ*) and Bridge Information Systems.

Table 8.3 presents the profile and share structure of these seventeen companies. All of them issued H shares in Hong Kong first, and issued A shares in mainland China at a later date. In the Chinese shareholding system, there are capital contributions by the state or by state-owned legal entities, by domestic investors, and by foreign investors. State and state-owned legal-person shares are not tradable, while domestic shares (A shares) and offshore shares (H and N shares) are floating shares. The Chinese shareholding system preserves the predominant portion of state ownership as state and state-owned legal-person shares account for 57 percent of company shares, while domestic and offshore shares account for 11 percent and 32 percent of company shares, respectively. The H shares of companies such as Eastern Airlines, Jilin Chemical, and Shanghai Petrochemical, are also cross-listed on the NYSE as N shares. The average market capitalization of these companies is U.S.$457 million, and the average total asset is approximately U.S.$840 million, indicating that these are large cap companies with a substantial asset base.

In Table 8.4, the market microstructures of A and H shares are compared. China's two domestic exchanges and the SEHK all trade Monday through Friday with two trading sessions which are operated in a continuous auction environment with no specialist making the market. Limit orders are matched and executed through a computerized matching system. The average daily trading volume of H shares in Hong Kong is

Table 8.3

Profiles and Ownership Structure of Chinese Companies That Issued Both A and H Shares

Company Name	Exchange	A-share security code	H-share security code	A-share listing date	H-share listing date	Total company shrs. (millions)	State shrs. %	Legal pers. shrs. %	Domestic floating shrs. %	Offshore floating shrs. %	Market capitalization (in US$ millions)	Total assets (in US$ millions)
Angang New Steel	SZSE	0898	0347	12/25/97	07/24/97	2,509.00	52.6	0.0	12.0	35.5	656.03	841.95
Beiren Printing	SHSE	600860	0187	05/06/94	08/06/93	400.00	62.5	0.0	12.5	25.0	121.26	132.22
Dongfang Electric	SHSE	600875	1072	10/10/95	06/06/94	450.00	48.9	0.0	13.3	37.8	140.84	281.41
Eastern Airlines	SHSE	600115	0670	11/05/97	02/05/97	4,866.95	61.6	0.0	6.2	32.2	807.30	3,184.43
Guangzhou Shipyard	SHSE	600685	0317	10/28/93	08/06/93	494.68	42.6	0.0	25.6	31.8	163.30	366.68
Jilin Chemical	SZSE	0618	0368	10/15/96	05/23/95	3,411.08	67.3	0.0	5.6	27.1	735.42	1,900.16
Jingwei Textile	SZSE	0666	0350	12/10/96	02/02/96	423.80	51.9	0.0	5.4	42.7	99.75	183.74
Kunming Machine	SHSE	600806	0300	01/03/94	12/07/93	245.01	41.8	7.2	24.5	26.5	61.08	69.55
Luoyang Glass	SHSE	600876	1108	10/31/95	07/08/94	700.00	36.4	36.4	4.6	22.7	179.56	311.11
Maanshan Iron & Steel	SHSE	600808	0323	01/06/94	11/03/93	6,455.30	62.5	1.4	9.3	26.9	1,431.61	2,080.82
Northeast Machinery	SZSE	0585	0042	12/13/95	07/06/95	873.37	51.6	2.4	16.4	29.5	187.28	248.50
Panda Electronics	SHSE	600775	0553	11/18/96	05/02/96	655.02	54.2	0.0	8.9	37.0	77.64	178.86
Shanghai Petrochem	SHSE	600688	0338	11/08/93	07/26/93	7,200.00	55.6	2.1	10.0	32.4	1,565.07	2,328.86
Tianjin Bohai Chem	SHSE	600874	1065	06/30/95	05/17/94	1,330.00	63.1	2.9	8.5	25.6	157.43	216.39

Tsingtao Brew	SHSE	600600	0168	08/27/93	07/15/93	900.00	44.4	5.9	11.1	38.5	273.82	450.86
Xinhua Pharmaceut- ical	SZSE	0756	0719	08/06/97	12/31/96	427.31	50.9	3.9	10.1	35.1	107.58	167.01
Yizheng Chemical Fiber	SHSE	600871	1033	04/11/95	03/29/94	4,000.00	0.0	60.0	5.0	35.0	1,008.64	1,347.62
Cross-sectional Mean						2,078.91	49.9	7.2	11.1	31.8	457.27	840.60
Cross-sectional Total						35,341.47	49.9	7.2	11.1	31.8	7,773.59	14,290.20

Notes: This table includes all Chinese companies that have issued both A shares (on the SHSE or SZSE) and H shares (on the SEHK) by the end of 1997. The data on company-ownership structure, total number of shares, total market value, and total assets are based on the year end 1999. State shares % indicates the percentage of company shares that are not floating shares and are held by the state. Legal person shares % indicates the percentage of shares that are not floating shares and are held by state-owned legal persons. Domestic floating shares % indicates the percentage of company shares held by Chinese domestic investors—A shares listed and traded on the SHSE or SZSE. Offshore floating shares % indicates the percentage of company shares held by offshore investors—H shares listed and traded on the SEHK (some H shares, such as Eastern Airlines, Jilin Chemical, and Shanghai Petrochem, are also cross-listed on NYSE as N shares).

Table 8.4

The Market Microstructure of A and H Shares: Volume, Spread, Return, and Volatility

Company name	Average daily trading volume (in 000 shares)		Average bid-ask spread (in RMB)		Average daily stock return (%)		Standard deviation of daily stock return (%)		Correlation between daily H- and A-share returns	
	A share	H share	A share	H share	A share	H share	A share	H share	(R_h, R_a)	(R_h, R_{a-1})
Angang New Steel	5,303	22,049	0.011	0.011	0.098	0.027	2.274	5.494	0.134	-0.063
Beiren Printing	1,084	542	0.016	0.033	0.150	-0.107	2.865	4.362	0.102	-0.045
Dongfang Electric	1,106	1,158	0.016	0.024	0.146	-0.129	2.874	5.318	0.090	-0.017
Eastern Airlines	4,884	17,772	0.011	0.012	0.112	0.041	2.946	4.897	0.156	0.066
Guangzhou Shipyard	2,076	1,036	0.012	0.027	0.150	-0.153	2.825	5.316	0.104	0.041
Jilin Chemical	2,076	15,253	0.016	0.012	0.098	-0.074	3.422	5.935	0.075	-0.014
Jingwei Textile	1,034	2,134	0.021	0.022	0.095	0.066	3.150	5.926	0.056	0.033
Kunming Machine	2,545	203	0.016	0.039	0.266	-0.074	3.881	6.091	0.165	0.076
Luoyang Glass	1,340	2,683	0.015	0.015	0.144	-0.067	2.920	5.847	0.112	0.080
Maanshan Iron & Steel	10,833	23,404	0.011	0.009	0.104	-0.139	2.717	5.711	0.085	0.026
Northeast Machinery	1,609	3,242	0.016	0.017	0.113	-0.092	2.766	5.786	0.099	-0.009
Panda Electronics	713	2,902	0.022	0.027	0.161	0.272	2.871	6.759	0.090	0.058
Shanghai Petrochem	8,360	25,912	0.011	0.014	0.073	-0.023	2.406	5.438	0.101	0.017
Tianjin Bohai Chem	2,612	7,128	0.012	0.014	0.227	0.037	2.939	6.543	0.049	0.005
Tsingtao Brew	1,629	1,126	0.015	0.038	0.117	0.015	2.526	5.027	0.062	-0.005

Xinhua Pharmaceutical	404	986	0.030	0.029	0.161	−0.093	3.159	4.385	0.070	0.020
Yizheng Chemical Fiber	4,074	32,944	0.012	0.017	0.104	0.061	2.788	6.073	0.163	0.008
Cross-sectional mean	3,040	9,440	0.015	0.021	0.137	−0.025	2.902	5.583	0.101	0.016
Cross-sectional median	2,076	2,902	0.015	0.017	0.117	−0.067	2.871	5.711	0.099	0.017
Cross-sectional standard deviation	2,870	10,928	0.005	0.010	0.049	0.106	0.372	0.664	0.036	0.040

Notes: The above market-microstructure statistics for each company on trading volume (thousand shares traded daily), bid-ask spread (the difference between daily closing bid and ask prices, both expressed in RMB), and stock return (the daily percentage change in closing price) are based on daily data from August 1, 1997, to August 31, 2000. The standard deviations of daily stock A- and H-share returns are used as measures of the return volatility for A and H shares, respectively. The last two columns represent the contemporaneous correlation between daily H- and A-share returns and the correlation between H-share return on day t and A-share return on t-1.

Table 8.5

Annual Earnings, Prices, and Financial Ratios of Chinese Companies That Issued Both A and H Shares

Company Name	1993 EPS	1993 A price	1993 H price	1994 EPS	1994 A price	1994 H price	1995 EPS	1995 A price	1995 H price	1996 EPS	1996 A price	1996 H price	1997 EPS	1997 A price	1997 H price	1998 EPS	1998 A price	1998 H price	1999 EPS	1999 A price	1999 H price
Angang New Steel										0.22		1.23	0.20	4.74	1.26	0.05	2.89	0.49	0.12	3.00	0.55
Beiren Printing	0.14	7.22		0.27	3.83	2.30	0.22	3.73	1.50	0.18	5.12	2.03	0.16	5.06	1.09	0.14	5.06	0.81	0.12	6.57	0.75
Dongfang Electric				0.42		3.77	0.20	7.1	2.02	0.13	6.38	2.63	0.12	5.58	1.10	0.09	5.27	0.43	0.01	6.91	0.49
Eastern Airlines										0.11			0.07	5.13	0.92	-0.13	3.24	0.37	0.04	3.90	0.45
Guangzhou Shipyard	0.36	6.98	5.89	0.32	3.05	2.97	0.26	2.90	2.10	0.07	5.20	2.10	0.08	4.00	1.23	0.04	3.76	0.57	0.00	4.70	0.66
Jilin Chemical							0.22		1.71	0.07	10.80	1.28	0.03	6.66	1.94	0.02	5.93	0.89	0.04	6.21	2.54
Jingwei Textile										0.19	12.24	1.48	0.08	6.66	1.13	0.02	6.38	0.47	0.21	8.61	0.72
Kunming Machine	0.46	6.37		0.16	2.56	4.96	0.03	2.73	2.48	0.01	3.83	3.01	0.00	3.41	1.08	-0.10	5.13	0.37	-0.19	7.70	2.09
Luoyang Glass				0.48	3.16		0.35	6.95	1.94	0.03	5.65	2.31	-0.31	4.12	0.68	-0.52	4.24	0.24	0.07	5.75	0.39
Maanshan Iron & Steel	0.17	4.60		0.12	1.75	1.74	0.01	1.94	1.16	0.01	3.60	1.78	0.01	2.87	1.34	-0.03	2.33	0.57	0.00	2.58	0.98
Northeast Machinery							0.23	4.65		0.10	6.97	1.44	0.10	7.02	0.94	0.01	6.58	0.55	-0.19	4.78	0.43
Panda Electronics	0.18	4.48	3.48	0.23	1.84	2.35	0.32	2.31	2.38	0.27	10.23	1.82	-0.53	7.50	0.96	-0.77	7.26	0.43	0.05	11.10	0.63
Shanghai Petrochem							0.13	3.90	0.58	0.16	6.10	2.51	0.10	4.07	0.81	0.03	2.92	0.36	0.10	3.54	0.86
Tianjin Bohai Chem				0.13	1.00					0.05	4.16	0.98	-0.46	3.56	1.02	-0.28	3.15	0.37		6.03	0.63
Tsingtao Brew	0.38	7.90	10.43	0.18	4.08	4.55	0.16	3.63	1.92	0.08	6.20	3.16	0.07	5.93	1.29	0.11	5.41	0.75	0.10	8.17	1.31

Xinhua Pharmaceutical			0.21		2.46	0.20	8.70	1.09	0.12	9.60	0.77	0.15	12.59	1.14			
Yizheng Chemical Fiber	0.27	3.08	0.26	3.00	1.86	0.04	4.51	2.01	0.00	4.57	1.50	-0.06	3.40	0.76	0.19	4.87	2.33
Cross-sectional mean	0.28	6.45	6.33	0.26	2.85	2.99	0.20	3.89	1.75	0.11	6.50	2.04	0.02	5.27	1.14	-0.08	4.86
												0.54	0.03	6.30	1.00		
Cross-sectional median	0.27	6.98	6.13	0.25	2.81	3.03	0.22	3.63	1.89	0.10	5.88	2.02	0.07	5.06	1.10	0.02	5.06
												0.49	0.05	6.03	0.72		
Cross-sectional standard deviation	0.13	1.77	2.40	0.12	0.98	1.22	0.10	1.72	0.53	0.07	2.71	0.64	0.18	1.61	0.32	0.26	1.91
												0.19	0.14	2.73	0.68		

Other key balance sheet items and financial ratios	1996		1997		1998		1999	
	Mean	Std Dev	Mean	Std Dev	Mean	Std Dev	Mean	Std Dev
Debt (in million RMBs)	3,201	4,845	3,339	4,825	3,448	5,121	3,174	4,986
Equity (in million RMBs)	3,416	3,584	3,785	3,801	3,655	3,785	3,786	4,059
Total assets (in million RMBs)	6,617	7,401	7,124	7,876	7,103	7,973	6,960	7,951
Net income (in million RMBs)	186	273	96	244	-108	267	115	279
Debt ratio (=debt/total assets)	36.00%	20.35%	36.65%	19.99%	39.53%	20.30%	37.88%	17.93%
Return on equity (=net income/equity)	6.37%	5.54%	1.09%	9.64%	-7.98%	22.35%	0.78%	9.46%
Return on assets (=net income/total assets)	3.80%	3.38%	1.45%	4.47%	-2.83%	8.38%	0.08%	6.81%

Notes: The H-share prices are converted from Hong Kong dollars (HKD) to renminbi (RMB) for the purpose of comparison. Both A- and H-share prices presented in the above table are in RMB. The A- and H-share prices are based on year-end closing prices of A and H shares from 1993 to 1999. The EPS (earnings per share) statistics are based on the companies' annual financial statements from 1993 to 1999. The EPS is in RMB.

Table 8.6

Discount Ratios of H Shares Over A Shares Issued by the Same Chinese Companies

Company name	1994	1995	1996	1997	1998	1999	2000
Angang New Steel	39.9			73.4	83.0	81.8	89.0
Beiren Printing		59.8	60.3	78.4	83.9	88.6	90.7
Dongfang Electric		71.6	58.8	80.3	91.9	93.0	95.8
Eastern Airlines				82.1	88.4	88.5	90.7
Guangzhou Shipyard	2.6	27.7	59.7	69.2	84.9	85.9	85.3
Jilin Chemical			88.1	70.9	85.0	59.1	65.6
Jingwei Textile			87.9	83.0	92.7	91.7	92.1
Kunming Machine	-93.9	9.1	21.3	68.3	92.7	72.9	82.5
Luoyang Glass		72.1	59.1	83.5	94.4	93.2	94.3
Maanshan Iron & Steel	0.3	40.4	50.7	53.4	75.7	61.8	66.9
Northeast Machinery		71.0	79.3	86.6	91.7	91.0	94.2
Panda Electronics			82.2	87.2	94.0	94.3	96.3
Shanghai Petrochem	-27.9	-3.1	58.8	80.0	87.5	75.8	71.4
Tianjin Bohai Chem		85.2	76.3	71.4	88.1	89.5	92.6
Tsingtao Brew	-11.5	47.2	49.1	78.2	86.2	84.0	87.1
Xinhua Pharmaceutical				79.6	92.0	90.9	90.6
Yizheng Chemical Fiber		37.9	55.4	67.2	77.7	52.2	67.6

Cross-sectional statistics:	1994	1995	1996	1997	1998	1999	2000
No. of companies	6	11	14	17	17	17	17
Mean	−15.1	47.2	63.4	76.5	87.6	82.2	85.5
Median	−5.6	47.2	59.4	78.4	88.1	88.5	90.6
Standard deviation	44.7	28.1	18.1	8.6	5.5	13.1	10.7
Minimum	−93.9	−3.1	21.3	53.4	75.7	52.2	65.6
1st quartile (25%)	−44.4	27.7	54.2	70.1	84.4	74.4	77.0
3rd quartile (75%)	12.0	71.6	80.0	82.5	92.3	91.4	93.4
Maximum	39.9	85.2	88.1	87.2	94.5	94.3	96.3

Notes: H-share discount ratio = (A-share price in RMB—H-share price in RMB) / A-share price in RMB * 100%. A negative discount ratio indicates that the H shares are traded at a premium over the corresponding A shares.

The H-share prices are converted from HKD to RMB in computing the H-share discount ratios.

The above table presents cross-sectional statistics that are based on year-end closing prices of A and H shares from 1994 to 1999. The statistics for the year 2000 are based on the monthly closing prices of August 2000.

three times the volume of corresponding A shares in mainland China, indicating that H shares of the same companies are more frequently traded. Xu and Liu (2000) document that B shares are on average traded at only 10 percent of the volume of corresponding A shares. Given that B shares are foreign shares traded domestically while H shares are foreign shares traded in Hong Kong, the results seem to indicate that the Hong Kong market provides better liquidity for China-backed securities than the domestic market. The bid-ask spread for H shares, however, is slightly higher than the spread for A shares of the same listed firm. This might be due to excessive volatility related to H-share returns. The H-share daily stock return standard deviation is on average 5.58 percent, which is almost twice the level of the corresponding A shares. The daily contemporaneous correlation between H- and A-share returns is only about 10 percent, reflecting strong market segmentation between the domestic and foreign share classes. The extremely low correlation between H-share return and the previous day's A-share return further indicates that the two share returns might be driven by different fundamental forces.

Table 8.5 presents the annual data on EPS, A-share closing prices, and H-share closing prices for the seventeen sample firms from 1993 through 1999. All data have been adjusted for any company's capital changes (such as rights offerings and stock dividends). A cross-sectional summary of other key financial figures is also described in Table 8.5. The profitability of listed H-share companies has deteriorated substantially over the years, with the cross-sectional median EPS ranging from RMB 0.25 in 1994, RMB 0.22 in 1995, RMB 0.10 in 1996, RMB 0.07 in 1997, to RMB 0.02 in 1998. The median EPS slightly rebounded to RMB 0.05 in 1999, but was still far below the listed H-share firms' pre-IPO EPS level. Similar patterns can be observed from the return on equity and return on assets. The A-share prices of these firms, however, have been on an upward trend over the years despite short-run fluctuations and disappointing earnings. Unlike Chinese domestic investors, H-share investors place stronger emphasis on the listed company's ability to generate earnings. In addition, this stronger emphasis on earnings valuation by H-share investors might be due to the differences in accounting earnings reported to domestic and foreign investors. Chen, Gul, and Su (1999) examined the difference between earnings based on Chinese GAAP—released to A-share investors—and those based on the International Accounting Standard (IAS)—released to foreign investors.

They found that earnings under Chinese GAAP are on average 20 to 30 percent higher than those reported under the IAS. Over the years, H shares have been largely clouded by bad earnings and deteriorating profitability, resulting in dramatically lower share prices.

Table 8.6 presents the discount ratio of H shares over A shares issued by the same Chinese companies. H shares were on average traded at 15 percent premium to A-share prices in 1994, but later traded at 47.2 percent discount to A shares in 1995, 63.4 percent discount in 1996, 76.5 percent discount in 1997, 87.6 percent discount in 1998, and 82.2 percent discount in 1999. Despite the fact that H shares have better liquidity than B shares, the magnitude of the H-share price discount to A share is similar to the B-share price discount to A share as documented by Xu and Liu (2000). Fundamental concerns over earnings and profitability have been key drivers in the price movements of both H and B shares.

Conclusion

Since their debut in July 1993, Hong Kong–listed Chinese H shares have experienced extreme market volatility. Currently, H shares are traded at a deep discount to corresponding A shares. Foreign investors were first attracted to H shares since they promised opportunities to cash in on China's alluring economic growth, but these investors were later deterred from H shares due to their lack of transparency, poor management, improper usage of funds in noncore businesses, and deteriorating profitability. Given the critical role of the Hong Kong capital market for China's economic growth, it is important to maintain a healthy primary market for new H-share issues and foster a strong secondary market for existing H shares. The H-share market is calling for listed state enterprises to rethink their approach to investor relations, financial transparency, and fund management in order to achieve greater efficiency, competitiveness, and profitability, and to recover credibility.

References

Bailey, W.; Y.P. Chung; and J.K. Kang. 1999. "Foreign Ownership Restrictions and Equity Price Premiums: What Drives the Demand for Cross-Border Investments?" *Journal of Financial and Quantitative Analysis* 34: 489–511.

Chen, C.J.P.; F.A. Gul; and X. Su. 1999. "A Comparison of Reported Earnings under Chinese GAAP vs. IAS: Evidence from the Shanghai Stock Exchange." *Accounting Horizons* 13: 91–111.

Chui, A.C., and C.Y. Kwok. 1998. "Cross-Autocorrelation between A Shares and B Shares in the Chinese Stock Market." *Journal of Financial Research* 21: 333–53.

Fung, H.G.; W. Lee; and W.K. Leung. 2000. "Segmentation of the A and B Share Equity Markets." *Journal of Financial Research* 23: 179–95.

Keenan, F. 1999. "H Is for Hazard." *Far Eastern Economic Review* 162: 56.

Loong, P. 1998. "Finding Trouble in the Footnotes." *Euromoney* 350: 227–28.

Mendelson, H. 1987. "Consolidation, Fragmentation, and Market Performance." *Journal of Financial and Quantitative Analysis* 22: 189–207.

Poon, W.P.H., and H.G. Fung. 2000. "Red Chips or H Shares: Which China-Backed Securities Process Information the Fastest?" *Journal of Multinational Financial Management* 10: 315–43.

Smith, C.S. 1997. "China's Markets Feel the Regional Heat: Asian Economic Crisis Clouds Listing of State Firms." *Wall Street Journal*, September 11: A12.

Su, D. 1999. "Ownership Restriction and Stock Prices: Evidence from Chinese Markets." *Financial Review* 34: 37–55.

Wang, G., and Z. Wei. 1996. *Legal Developments in China: Market Economy and Law*. Hong Kong: Sweet and Maxwell.

Xia, M. 1992. *The Re-emerging Securities Market in China*. Westport, Conn.: Quorum Books.

Xu, X.E., and J. Liu. 2000. "Short-Term Dynamic Transmission and Long-Term Foreign Share Discount: Evidence from the Chinese Stock Markets." *International Journal of Business*, forthcoming.

Yao, C. 1998. *Stock Market and Futures Market in the People's Republic of China*. Hong Kong: Oxford University Press.

Part III

Foreign Direct Investment

9

China's Inward FDI Boom and the Greater Chinese Economy

Kevin H. Zhang

I. Introduction

In the two decades since 1979, China, Taiwan, and Hong Kong have become one integrated economic region, driving the dramatic growth of investment, production, and trade in East Asia. Often referred to as "the greater Chinese economy," this region represents in certain respects the triumph of economics over politics, in the sense that the three very different political entities have today become an economic trading, investing, and producing region, despite political and military conflict and long-standing, deep-seated suspicion and mistrust. FDI has been the engine driving these three entities into an increasingly intimate relationship (Ash and Kueh 1993; Naughton 1997).

Few developments in the world economy in recent years have elicited more interest or stirred more controversy than the sudden emergence of China as the most attractive site of FDI. In fact, China has become the largest recipient of FDI among developing countries and since 1993 has been second in the world only to the United States (UNCTAD 1999). The FDI boom in China has been considered a puzzle because foreign investors have traditionally had little legal security in China since the Communists took control in 1949 (Perkins 1994). More important, most FDI received in China did not come from the industrial countries that supply over 90 percent of global FDI, but from Hong Kong and Taiwan. As shown in Table 9.1, Hong Kong (the largest investor in China) invested as much as $138.5 billion during the

Table 9.1

FDI in China by Origin, 1979–1991 and 1992–1998 (U.S.$ millions)

Country/region origins	Rank	1992–98 Total inflows	%	Rank	1979–91 Total inflows	%
Hong Kong	1	125,300	53.57	1	13,208	57.17
Taiwan	2	19,458	8.32	6	199	0.86
Subtotal		144,758	61.89		13,407	58.03
Japan	3	18,890	8.08	4	1,740	7.53
United States	4	17,963	7.68	2	2,382	10.31
European Union	5	14,462	6.17	3	1,953	8.50
Singapore	6	11,626	4.97	5	628	2.72
South Korea	7	8,005	3.42	7	51	0.22
Others		26,205	11.20		2,942	12.73
Total		233,906	100.00		23,103	100.00

Sources: Data for 1992–97 are from *International Trade* (various issues), MOFERT. Others are from *Almanac of China's Foreign Economic Relations and Trade* (various issues) and *China Statistical Yearbook* (various years).
Note: All numbers of FDI flows and stock are realized investment in current values.

period 1979–1998, which is 55 percent of the total FDI received by China. Investment from Hong Kong and Taiwan (the second-largest investor in China) together constituted over 60 percent of FDI in China. The large amount of FDI from Hong Kong (HKDI) and Taiwan (TDI) raises the question of how well the theory of FDI explains China's emergence as a major FDI host and the rise of FDI from developing economies.

While there is considerable literature on inward FDI in China (e.g., Casson and Zheng 1991; Pomfret 1991; Kueh 1992), the puzzle of large amounts of HKDI and TDI in China has not been addressed. This paper thus investigates the issue by assessing China's location advantages and disadvantages in attracting HKDI and TDI relative to other developing countries. Shedding light on the issue should have important policy implications. The three economies of Hong Kong, Taiwan, and China, working in concert, have enormous potential, because there are substantial opportunities to improve productivity and profit from flows of direct investment among the three economies. For China, keeping large FDI flows—including both HKDI and TDI—will not only enhance its economic growth, but will also necessarily upgrade its industrial structure through the absorption of the advanced technology embodied in such investment.

This chapter investigates the determinants of China's FDI boom in the context of the greater Chinese economy. The growing interactions between mainland China, Hong Kong, and Taiwan have been driven by trade in goods and services and flows of capital and labor. Evidence presented in the paper indicates that the large amount of HKDI and TDI has been associated with the greater Chinese economy and "Chinese connections." We test for determinants of HKDI and TDI through a relative-demand model with time-series data. The behavior of investors in Hong Kong and Taiwan is especially analyzed in comparison with that of developed-country investors. The evidence suggests that China's location advantages and disadvantages have received unique responses from Hong Kong–Taiwan investors. While HKDI and TDI are attracted primarily by China's cheap labor, they also intend to increase investment oriented toward China's potentially huge market. China's FDI incentive and the special links (Chinese connections) of Hong Kong and Taiwan with China have contributed substantially to these large amounts of HKDI and TDI.

Section 2 briefly explains the theory of why FDI from developing economies exists, and derives a conceptual framework within which the determination of HKDI and TDI may be analyzed. Section 3 discusses the patterns of HKDI and TDI and their stylized facts in comparison with FDI from developed countries. Section 4 develops empirical models and presents estimation results of HKDI–TDI determinants. We summarize the conclusions and suggest some policy implications in Section 5.

II. Conceptual Framework

According to Dunning (1981), a firm with certain ownership advantages (patent or brand name) would open a subsidiary in a foreign country with location advantages (cheap labor or growing market) to maximize its profits. Both advantages of ownership and location can best be captured by the internalization of production (not exporting or licensing) via direct investment in the foreign country.

The growth of FDI from developing economies such as Hong Kong and Taiwan in the last two decades has raised such questions as how well traditional theories of multinational enterprise (MNE) explain the rise of their FDI. In particular, the most intriguing question has been the source of their competitive edge in world markets for investment.

Theory has established that some advantage in intangible assets (ownership advantages) must exist if a firm is to become transnational. Yet, on the surface, developing-economy firms appear to lack such assets; they possess no advanced proprietary technology, established brand names, or special marketing or organizational skills. Moreover, their competitors include not just local enterprises in the host countries, but established MNEs from developed countries, with global production and communication networks.

There have been two approaches to this question. One has its origins in the product-life-cycle literature (Vernon 1979); the other, called the capability-building approach, is based on microlevel analyses of a firm's technology (Lall 1982). The product-life-cycle approach views developing-economy enterprises as relatively passive recipients of technology and skills at the mature stage of their life cycle. The competitive edge of developing-economy MNEs thus can be derived from one of three possible sources: (1) the possession of technologies so mature that they have been phased out by developed-country firms, but not yet mastered by countries lower on the industrialization scale; (2) an advantage gained by downscaling the technology, making production more labor-intensive, or adapting it to local raw materials; and (3) a cost advantage arising from lower wages.

The product-life-cycle approach suggests several conclusions. Developing-economy MNEs will specialize in relatively labor-intensive, low-skill, and low-technology activities; their operations will tend to be modest in scale; their products will tend to be undifferentiated and sold mainly on the basis of price rather than distinct design or performance characteristics.

The second approach to the problem focuses on how technological mastery is acquired, and covers both simple and complex activities. Technological capabilities in both are built up by a gradual accumulation of skills, information, and technological effort. The nature of the effort is very sensitive to the policy regime and to the local availability of the necessary technical skill, infrastructure, science and technology support, and other relevant institutions (Lall 1990). Thus, different settings and regimes produce very different sets of competitive capabilities.

This capability-building approach has evident overlaps with the theories of the product life cycle and the investment-development path. If a comparison were made of the capability-building and product-life-cycle approaches with respect to low and mature technologies, we would find that the sources of competitive advantage are similar: mastery of the relevant technology, and the subsequent ability to adapt it. The capability-building approach emphasizes the accumulation of special marketing and engineering skills; the product life cycle emphasizes cost advantages from cheaper technical manpower. What primarily distinguishes the two approaches is their application to more advanced activities. These do not fit comfortably in the product-life-cycle approach, which focuses on low and mature technology; by contrast, the capability-building approach provides several insights into how these activities are acquired and why they may yield unique firm-specific assets.

Other possible sources of ownership advantage for developing-country MNEs can also be considered, including ethnic connections, participation in a conglomerate business group, and specialization in products not made by traditional MNEs. Scattered examples of such advantage are offered by empirical research, but they do not add up to a comprehensive or persuasive theory of ownership advantage for developing-country MNEs.

Focusing on location factors, we can distinguish between export-oriented and market-oriented FDI on the basis of multinationals' motivations.[1] Export-oriented FDI involves fragmenting the production process geographically by different stages based on labor intensities, while market-oriented FDI is made to build plants in multiple countries to serve local markets (Zhang and Markusen 1999). Location factors that influence export-oriented FDI include labor cost and infrastructure (e.g., transportation conditions). Due to its "footloose" feature, this type of FDI is largely attracted to the location with favorable fiscal policies (e.g., tax holidays) and other incentives (e.g., low land fees).

Market-oriented FDI is essentially motivated by gaining access to local markets. A host country's FDI regime regulating the entry and scope of this type of FDI would be a prerequisite for the presence of multinationals. If subsidiaries of multinationals are allowed to sell their products in a host country, the size of local markets is expected to be a

critical determinant because larger market size offers greater opportunities to realize effective economies of scale (Zhang 2000). Since
this type of FDI involves advanced technology, it generally requires
a certain level of human capital or skilled labor and good infrastructure conditions in the host country.

III. HKDI and TDI in China and the Greater Chinese Economy

The most impressive characteristic of the FDI trend in China over the
period 1979–98 is the sharp FDI boom in the 1990s contrasted with the
moderate growth during the 1980s (Table 9.1). In the early period,
1979–83, there was great interest in China, but not much investment, due to limited understanding between China and foreign investors. In the period 1984–91, FDI grew steadily and by a relatively
large amount, due in part to the extension of the special economic
zones (from four cities to another fourteen in 1984) and the increased
FDI incentives introduced in 1986. The Tiananmen Square incident
in 1989 hurt FDI inflows because investors began to doubt China's
political stability. The period 1992–98 witnessed an FDI boom with
a sharp rise in volume. The seven-year (1992–98) inflows amounted
to $240 billion, which constituted 92 percent of total FDI ($260
billion) over the entire period, 1979–98 (SSB 1999).

Considering that 95 percent of global FDI originates from industrial
countries (UNCTAD 1996), it is striking that the majority of FDI in
China did not come from industrial countries, but was received from
Hong Kong and Taiwan. Table 9.1 shows the origination of FDI into
China over the period 1979–1998. During the boom years, 1992–
97, HKDI and TDI ranked first and second, together accounting for
63 percent of that period's total FDI flows into China. With the exception of Japan (ranked third) and the United States (fourth), other
industrialized countries played a minor role.

As by far the largest investor, Hong Kong invested as much as $154.9
billion in the years 1979 to 1999, making up over 50 percent of total
FDI received by China in that period (Tables 9.1 and 9.2).[2] In fact, HKDI
has constituted over one-half of China's inward FDI in almost every
single year since 1979. The dominant role of Hong Kong reflects the
fact of its fundamental connections and cultural proximity with China.
With similar connections, Taiwan has also made a substantial invest-

ment in China, amounting to $23.75 billion in the period 1990–99 (Table 9.2). Since the early 1990s, Taiwan has emerged as the second-largest source of China's FDI due to relaxation of the government's restrictions on TDI and rising domestic wages. Production efficiencies resulting from lower labor costs are obviously a key motive for firms in Hong Kong and Taiwan to move to or build production facilities in China (Wells 1993).

The large flows of FDI from Hong Kong and Taiwan into China have been strongly associated with the formation of the ongoing greater Chinese economy, in which growing economic interactions among the three partners have taken place. The quietest aspect of such interactions is China's trade with Hong Kong and Taiwan, as shown in Table 9.3. Significant differences in factor endowments, economic structure, and technology among China, Hong Kong, and Taiwan have produced great potential for economic complementarities. This has created many opportunities for economic cooperation through trade in goods and services. Hong Kong was China's largest trading partner for a long time until 1992 (over 40 percent of China's exports went to Hong Kong, and nearly 30 percent of its total imports came from Hong Kong). Since then, Hong Kong's share of total Chinese trade with China has fallen. At the same time, trade between Taiwan and mainland China has risen dramatically—from less than 5 percent in 1990 to nearly 14 percent. The large trade flows in the greater Chinese economy not only stimulated FDI flows from Hong Kong and Taiwan to China, but also were largely influenced by such direct investment.

The patterns of HKDI and TDI have been affected substantially by China's FDI regime. Though many FDI incentives were introduced in the early 1980s, FDI was invited exclusively for exports— except offshore-oil exploration and the real-estate sector (hotels and other tourism-related projects in particular). As a result, HKDI and TDI that are export-oriented were encouraged and rose steadily relative to FDI from industrial countries that were market oriented. The "export-promotion" FDI regime did not change much until 1992, when China gradually began to open its domestic market to multinational firms in certain sectors, including services such as telecommunications, transportation, banking, and insurance. Institutional changes, along with the growing market, induced dramatic increases in overall FDI as well as HKDI and TDI.

Table 9.2

FDI in China from Hong Kong and Taiwan, 1990–99 (flows in U.S.$ millions and shares as percentages of total)

Year	Hong Kong Flows	Hong Kong Share	Taiwan Flows	Taiwan Share	Share of FDI from Hong Kong &Taiwan
1990	2,018	57.87	372	10.67	68.54
1991	2,444	55.98	472	10.81	66.79
1992	7,706	70.01	1,051	9.55	79.56
1993	17,609	64.00	3,025	10.99	74.99
1994	19,823	58.71	3,391	10.04	68.75
1995	20,185	53.80	3,162	8.43	62.22
1996	21,257	50.94	3,475	8.33	59.27
1997	20,632	45.59	3,289	7.27	52.86
1998	18,508	40.71	2,915	6.41	47.12
1999	16,363	40.58	2,599	6.45	47.03
1990–99	146,545	50.46	23,751	8.18	58.64

Sources: China Foreign Economic Statistical Yearbook (SSB 1994, 1996, and 1999) and *China Statistical Yearbook 2000* (SSB 2000).

Table 9.3

China's Trade with Hong Kong and Taiwan, 1990–99
(amounts in U.S.$ millions and shares as percentages of total)

Year	Hong Kong Exports	Share (%)	Hong Kong Imports	Share (%)	Taiwan Exports	Share (%)	Taiwan Imports	Share (%)
1990	26,650	42.92	14,254	26.72	320	0.52	2,255	4.23
1991	32,137	44.73	17,463	27.38	595	0.83	3,639	5.70
1992	37,512	44.16	20,534	25.48	694	0.82	5,866	7.28
1993	22,050	24.03	10,446	10.05	1,462	1.59	12,931	12.44
1994	32,361	26.74	9,442	8.17	2,242	1.85	14,086	12.18
1995	35,983	24.19	8,591	6.50	3,098	2.08	14,784	11.19
1996	32,906	21.79	7,827	5.64	2,802	1.86	16,180	11.65
1997	43,783	23.95	6,990	4.91	3,397	1.86	16,441	11.55
1998	38,742	21.08	6,658	4.75	3,869	2.10	16,631	11.86
1999	36,863	18.91	6,892	4.16	3,950	2.03	19,527	11.78

Sources: China Foreign Economic Statistical Yearbook (SSB 1994, 1996, and 1999) and *China Statistical Yearbook 2000* (SSB 2000).

There are many aspects of HKDI and TDI in China that cannot be fully assessed without understanding their basic characteristics. HKDI and TDI in China exhibit different sectoral distributions relative to FDI from developed countries. Table 9.4 suggests that, compared to HKDI and TDI, developed countries have placed less emphasis on export-oriented light industries and textile projects in China. While the share of HKDI and TDI in these two industry groups is as high as nearly 48 percent, that of developed-country FDI is only 28 percent. HKDI and TDI are concentrated in labor-intensive and relatively low-technology goods (such as garments, toys, shoes, and consumer electronics) aimed at the international market. Developed-country FDI aims at China's domestic market in capital-intensive goods such as machinery, chemicals, health-care products, and services.

HKDI projects are in general smaller than those of developed countries. According to a survey study (Pearson 1991), the average project size of HKDI was $2.9 to $3.4 million during 1979–1988, while the average size for developed-country FDI projects ranged from $4 to $8.7 million. In particular, the average equity committed by U.S. partners to equity joint ventures in the 1980s was nearly twice as high as that from Hong Kong (United States–China Business Council 1990). The relatively small size of Hong Kong commitments may be explained by the fact that these investors tend to be involved in small export-processing (assembly) plants.

The destinations of the investments from Hong Kong and Taiwan reflect ethnic factors, and the "Chinese connection" is pervasive. All four special economic zones established in 1980 are located in Guangdong and Fujian provinces to facilitate FDI, mainly from Hong Kong.[3] The Taiwanese placed a substantial portion of their investments in Fujian province, which is not only the part of China closest to Taiwan, but also the one that includes their hometowns. As shown in Table 9.5, the share of developed-country FDI in metropolitan cities was 34 percent in 1990, which is nearly three times as high as that of HKDI and TDI.

IV. Empirical Analysis

The preceding discussions of the theoretical framework and the patterns of HKDI and TDI in comparison with FDI from developed countries suggest that large HKDI and TDI might be a result of two

Table 9.4

FDI Sector Distribution in China in 1990, by Source of FDI and Projects

Sector	FDI from Hong Kong & Taiwan		FDI from developed countries	
	Number	Percent	Number	Percent
Energy & transportation	100	5.45	52	7.92
Medical	35	1.90	43	6.55
Agriculture and food	144	7.85	96	14.64
Electronics & heavy industry	273	14.87	141	21.49
Printing	14	0.76	8	1.22
Building materials	90	4.90	35	5.34
Textiles & light industry	873	47.57	182	27.74
Property development	53	2.89	17	2.59
Services	68	3.71	22	3.35
Chemicals	146	7.96	51	7.77
Miscellaneous	39	2.13	9	1.37
Total	1,835	100.00	656	100.00

Source: U.S.–China Business Council, *Special Report on U.S. Investment in China*, 1990.

Table 9.5

FDI Regional Distribution in China in 1990, by Source of FDI and Projects

Region in China	FDI from Hong Kong & Taiwan		FDI from developed countries	
	Number	Percent	Number	Percent
Metropolitan	223	12.15	222	33.84
Coastal	1,234	67.24	336	51.22
Near inland	265	14.44	51	7.78
Far inland	113	6.16	47	7.16
Total	1,835	100	656	100

Source: U.S.–China Business Council, *Special Report on U.S. Investment in China*, 1990.

broad sets of factors. One is related to U.S. investors' preferences and technological features such that USDI aims primarily at China's domestic market. These include U.S. firms' special ownership advantages that require large market size for economies of scale, and U.S. investors' strong interest in gaining market access rather than the benefits of cheap labor. The other is associated with China's location advantages that were more significantly attractive to export-oriented (vertical) FDI than to market-oriented (horizontal) FDI. Among them are China's export-promotion FDI regime, its huge pool of cheap labor, and its fast-growing market. The small USDI and the dominant HKDI suggest that the two investor groups did not respond equally to China's location characteristics. To best understand why USDI in China is so small, we cannot overlook the factors that led to large HKDI.

The above reasoning, along with the discussions of theory and the pattern of USDI, suggest the following determinants of USDI and HKDI: (a) *market size*: China's growing market with 1.2 billion people is bound to be extremely attractive to foreign investment, particularly USDI. The larger the market size, the more FDI is likely to be received; (b) *economic growth*: China's growing economy would create a greater demand for FDI and greatly improve conditions of infrastructure; (c) *labor costs*: China's cheap labor should encourage FDI, especially HKDI and TDI, with labor-intensive production; (d) *trade barriers*: higher import tariffs would reduce export-oriented FDI but induce market-oriented FDI; (e) *FDI incentives*: many fiscal incentives adopted since 1986 would increase HKDI and TDI; (f) *political instability*: the incidents of 1987 and 1989 led to political instability, which is postulated to have had a negative effect on FDI inflows during the period 1987–90.

Correspondingly, two models are specified for the determination of USDI and HKDI, as follows:

$$HKTDIR_t = \alpha_0 + \alpha_1 GDPR_t + \alpha_2 GDPRATED_t + \alpha_3 WAGER_t + \alpha_4 TARIFTR_t + \alpha_5 D1_t + \alpha_6 D2_t + \alpha_7 T_t + \varepsilon_t$$

where $HKTDIR_t$ = ratio of sum of HKDI and TDI in China to total FDI in all developing countries in year t,

$GDPR_t$ = share of China's gross domestic product (GDP) in all developing countries in a given year t, and the expected sign is positive,

$GDPRATED_t$ = difference between GDP growth rate in China and average GDP growth rate in all other developing countries in year t, and the expected sign is positive,

$WAGER_t$ = ratio of China's real wage to the average real wage of Hong Kong and Taiwan in year t, and the expected sign is negative with HKDI,

$TARIFFR_t$ = ratio of China's tariff rate to the average tariff rate of selected Asian countries[4] in year t, and the expected sign is negative,

$D1_t$ = dummy for FDI incentives. $D1 = 1$ for 1986–97, and $D1 = 0$ for the rest. A positive sign is expected,

$D2_t$ = dummy for China's political instability. $D2 = 1$ for 1987–90, and $D2 = 0$ for the rest. A negative sign is expected,

T_t = time-trend variable which takes the values 1 through 21 from 1977 to 97,

ε_t = stochastic disturbance term.

It should be noted that: (1) both dependent and independent variables are measured relatively such that China's location conditions could be assessed in comparison with other potential host countries; (2) the "Chinese connections" linked to HKDI and TDI are not included in the models, due to their time invariance, although the factor has played a key role in the predominant HKDI and TDI; and (3) the trend variable (T) is included in the models to take account of an upward trend in FDI flows that cannot be explained by the variables in the models.

The data sources and definitions of variables used in the analysis are as follows: data on HKDI and TDI in China are taken and calculated from *China Statistical Yearbook* (SSB, various years), *Almanac of China's Foreign Economic Relations and Trade* (various years) and *International Trade* (various issues) by the MOFERT of China; data on FDI in all developing countries are from *International Financial Statistics Yearbook* (various years) by International Monetary Fund (IMF); data on GDP for China are taken from *China Statistical Yearbook* (various issues) and *International Financial Statistics Yearbook* (various years); data for GDP for all developing countries are taken and computed from *International Financial Statistics Yearbook* (various years); data on WAGE for China, Hong Kong, and Taiwan are computed from *Yearbook of Labor Statistics* (various years) by International Labor Office (ILO); all wage rates are converted into U.S. dollars by the current exchange rates, which are from *International Financial Statistics Yearbook* (various years); data on TARIFF for China and selected Asian countries are computed based on values of the ratio of custom duty to imports; data on the custom duty and imports for China and selected

Table 9.6

Estimates of Determinants of FDI from Hong Kong and Taiwan (HKTDI)

Independent variables	Estimated coefficients	t - statistics
$GDPR_{t-1}$	1.65**	2.44
$WAGEHKTR_{t-1}$	−0.13**	−2.86
$TARIFFR_{t-1}$	0.02	1.09
$TREND_t$	0.02	−1.00
$D1_{t-1}$	0.25**	2.57
$D2_{t-1}$	−0.17**	−2.65
Adjusted R^2	0.92	
Durbin-Watson	1.89	
F-statistics	120.70***	

Note: Dependent variable is $HKTDIR_t$. The asterisks *** and ** indicate significance at 1 percent and 5 percent levels, respectively. The coefficient estimate of the constant term is omitted to save space.

Asian countries are from *International Financial Statistics Yearbook* (various years).

The empirical estimates for the model are obtained by the ordinary-least-squares technique, using all independent variables lagged by one year so as to make the regressors predetermined and allow a one-year lag between the regressors and the actual investment. The results from the three models are presented in Table 9.6.

We begin with a summary of major findings from the estimates, to be followed by a discussion and interpretation of these findings. The values adjusted R^2 is 92 percent, suggesting that the explanatory power of the model is very good. The Durbin-Watson statistics show an absence of first-order serial correlation in all equations.

The significantly positive effect of *GDPR* is somewhat unexpected with regard to the fact that dominant HKDI and TDI are export oriented. There are two possible explanations for HKDI and TDI. One is that, though a large part of HKDI and TDI was related to production for export, investors from these two economies also intended to gain market access in the 1990s, thus responding positively to market size.[5] The other is based on the consideration that a huge pool of cheap labor in China encouraged a variant of the vertical FDI that was labor-intensive in nature. In other words, the large relative GDP proxies the large market size in terms of population as much as a huge pool of cheap labor, since per-capita income in China is still much lower than that in most developing countries.

As a proxy for infrastructure conditions, high growth rates may be expected to induce more FDI. Mixed results about the significance of the coefficient of *GDPRATED* for HKDI and TDI may be due to its relatively low requirements for human capital and infrastructure.

The insignificance of the coefficients of relative wage rates is somewhat surprising. China indeed has advantages in labor costs in the sense that the relative real-wage rate in China had a falling trend during the period, although its absolute wage rate rose. Low labor costs should be an attraction to HKDI and TDI. A possible explanation is that China's relative wage rate did not vary much over the period, and thus its effect is hard to capture in the sample used. Like the important role of Chinese connections in HKDI and TDI, the advantage of labor costs in China did exist in the period and its small changes may not have generated a significant response in the regression estimates.

The significantly negative coefficients suggest that trade barriers, which reduce costs of imported equipment and intermediate inputs from the source country, make China more attractive to HKDI and TDI. China's FDI policy has generally been export oriented in the sense that FDI projects are expected to aim not at domestic but at foreign markets.[6]

The estimates of D1 and D2 are expected. China's more open FDI policy indeed increases HKDI and TDI flows, and investors from Hong Kong and Taiwan seem very sensitive to political instabilities like the 1989 Tiananmen Square incident.

In short, we conclude that China's large market, improvements in infrastructure, and liberalized FDI policy encourage HKDI and TDI flows. Tariffs and political instability reduce HKDI and TDI.

V. Summary and Concluding Remarks

The substantial amount of direct investment from Hong Kong and Taiwan into China has played an extremely important role in the emergence of the greater Chinese economy. Moreover, the potential benefits from future HKDI and TDI in China are huge. These benefits may be divided into static and dynamic benefits. The static benefits accrue primarily from the relocation of production chains to take advantage of lower costs, especially lower labor costs. In the long run, the more important dynamic benefits for direct investment accrue primarily through the learning process: they accumulate when individuals imitate and learn to begin new activities and make existing activities better. Both static and dynamic benefits of HKDI and TDI would be truly impressive.

This study has attempted to address the phenomenon of the FDI boom in China in the context of the greater Chinese economy. The evidence presented here makes it clear that we would have a better understanding of FDI from Hong Kong and Taiwan in China by comparing it with FDI from developed countries. The FDI boom in the 1990s and the dominant position of HKDI and TDI merit particular attention relative to China's unique advantages, such as its fast economic growth and its Chinese connections in attracting FDI.

The main findings may be summarized as follows. First, China's FDI position among developing countries in the past two decades has been substantially determined by its market size, rapid income growth, and liberalized FDI regimes. This argument is quite consistent with the widely accepted belief that growing market size and better infrastructure create an incentive for Hong Kong–Taiwan investors to gain market access. Second, HKDI and TDI seem encouraged by the liberalized trade policy, the huge pool of cheap labor, and political stability in China.

Notes

1. In the literature, export-oriented MNEs are often called vertical multinationals, while market-oriented MNEs are called horizontal multinationals.

2. It is well known that a part of reported HKDI is actually either industrial countries' investment through subsidiaries based in Hong Kong, or TDI under the name of Hong Kong for political reasons, or investment carried out by subsidiaries located in Hong Kong but owned by Chinese central or local governments to take advantage of preferential FDI treatment (UNCTAD 1996).

3. With close links to Guangdong province, Hong Kong's direct investment made up over 90 percent of that area's foreign investment. Chinese connections provide Hong Kong investors with much easier access to the Chinese market than for non-Chinese investors elsewhere. Moreover, Hong Kong investors were also motivated by the desire to establish continuity and a strong base of operations that would benefit the colony after its transfer to China in 1997.

4. The countries include Hong Kong, Indonesia, Malaysia, Singapore, South Korea, Thailand, and Taiwan.

5. Recent evidence shows that the share of local sales of Hong Kong– and Taiwan-based multinational firms rose significantly as the Chinese govern-

ment allowed local sales and reduced export requirements of multinational firms (UNCTAD 1996).

6. The export requirement set up in China ranged from 90 percent to 100 percent, as stated in the Chinese government's "Twenty-Two Provisions to Encourage Foreign Investment" (MOFERT 1994).

References

Ash, Robert, and Y.Y. Kueh. 1993. "Economic Integration Within Greater China: Trade and Investment Flows Between China, Hong Kong, and Taiwan." *China Quarterly* 136: 711–45.

Casson, Mark, and J. Zheng. 1991. "Western Joint Ventures in China." *Journal of International Development* 3, no. 3: 293–323.

Caves, Richard. 1996. *Multinational Enterprise and Economic Analysis.* 2d ed. Cambridge: Cambridge University Press.

Dunning, John. 1981. *International Production and the Multinational Enterprise.* London: Allen and Unwin.

International Labour Office (ILO). *Yearbook of Labor Statistics* (various years).

International Monetary Fund (IMF). *International Financial Statistics Yearbook* (various years).

Jones, Randall. 1992. *The Chinese Economic Areas: Economic Integration Without a Free Trade Agreement.* Paris: Organisation for Economic Co-operation and Development (OECD), Department of Economics and Statistics.

Kueh, Y. Y. 1992. "Foreign Investment and Economic Change in China." *China Quarterly* 131: 637–90.

Lall, Sanjaya. 1982. "The Emergence of Third World Multinationals." *World Development* 10, no. 2: 127–46.

———. 1990. *Building Industrial Competitiveness in Developing Countries.* Paris: OECD Development Centre.

Lardy, Nicholas R. 1992. *Foreign Trade and Economic Reform in China: 1978–1990.* Cambridge: Cambridge University Press.

Ministry of Foreign Economic Relations and Trade (MOFERT) of China. 1994. *Almanac of China's Foreign Economic Relations and Trade.* Beijing: MOFERT Press.

———. *International Trade* (various issues).

Naughton, Barry. 1997. *The China Circle: Economics and Electronics in the PRC, Taiwan, and Hong Kong.* Washington, DC: Brookings Institution.

Pearson, Margaret M. 1991. *Joint Ventures in the People's Republic of China: The Control of Foreign Direct Investment under Socialism.* Princeton: Princeton University Press.

Perkins, Dwight. 1994. "Completing China's Move to the Market." *Journal of Economic Perspectives* 8, no. 2 (spring): 23–46.

Pomfret, Richard. 1991. *Investing in China: Ten Years of the Open Door Policy.* Ames: Iowa State University Press.

State Statistical Bureau (SSB) of China. 2000. *China Statistical Yearbook.* Beijing: China Statistics Press.

————. 1994, 1996, 1999. *China Foreign Economic Statistical Yearbook.* Beijing: China Statistics Press.

United Nations Conference on Trade and Development (UNCTAD). 1996. *World Investment Report: 1996.* New York: United Nations.

————. 1999. *World Investment Report: 1998.* New York: United Nations.

United States–China Business Council. 1990. *Special Report on U.S. Investment in China.* Washington, DC: China Business Forum.

Vernon, Raymond. 1979. "The Product Cycle Hypothesis in a New International Environment." *Oxford Bulletin of Economics and Statistics* 41, no. 4: 255–67.

Wells, Louis T., Jr. 1993. "Mobile Exporters: New Foreign Investors in East Asia." In *Foreign Direct Investment*, ed. K.A. Froot. Chicago: University of Chicago Press.

Zhang, Kevin H. 2000. "Human Capital, Country Size, and North–South Manufacturing Multinational Enterprises." *Economia Internazionale/International Economics* 53, no. 2 (May): 237–60.

Zhang, Kevin H., and James R. Markusen. 1999. "Vertical Multinationals and Host-Country Characteristics." *Journal of Development Economics* 59, no. 2: 233–52.

10

Taiwan's Outward Investment
in Mainland China

Jack W. Hou and Kevin H. Zhang

1. Introduction

As we begin the new millennium, there can be no doubt that Asia will be one of the most economically vibrant areas in the world. Indeed, this has been a continuous development for the past four decades. Since the resurrection of Japan in the 1960s and 1970s, Asia (especially East Asia) has shown an uncanny ability for almost unbridled growth and development. In the 1980s, the Four Small Tigers (Hong Kong, Singapore, Taiwan, and Korea) took off and created a new terminology, newly industrialized countries (NICs), while the spectacular growth of China has made her the second largest economy in the world (the Four Small Tigers were reclassified as "advanced economies" in 1997 by the International Monetary Fund). In between, we also see the emergence of successors to the Four Small Tigers: Thailand, Malaysia, Indonesia, the Philippines, and Vietnam.

Though the area has seen some hard times recently, from the burst of Japan's bubble economy to the Asian financial crisis, recovery is well under way, and most economists would agree that Asia will emerge stronger than before as its economic institutions have undergone significant reform (for the better). Nowhere else in the world can one see the bustling markets and the vibrant demonstration of entrepreneurial spirit.

These are all well documented and have contributed to the phenomenal success of the growth in the region, especially in terms of trade (Hou et al. 1995). What is perhaps less understood or emphasized is the unique multilateral interdependency of the economies that is continuously accelerating. This involves not just trade of goods and services, but increasingly capital movements, especially in foreign direct investment (FDI). Japan has always been the largest investor, but recently the NICs are also exhibiting significant capital outflow. For example, Hong Kong is the largest "foreign" investor in China, while Taiwan is the largest investor in Malaysia and among the top three FDI providers for Vietnam and the second largest investor in China.

The main driving force for such behavior is the fact that Asia has a very complete system of economies in the sense that on the top we have the fully mature industrialized countries like Japan, flanked by the NICs (Hong Kong, Singapore, South Korea, and Taiwan), complemented by the rest of the "upwardly mobile" economies of the region (Indonesia, Malaysia, Philippines, Thailand, Vietnam, etc.). Much like the tropical forests of the Amazon River Basin, Asia is almost a complete ecosystem economically speaking. This is absent in most of the other regions in the world, with the exception of perhaps the European Union and the former socialist economies, though the intimacy in their interdependence is still at a much earlier stage of development.

Just as it is hopeless for any individual biologist to unravel the interdependencies of the Amazon ecosystem, it is impossible for any economist to fully characterize the multilateral trade/investment relationships among the Asian economies. In this study, with this big picture in mind, we take a small first step toward understanding these relationships by examining the causal effect of the capital flows from Taiwan to mainland China. More specifically, we will focus on Taiwan firms' direct investment in China. We will term such investment Taiwanese direct investment (TDI), so as to differ from the broader foreign direct investment (FDI) in China.

Over the last two decades (1979–1998), China has emerged as the largest FDI recipient among the developing countries and, next to the United States, second in the world (UNCTAD 1999). TDI in China has contributed significantly to China's FDI boom. In fact, Taiwan was the second largest investor in China during most of the 1990s, next to Hong Kong (SSB 1998). There is some suspicion that Taiwan may indeed be the largest "true" investor, as a nontrivial portion of Hong Kong FDI in China may be a form of "money laundering"; that is, funds that belong to China's state-owned–enterprises are diverted to Hong Kong and then returned to China as Hong Kong FDI.

While there is a growing literature on determinants of aggregate FDI flows in China (for example, Pearson 1991; Pomfret 1991; Kueh 1992; and Zhang 2000), the number of studies on TDI in China has been limited. The purpose of this chapter is to investigate the influences of both macroeconomic and microeconomic factors of TDI in mainland China and the salient characteristics of TDI. The study shows that, given different macroeconomic conditions on both sides of the strait, the direct-investment flows across the Taiwan Strait have been motivated by different factors. It was found that TDI has been attracted most to the other side by China's huge market size, low labor costs, and cheap and abundant resources such as raw materials and land.

We will pay special attention to the evolutionary process of China's attitude toward FDI as reflected in her economic policies. At the same time, we will acknowledge the parallel economic development of Taiwan during China's changing disposition toward foreign capital and market economic reform in general. The switch in China's FDI policy was a perfect match in terms of timing as far the TDI was concerned. This seemingly fortuitous timing is no coincidence. Much as the fusion of two hydrogen atoms and an oxygen atom into the molecule called water is no accident, the complementarity between China's FDI policy and the influx of TDI is caused by a complex interactive dynamic that warrants serious attention. This chapter, however, is not an attempt to understand this dynamism. Rather, our intention is modest: to characterize the sequence of events (both in China and in Taiwan) and their effects on TDI location choice. As TDI is on the rise, such understanding is paramount to the complete comprehension of the economic dynamics of greater China and may shed light on the development of similar interdependencies in other regional economic blocs.

The remainder of this essay is organized as follows. Section 2 discusses TDI against a broad background in which key macroeconomic factors in both Taiwan and China that influence TDI are identified. Section 3 explores microeconomic factors that contribute to large TDI flows into China and discusses the main characteristics of TDI in China. Section 4 provides a brief summary and some conclusions.

2. Capital Flows Across the Taiwan Strait: Pull and Push Forces

The historical development and recent trends of TDI in mainland China are best illustrated by the statistics in Table 10.1. It is obvious that the two

Table 10.1

Taiwanese Investment in Mainland China: 1991–98 (millions of U.S.$)

Year	Approved by Taiwan			Official Data from Mainland China				
	Cases	Amount	Average Amount	Cases	Contracted Amount	Average Amount	Realized Amount	Realization Ratio
1991	237	174	0.73	3,446	2,783	0.81	844	30.33
1992	264	247	0.94	6,430	5,543	0.86	1,050	18.94
1993	9,329	3,168	0.34	10,948	9,965	0.91	3,139	31.50
1994	934	962	1.03	6,247	5,395	0.86	3,391	62.85
1995	490	1,093	2.23	4,778	5,777	1.21	3,162	54.73
1996	383	1,229	3.21	3,184	5,141	1.61	3,475	67.59
1997	8,725	4,334	0.50	3,014	2,814	0.93	3,289	116.88
1998	1,284	2,035	1.58	2,970	2,982	1.00	2,915	97.75
1991-98	21,646	13,243	0.61	41,017	40,400	0.98	21,265	52.64

Source: Liang'an jingji tongji nianbao (Taiwan-China Economic Statistics Yearbook); Taipei: Chunghwa Institute for Economics Research, 1999.

Notes: The figure for 1991 includes investments in years before 1991. Due to political reasons, Chinese figures are in general larger and more accurate than Taiwanese figures because many Taiwanese investors did not report their investment to their government.

statistical sources (the official data from both Taiwan and China) differ substantially. The main reason for the differences is the restrictions (on Taiwan foreign investment) imposed by the Taiwan government forced many Taiwan investors to avoid documenting their cases to their government. Such behavior is so rampant that between 1991 and 1998, the number of cases and value of realized investment from the official data of China amounts to twice the size of the official Taiwan statistics. The significant fluctuation of TDI over time also reflects such restrictions and the estranged relationship between Taiwan and China. Nevertheless, the cases and magnitude of TDI flows into China are large. TDI accounts for 10 percent of China's total FDI, both in terms of case numbers and in terms of dollar amount. This is second only to Hong Kong and slightly ahead of the U.S. and Japan (SSB 1999).

The broad spectrum of TDI in China can best be explained with the "pull" gravity of China and the "push" forces of Taiwan. The former enhanced the attractiveness of China to Taiwan firms, while the latter reflect structural changes in Taiwan's economy, which in turn led to capital outflows. Understanding these two separate, yet intimately related factors, is instrumental to an understanding of the growth and evolution of TDI.

Prior to the comprehensive economic reform, China was essentially a closed economy and conducted the bulk of its international trade with other communist nations. Under the leadership of Deng Xiaoping, China embarked on the historical journey toward a socialistic market system with Chinese characteristics (Fei and Hou 1994). To date, we have witnessed over two decades of such effort, and the economic result is impressive by any standard.

One of the main objectives of China's reform is to open the Chinese economy to both international trade and foreign investment. To this end and to further the degree of reform, China formally requested reinstatement to membership in GATT (now WTO) in July of 1986 and petitioned the WTO in November of 1995. However, both organizations have strict guidelines in terms of market access, both in trade and in capital investment. It is this latter issue that is the focus of this chapter. Table 10.2 summarizes the evolution of China's main FDI policy. In terms of inward FDI flows, China's first steps were gingerly and cautious (Zhang 2000). Foreign investors appeared modestly in China after the passage of the Law on Joint Ventures in 1979. While permitting entry of foreign firms, the law did not create a clear legal framework to facili-

Table 10.2

The Evolution of China's FDI Policy

July 1979	The "Law of the People's Republic of China on Joint Ventures Using Chinese and Foreign investment" ("Law of Sino-Foreign Joint Ventures") was adopted, granting foreign investment a legal status in China.
August–October 1980	Four special economic zones (SEZ) were established on the southeast coast to attract foreign capital and advanced technology. One of them is Xiamen in Fujian province, which was not only intended to attract TDI but also to facilitate the eventual reunification of China.
October 1986	New provisions (called "Twenty-two Provisions on the Encouragement of Foreign Investment") were established. The new incentives included: reducing fees for labor and land use; establishing a limited foreign currency market for joint ventures; and extending the maximum duration of a joint-venture agreement beyond fifty years.
March 1990	Amendments to the 1979 "Joint-Venture Law" were passed, greatly improving the investment climate in China. The stipulation that the chairman of the board of a joint venture should be appointed by Chinese investors, for example, was abolished. Also significant was the provision of protection from nationalization.
April 1990	The concept of SEZ was extended to the Shanghai Pudong New Development Area, which is about the size of Singapore.
January 1997	Shenzhen (the most important SEZ) allowed foreign-invested enterprises with advanced technology to sell 100% of their products on the domestic market.

Source: Based on information compiled by the author.

tate the complicated issues involved in foreign direct investments. As a result, problems like the lack of currency convertibility and the overwhelming red tape caused many would-be investors to hesitate.

In 1986, a new provision (called the Twenty-Two Provisions) was introduced. The timing, in terms of China's petition to be reinstated into GATT, is unmistakable. The main theme was the use of preferential tax policies to encourage or induce FDI. The goal is to attract export-oriented ventures, with the exception of offshore oil exploration and the real estate sector (hotels and other tourism-related projects in particular). Under such an export-promotion FDI regime, the biggest difficulty facing most foreign firms was how to reconvert their investment and repatriate their earnings, as Chinese currency (the RMB) was not convertible.

Indeed, much of the FDI that is at least partially market-oriented (e.g., the tourist hotels, etc.) was unable to earn sufficient foreign exchange to cover its obligations at home, including distribution of profits to investors. On the other hand, firms in Taiwan (and perhaps Hong Kong) were almost 100 percent export oriented and were hence able to earn foreign exchange directly and were the most successful in avoiding serious foreign-exchange deficits. Besides, the common culture and language provided links for "connections" and back-door channels to bypass many of the official restrictions. As a result, Taiwanese direct investments and those of others with export orientation rose steadily, but Western investors, for the most part, did not view China as attractive relative to other developing countries.

This "export promotion" FDI regime persisted until 1992. That was when China exhibited a shift in paradigm and gradually began to open certain sectors of its domestic market to multinational firms, including services such as telecommunications, transportation, banking, and insurance. This change in regime is due to many reasons. Among them was that China's economy had reached a stage of maturity and confidence by 1992, as the real GDP was over five times as large as that in 1979, and its annual GDP growth rate was 11 percent during the period 1992–97 (SSB 1998). Years of export orientation had led to significant accumulation of foreign exchange, which allowed partial convertibility of the renminbi. The most important consideration was undoubtedly to send a signal of sincerity and commitment to the WTO. With this and the increasing pressure from the West, China finally allowed FDI firms access to (though only partially) her domestic market. This institutional change, along with the increased purchasing power of the general population, led to a dramatic rise in TDI and the broader FDI.

Now let us turn our attention briefly toward the other side of the Taiwan Strait. During this same period, Taiwan has taken great strides both in terms of her economic development and of political pluralism. It is not the intention of this chapter to examine the political climate. The focus is on economic issues. It is generally believed that Taiwan achieved economic takeoff, in Rostow's terminology, in the mid-1980s. Undoubtedly, the economic and industrial structure of Taiwan must have undergone major transformations as the old "sunset" industries gave way to the new generation of technology-oriented industries. Three macroeconomic factors have been identified as important to the TDI boom: (a) Taiwan's currency appreciated sharply in the late 1980s; (b) wages rose substantially, and at the same time there were labor shortages; and (c) since 1987, the Taiwan government has become increasingly liberal about FDI outflows.

Taiwan appears to be the fastest-growing overseas investor in the developing world. Its outward FDI stock grew at an annual rate of 42 percent over 1980–91. The latest investment surge started in 1987, when the Taiwanese dollar appreciated by about 20 percent over the previous year and foreign exchange regulations were liberalized. In the 1980s, TDI was roughly distributed equally among developing countries (Southeast Asia) and developed countries (the United States). After that, TDI was unmistakably biased toward China and other Asian developing economies. About 60 percent of TDI stock had gone into manufacturing by 1991; electrical equipment and chemicals ranked as the largest industries, together accounting for 70 percent of manufacturing investments (UNCTAD 1990).

The bulk of TDI is undertaken by small- and medium-sized enterprises. Numerous factories have been established throughout China and Southeast Asia; most are labor-intensive small- and medium-sized enterprises targeted at low-end markets. Small- and medium-sized enterprises are the norm in (and indeed, the backbone of) Taiwan's industry, covering the entire spectrum of production categories, from simple labor-intensive activities to high-skill, technology-intensive processes. The TDI mainly comes from a broad cross-section of small- and medium-sized enterprises in traditional industries. Rising costs at home, currency appreciation, small size, and the consequent handicaps in adjusting to competitive pressures are now leading low-technology small- and medium-sized enterprises to shift part of their production overseas.

Due to rising costs and loss of international comparative advantage, the need for industrial upgrading is very real in Taiwan. Many firms, unable to meet the challenge of upgrading, took the low road and actively promoted TDI, or exporting "factories." Such investments by small- and medium-sized enterprises are one of the salient features of TDI. However, there are also other players: large enterprises with differentiated products, advanced technological capabilities, and far-reaching sales networks. Such TDI has been invested partly in developing countries (China and Southeast Asia) to take advantage of cheaper labor or natural resources, and partly in developed countries (mainly in the United States) to establish market positions, promote brand-name products, and to gain access to advanced technologies.

Growing faster than the FDI from other countries, TDI in China has risen substantially since 1987 when the New Taiwan dollar started to appreciate against the U.S. dollar. The amount of cumulative TDI approved in China was merely $20 million before 1987, but TDI in 1987 alone was $100 million (clearly the effect of the Twenty-Two Provisions) and reached $420 million the next year (SSB 1994). Under pressure from Taiwan's business communities and industrial organizations, the Taiwan government finally allowed TDI in China via a third country in 1990 (MOFERT 1987–1997). The amount of TDI approved in 1993 pushed close to U.S. $10 billion (9,965 million, to be exact), equivalent to 4.6 percent of Taiwan's GDP (SSB 1997). Up to the end of 1998, the contract amount of TDI was $40 billion, and the realized TDI in China totaled $21.3 billion (SSB 1999). Taiwan has become the second largest source of foreign direct investment in China.

Several distinguishing features characterize TDI in China. In addition to the small and medium size of TDI projects relative to FDI from industrial countries (the United States, Japan, and the European Union), the industrial distribution of TDI in China is characterized by the domination of electronics, food/beverage processing, metals and plastic products (Table 10.3). These four sectors constitute 46.55 percent of total TDI in value in the period of 1991–98. Investments in chemicals, nonmetallic minerals, textiles, and precision instruments are also significant (making up 24.11 percent in total). Table 10.4 breaks down the regional distribution of TDI within China. Coastal areas (Guangdong, Jiangsu including Shanghai, Fujian, Hebei including Beijing and Tianjin, Zhejiang, Shandong, and Liaoning) received a lion's share of TDI (91.21 percent in total), and the vast inland areas hosted only less than 10 percent of total TDI. Both industrial and regional distributions reflect the fact that TDI is strongly export oriented, a subject we will discuss in detail in the following section. The changing regional pattern of TDI over the three time periods (Table 10.4) clearly suggest an increasing trend based on market orientation, e.g., more TDI took place in large cities (Shanghai, Beijing, and Tianjin) rather than in export-promotion-base provinces (Guangdong and Fujian).

Table 10.3

Industrial Distribution of Taiwanese Investment in China: 1991–1998

Industry	Cases	Amount	Percentage
Electronics and electric appliances	3,078	2,793,819	21.10
Food and beverage processing	2,180	1,178,391	8.90
Basic metals and metal products	1,848	1,134,556	8.57
Plastic products	1,999	1,056,349	7.98
Chemicals	1,411	862,703	6.51
Non-metallic minerals	1,137	832,704	6.29
Textiles	983	753,067	5.69
Precision instruments	2,137	743,869	5.62
Transport equipment	664	638,815	4.82
Rubber products	472	461,251	3.48
Others	5,737	2,787,134	21.05
Total	21,646	13,242,658	100.00

Source: Liang'an jingji tongji nianbao (Taiwan-China Economic Statistics Yearbook), Taipei: Chunghwa Institute for Economics Research, 1999.

Notes: Cases indicate number of investment projects, and amount is in thousands of US dollars.

3. Seeking Explanations for TDI in China

FDI arises from activities of multinational firms that operate across countries. A firm that goes multinational must possess some special advantages to overcome the inherent disadvantages and high costs of foreign production. The orthodox theory on the existence of FDI, the "OLI" paradigm that emanates from Hymer's work (1976), asserts that a firm with certain Ownership advantages (patent or brand name) would open a subsidiary in a foreign country with Location advantages (cheap labor or growing market) to maximize its profits. Both advantages of ownership and location can best be captured by the Internalization of production (not exporting or licensing) via direct investment in the foreign country (Dunning 1981).

The OLI theory is based primarily on the behavior of large multinational firms from developed countries. FDI from these countries thus has been associated with such intangible assets as leading-edge technology and brand names. Taiwan multinationals may not be on world frontiers of technology and organizational sophistication. In fact, the ownership advantages of TDI might be derived from either marketing skills that make investors specialize in delivering timely, international marketing networks, uniform quality products to Western markets (Wells

Table 10.4

Regional Distribution of Taiwanese Direct Investment in Mainland China, 1987–98 (value in millions of U.S.$)

Provinces in China	1987–98		1987–90		1991–94		1995–98	
	Value	%	Value	%	Value	%	Value	%
Guangdong	4,310	33.41	328	43.50	1,464	32.17	2,518	33.16
Jiangsu	4,053	31.42	25	3.32	1,284	28.21	2,744	36.13
Fujian	1,498	11.61	179	23.74	656	14.41	663	8.73
Hebei	780	6.05	4	0.53	281	6.17	495	6.52
Zhejiang	572	4.43	15	1.99	205	4.50	352	4.64
Shandong	363	2.81	18	2.39	124	2.72	221	2.91
Liaoning	191	1.48	10	1.33	102	2.24	79	1.04
Sichuan	182	1.41	2	0.27	94	2.07	86	1.13
Hubei	156	1.21	5	0.66	66	1.45	85	1.12
Hunan	116	0.90	2	0.27	61	1.34	53	0.70
Others	678	5.26	166	22.02	214	4.70	298	3.92
Total	12,899	100.00	754	100.00	4,551	100.00	7,594	100.00

Source: Liang'an jingji tongji yuebao (Taiwan-China Economic Statistics Monthly Bulletin) (various issues). Taipei: Chunghwa Institute for Economics Research.

Notes: Regarding regional distribution of TDI within China, only Taiwanese statistics are available, although TDI is understated in the statistics in general.

Table 10.5

Distribution of Approved Taiwanese FDI Destinations: 1952–1998

Area	Cases	Amount	Share in total (%)
Mainland China	21,646	13,243	41.57
USA	1,683	4,123	12.95
Malaysia	229	1,388	4.36
Hong Kong	477	974	3.06
Thailand	258	881	2.77
Singapore	257	847	2.66
Vietnam	171	709	2.23
Philippines	130	533	1.67
Indonesia	160	529	1.66
United Kingdom	78	327	1.03
Japan	172	181	0.57
British Central America	523	5,583	17.53
Others	1,129	2,534	7.95
Total	26,298	31,853	100.00

Sources: Liang'an jingji tongji nianbao (Taiwan-China Economic Statistics Yearbook), Taipei: Chunghwa Institute for Economics Research, 1999.

Notes: Figures are based on official data of Taiwanese government. Cases indicate number of investment projects, and amount is in millions of US dollars.

1993), or the adaptation of mature technologies to more labor-intensive contexts and to local raw materials (Vernon 1979). Another unique ownership advantage is Taiwan's ethnic connections with China: sharing the same language and culture makes TDI much easier in negotiation and operation.

Table 10.5 shows distribution of approved TDI among host countries from 1952 to 1998. The pattern of TDI destinations reveals the motives of Taiwan investors. Except for investments in the United States (12.95% in total) and Japan (0.57%), which are driven by market access, all other investments, which take place in developing countries like China (41.57%), are attracted by the availability of cheap labor and raw materials, in addition to market access. Cultural and linguistic affinity between Taiwan and China make it much easier for TDI to cross the strait than investments from industrial countries. In fact, linguistic and cultural affinity, and low labor and land costs, were recognized as the top motivations for most TDI in China. More important, Taiwan's economic structural adjustment (Fuess and Hou 2000) may have played an important role in the TDI boom in China. Combined, Taiwan's changing industrial specialization and loss of certain international comparative advantages have led her to shift many production operations overseas. The geographic proximity, cultural/linguistic linkages, and the relative stages of development between the two economies have led to Taiwanese firms' preference for investing in China.

In general there are five main motives for understanding FDI: market-seeking, export-orientation, resource-seeking, technology-seeking, and efficiency-seeking. These motives apply to all investors, but the first three are of particular relevance to FDI made by Taiwanese investors. The three motives are related to three types of FDI: export-oriented, market-oriented, and resource-oriented investment. Export-oriented FDI, motivated by cheap foreign labor, fragments the production process across countries by production stages based on labor intensity, while market-oriented FDI, induced by foreign-market access, builds plants in many countries to serve local markets. Export-oriented FDI is more likely to be attracted to host regions with cheap labor (Zhang and Markusen 1999). Due to its "footloose" feature, this type of FDI is also attracted to countries that offer favorable incentives such as tax holidays.

Export-oriented FDI has been the most salient feature of investments by Taiwanese firms. The main motive behind such TDI is the classic location edge of low-cost labor in China, with investors being forced to seek more economical bases to service established export markets (mainly the United States) as costs rise at home. The main activities subject to such relocation are relatively simple, labor-intensive manufacturing where skills are easily transferred and facilities are relatively small-scale. Garments, footwear, light electronics, and similar consumer goods are the prime candidates.

In addition to cheap labor, China also needs to offer more. The labor must be productive (disciplined, literate, easily trainable); physical infrastructure must be excellent to facilitate low-cost imports and exports; bureaucratic impediments to offshore processing activity must be minimal; and the business climate must be conducive to investment (competitive tax incentives, political stability, etc.). In the garment industry, there has been another strong location factor—the existence of under-utilized quotas under the Multi-fiber Arrangement, which has proved an important incentive to firms from countries whose import quotas are fully used up.

The dominant position of the export-oriented FDI in China can be

Table 10.6

Trade Across the Taiwan Strait: 1990–97 (millions of U.S.$)

Year	Based on Chinese Statistics			Based on Taiwanese Statistics		
	Exports	Imports	Total	Exports	Imports	Total
1990	2,255.0	319.7	2,574.6	4,394.6	765.4	5,160.0
1991	3,639.0	594.8	4,233.9	7,493.5	1,125.9	8,619.4
1992	5,881.0	698.0	6,579.0	10,547.6	1,119.0	11,666.6
1993	12,933.1	1,461.8	1,4394.9	13,993.1	1,103.6	15,096.7
1994	14,084.8	2,242.2	1,6327.0	16,022.5	1,858.7	17,881.2
1995	14,783.9	3,098.1	17,882.0	19,433.8	3,091.4	22,525.2
1996	16,182.2	2,802.7	18,984.9	20,727.3	3,059.8	23,787.1
1997	16,441.7	3,396.5	19,838.2	22,455.2	3,915.4	26,370.6

Source: Liang'an jingji tongji nianbao (Taiwan-China Economic Statistics Yearbook). Taipei: Chunghwa Institute for Economics Research, 1998.

seen from the growing share of exports by foreign-invested enterprises in China's total exports. In 1999, foreign-invested enterprises in China produced exports of US $88.6 billion (45.5% of total exports); most of such foreign affiliates are from Hong Kong and Taiwan. Tables 10.6 and 10.7 present the pattern of trade across the Taiwan Strait. The most prominent feature revealed in the tables is the large and growing trade surplus of Taiwan. Such a surplus is simply a result of relocating assembling plants from Taiwan to mainland China, since Taiwan firms moved their labor-intensive production to the other side of the Taiwan Strait. The huge Taiwan exports are mainly mid-products used for final-assembly stages of production and equipment. Since large portions of final products are re-exported to third markets (mainly the United States), Taiwan has switched its trade surplus with the U.S. to China because of the low value-added in the assembling plants. As a result, China's trade surplus with the U.S. rose substantially in the 1990s.

The market-oriented FDI involves building up similar production facilities abroad for economies of scale to gain access to local markets. The size of the local market plays a key role in attracting this type of FDI because the larger market offers greater opportunities to realize economies of scale (Zhang 2000). Since this type of FDI involves relatively advanced technology, it generally has higher requirements for human capital and infrastructure in the host regions. The resource-oriented FDI needs no explanation: it goes where the resources are located if the conditions in the sector call for vertical integration.

Table 10.7

Taiwan's Trade Surplus with China: 1990–97 (millions of U.S.$)

| Year | Taiwan net trade to China through Hong Kong | | | | Taiwan net trade to Hong Kong | | Taiwan net trade to the world |
| | Based on Hong Kong | | Based on Taiwan | | | | |
	Amount	%	Amount	%	Amount	%	Amount
1990	2,512.9	20.11	3,629.2	29.04	7,110.4	56.90	12,495.2
1991	3,541.2	26.63	6,367.6	47.88	1,0436	78.47	13,299.1
1992	5,169.0	54.53	9,428.6	99.47	13,635.1	143.80	9,479.3
1993	6,481.9	82.36	12,889.5	163.78	16,726.8	212.54	7,869.8
1994	7,224.9	93.86	14,163.8	184.01	19,730.0	256.33	7,697.2
1995	8,308.6	102.37	16,342.4	201.35	24,278.6	299.13	8,116.3
1996	8,135.2	55.32	17,667.5	120.15	25,100.1	170.70	14,704.4
1997	7,971.3	104.34	18,539.9	242.68	26,711.6	349.66	7,639.4

Sources: Liang'an jingji tongji nianbao (Taiwan-China Economic Statistics Yearbook). Taipei: Chunghwa Institute for Economics Research, 1998.

The particular motive of TDI in China depends on a number of factors and is greatly influenced by macro- and microeconomic conditions on both sides of the Taiwan Strait. The main force driving TDI in China, at least in the early stages, is the rise in Taiwan's labor costs and the apparent industrial policy of upgrading from labor-intensive to capital-technology–intensive production. This has forced the "sunset" industries to relocate their labor-intensive production to regions like China with lower labor costs. These old industries were the driving force in Taiwan's exports in the 1970s and early 1980s. By the mid 1980s, Taiwan had lost the comparative advantage in such labor-intensive manufacturing to other emerging economies such as Thailand and Malaysia. To maintain their profitability, these firms have only two options: one is to rely on cheap imported foreign labor (Hou 1997), and the other is to move the production plants overseas (the "push" forces).

This type of TDI is export-oriented, and the timing was perfect in the sense that the Chinese policy toward foreign investment was precisely limited to export-only ventures, so as to increase China's foreign exchange (the "pull" gravities). This type of TDI represents the first generation, and due to their export-oriented nature, investors will obviously choose to locate them in areas with good access to a port or good transportation conditions. In addition, geographic proximity and similarities ·in regional Chinese culture promote TDI in Fujian and other provinces where the hometowns of Taiwanese investors are located. This is especially important in the early stages, as much of the TDI is still in a tentative trial-and-error mode.

The increased liberalization of China's FDI regime in the 1990s (and of Taiwan's) combined with the fact that the experience of the TDI now inspires much more confidence, so the second generation of TDI tends to differ from the first generation of old "sunset" industries. The later TDI tends to be larger, newer (in technology), and slightly more capital intensive (e.g., Acer computers). In addition, besides export-orientation, some TDIs have started to aim at China's domestic market (market-oriented). This suggests a change in decision criteria, as both the "pull" and "push" factors have changed in nature.

Based on responses to survey questionnaires aimed at individual firms, TDI motivations can be quantified and summarized. Table 10.8 shows results of a survey of 2,311 firms in 1988 (Chen 1992). There are two waves of surveys, before and after 1987, with the relative importance of each TDI motivation measured as a percentage. Contrasting the two

Table 10.8

Reasons Cited for Taiwanese Outward Foreign Direct Investment

Reasons for Outward FDI	Before 1987 (%)	After 1987 (%)
1. Expansion of Markets	25.1	56.0
2. Low Cost of Labor	21.3	3.5
3. Raw Material Supplies	9.1	8.2
4. Tax Incentives	6.6	1.6
5. Avoidance of Trade Barriers	5.5	6.6
6. Collection of Market Information	2.1	6.9
7. Others	30.3	17.2
Total	100.0	100.0

Source: Adapted from Chen (1992).

surveys, it is quite obvious that the dominant reason for TDI before 1987 was to expand the market base and the second was to secure supplies of raw materials. After 1987, however, the importance of low-labor costs rose significantly and the weight of market expansion (although it remains important) fell to less than half. Tax incentives became more attractive to investors over time.

A recent (and hence more relevant) survey specifically targets the core industries of electronics, textiles, and food processing (CIER 1994). Table 10.9 summarizes what attracts Taiwan firms to invest in China. According to the survey, China's abundant supply of cheap labor, cultural and linguistic affinity with Taiwan, low land costs, and large domestic markets were the top four reasons for TDI in China. The results are quite consistent with the predictions of FDI theory in general and with widely held beliefs. The common culture and language on both sides of the Taiwan Strait have made it much easier for Taiwan firms to operate in China. For the electronics industry, tax breaks such as "tax holidays" are also attractive. Expanding production capacity and making use of redundant equipment are also major reasons for investors in textiles. Access to China's raw materials encouraged firms in the food processing industry.

A recent study by Hou and Zhang (2001) employed a conditional logit model to examine factors that influence the regional distribution of TDI within China. The main TDI determinants and regression results are summarized in Table 10.10. As succinctly outlined in the introduc-

Table 10.9

Key Motivations for Taiwanese Direct Investment in Mainland China

Motivations	Electronics manufactures	Textiles manufactures	Food processing industry
1. Abundant supply of cheap labor	95.12	100.00	100.00
2. Cultural and linguistic affinity	95.12	88.23	87.10
3. Low-cost land	73.17	76.47	80.65
4. Domestic markets	46.34	70.58	67.74
5. Expanding production capacity	34.15	44.11	25.81
6. Making use of redundant equipment	26.83	41.17	16.13
7. Spreading risk	34.15	23.52	29.03
8. Access to raw materials	19.51	17.64	38.71
9. Tax breaks	41.36	14.71	25.81
10. Favored nation treatment and quota	21.95	11.76	6.45
11. Low-cost research	9.76	5.88	6.45
12. Others	2.44	2.94	16.13

Source: Liang'an jingji tongji nianbao (Taiwan-China Economic Statistics Yearbook). Taipei: Chunghwa Institute for Economics Research, 1994, p. 160.

Notes: Figures represent the percentage of the total number of firms surveyed that chose each listed motivation for direct investment in mainland China.

tion section, there has been a natural evolution of China's FDI policy (the "pull"). This is matched by the changing needs of Taiwanese firms (the "push") and also has caused (we suspect) a shift in the decision structure of TDI location choice. To best capture this change in the decision structure, we propose to divide the time series into three different stages. The first stage (1987–90) represents the effect of the Twenty-Two Provisions; the third stage (1995–98) captures the second generation of TDI, which is relatively more technology/capital intensive and has been allowed to sell to China's domestic market; while the second stage (1991–94) is deemed a transitional period between the two FDI policy regimes of China.

The empirical estimates in Table 10.10 indicate that Taiwan investors prefer provinces with a superior infrastructure and basic industrial activities, along with a steady supply of skilled labor and a growing market size. This conclusion is quite consistent with the widely held belief that in general TDI in China is export-oriented based on cross-strait comparative advantages. Taiwanese cultural proximity to Fujian prov-

Table 10.10

Effects of TDI Determinants: 1987-98

TDI Determinants	1987–90	1991–94	1995–98
Labor costs	Significant	Not	Not
Market size	Not	Significant	Significant
Transportation	Significant	Significant	Significant
Education	Not	Significant	Significant
Agglomeration	Significant	Significant	Significant
Research and development	Not	Not	Not
FDI incentives	Significant	Significant	Significant
Cultural links	Significant	Significant	Significant

Source: Adapted from Hou and Zhang (2001).
Notes: Each of the determinants is defined as follows. *Labor costs* are the average annual real wage of manufacturing workers in a province of China. *Market size* is GDP of a particular region. *Transportation* is defined as railroad length adjusted for region size and is used as a proxy for transportation linkages. *Labor productivity* is measured by the share of secondary-school students in the total population in a province that will be used to measure education level that proxies for labor productivity. *Agglomeration* for a province in this study is measured by the share of manufacturing output in the province's GDP. *Research and development* is proxied by the share of spending on science in total fiscal expenditures in a province that will be a proxy of the variable. *FDI incentives* are defined as a dummy variable for coastal provinces which enjoyed favorable FDI policies. *Cultural links* are a dummy for Fujian province that not only is geographically adjacent to Taiwan, but whose population speaks the same dialect (Minnan).

ince is a key motivation for the large amount of TDI flow to that region. Favorable FDI incentives provided by the Chinese government in coastal areas have made significant differences in the regional distribution of Taiwanese manufacturing branch-plants. While low labor cost has been recognized as one of the major motives for TDI in China, cross-province differentials in manufacturing wages seem not to affect site-selection by Taiwanese firms.

4. Conclusions

This paper attempts (a) to demonstrate the pattern of Taiwanese direct investment in mainland China through identifying the main characteristics of such capital flows; and (b) to assess the main factors that influence the pattern of investment across the Taiwan Strait. Taiwanese direct investment has been not only a major source of FDI received in China between 1987 and 1999, but also the most dynamic one. The TDI boom in China is the result of an intimate interaction between Taiwanese push force and Chinese pull gravity. This is a typical story of conventional comparative advantages plus cultural and linguistic affinity across the Taiwan Strait. On the one hand, China is at a lower stage of development, with abundant cheap labor, vast amounts of land, and raw materials, which are attractive to foreign investors. On the other hand, Taiwan has already industrialized, with supplicated technology and a well-established international marketing network, but seeking industry upgrading because of changing international comparative advantages and continued growth. Such economic complementarities are conducive to large unilateral capital flows from Taiwan to China, as long as both governments do not impose too many restrictions that might hamper such movement.

The structural changes in the Taiwanese economy in the last two decades created a push force for outward investment flows. The push force was a result of three factors: a sharp appreciation of Taiwanese currency in the late 1980s, rising wages and labor shortages due to rapid economic growth for three decades, and gradual liberalization of government policy on capital outflows. The push force largely encourages outward investment flows to mainland China as well as to developing countries in Southeast Asia.

The open-door policy and outstanding performance in economic growth provided China with a strong gravitational pull in attracting foreign investors around the world, including Taiwan. China perhaps has become the world's most liberalized country in hosting foreign direct investment. In addition to the advantages of cheap labor and a huge market, the Chinese government has provided foreign investors with many favorable economic incentives to reduce risk and increase the chances of success in doing business in China. As a result, China has been the largest recipient of FDI among the developing world and the second largest overall. More than half of TDI flows went to China in the 1990s and an even larger share is expected in the next ten years, if political and military "accidents" can be avoided.

TDI in China is characterized by the dominant export-oriented investments, with a tendency toward market-seeking investment projects. Taiwanese investors prefer a region with a superior infrastructure for exporting and for basic industrial activities, along with a steady supply of skilled labor and a growing market size. The cultural proximity of individual investors with a host region is also a key motivation for TDI flows to that region. Favorable FDI incentives provided by the Chinese government in coastal areas have made significant differences in regional distribution of Taiwanese manufacturing branch-plants.

References

Chen, Tain-Jy. 1992. "Determinants of Taiwan's Direct Foreign Investment: The Case of a Newly Industrialized Country." *Journal of Development Economics* 39: 397–407.

CIER (Chunghwa Institute for Economics Research). 1994 and 1999. *Taiwan-China Economic Yearbook.* Taipei, Taiwan (ROC).

Dunning, J.H. 1981. *International Production and the Multinational Enterprise.* London: George Allen and Unwin.

Fei, John, and Jack W. Hou. 1994. "The Comprehensive Economic Reform of the PRC (1978–92)." In Shao-chuan Leng, ed., *Reform and Development in Deng's China*, volume 4. The Miller Center Series on Asian Political Leadership. New York: University Press of America, 19–64.

Fuess, Scott M. Jr., and Jack W. Hou. 2000. "Rapid Economic Development and Job Segregation: The Case of Taiwan, 1978–1997." Paper presented at the 75th Annual Conference of the Western Economic Association, Vancouver, Canada, July.

Hou, Jack W. 1997. "Foreign Labor Management Systems: An International Comparison." Monograph. Taiwan: Council of Labor Affairs.

Hou, Jack W., Shinichi Ichimura, Seiji Naya, Lars Werin, and Leslie Young. 1995. "Pacific Rim Trade and Development: Historical Environment and Future Prospects." *Contemporary Economic Policy* 13, 4:1–25.

Hou, Jack W., and Kevin H. Zhang. 2001. "A Location Analysis of Taiwanese Manufacturing Branch-Plants in Mainland China." *International Journal of Business.* Forthcoming.

Hymer, Stephen. 1976. *The International Operation of National Firms: Study of Direct Foreign Investment.* Cambridge, MA: MIT Press.

Kueh, Y.Y. 1992. "Foreign Investment and Economic Change in China." *China Quarterly*, no.131 (September): 637–90.

MOFERT (Ministry of Foreign Economic Relations and Trade). 1998. *Almanac of China's Foreign Relations and Trade* (1987–1997). Hong Kong: Chinese Resources Advertising Company.

Pearson, M.M. 1991. *Joint Ventures in the People's Republic of China.* Princeton, NJ: Princeton University Press.

Pomfret, R. 1991. *Investing in China: Ten Years of the Open Door Policy.* Ames: Iowa State University Press.

SSB (State Statistical Bureau). 1992–1999. *Statistical Yearbook of China.* Beijing: China Statistics Press.

UNCTAD (United Nations Conference on Trade and Development). 1999. *World Investment Report: 1999.* New York: United Nations.

Vernon, Raymond. 1979. "The Product Cycle Hypothesis in a New International Environment." *Oxford Bulletin of Economics and Statistics* 41, 4: 255–67.

Wells, Louis. 1993. "Mobile Exporters: New Foreign Investors in East Asia." In *Foreign Direct Investment*, K.A. Froot, ed. Chicago: University of Chicago Press.

Zhang, Kevin H. 2000. "Human Capital, Country Size, and North-South Manufacturing Multinational Enterprises." *Economia Internazionale / International Economics*, 53, 2 (May): 237–60.

————. 2001. "What Explains the Boom of Foreign Direct Investment in China?" *Economia Internazionale / International Economics* 53, 4. Forthcoming.

Zhang, Kevin H., and James R. Markusen. 1999. "Vertical Multinationals and Host-Country Characteristics." *Journal of Development Economics* 59: 233–52.

11

The Changing Trends of FDI Patterns in China

Changhong Pei

Foreign direct investments (FDIs) are making a significant contribution to China's economic growth. From 1979 to 1999 a large amount of realized FDI in the amount of U.S.$307.5 billion flowed into China, particularly into the industrial/manufacturing sector. This chapter discusses potential impacts of FDI on three Chinese industries: primary industry (related to agriculture such as farming, forestry, and husbandry); secondary industry (industrial mining, manufacturing, water supply, construction, among others); and tertiary industry (service sectors and others). In addition, it sheds light on industrial structural change resulting from FDIs.

It is most likely that China will adopt an active open-economy policy after China's entrance into the WTO, in order to attract foreign investments into that tertiary industry. The flow of FDI into the tertiary industry, especially into the service, financial, and telecommunication sectors, will benefit China and also make the service sectors better manage their resources and be more competitive.

Patterns of FDI in the Three Industries

Patterns of FDI

Table 11.1 indicates that, in the 1980s, 2.9 percent of the total contractual investment was in primary industry, 60.3 percent in secondary industry, and

36.8 percent in tertiary industry. In the 1990s, inward investment in primary industry dropped to 1.7 percent (which is small) and to 32.9 percent in tertiary industry, whereas it increased to 65.4 percent in secondary industry (i.e., 5 percent higher than in the 1980s). It is interesting to note that 62.4 percent of total inward investment was concentrated in the industrial sector (within secondary industry).

Changing Characteristics of FDIs

The pattern of FDI in China is changing, as Table 11.1 shows. From 1990 to 1991, the proportion of foreign investment in tertiary industry was lower (13.8 percent in 1990 and 16.7 percent in 1991), but the proportion of investment in secondary industry was higher (84.4 percent in 1990 and 81.5 percent in 1991). Meanwhile the industrial sector was at 81.7 percent in 1990 and at 80.4 percent in 1991. The proportion of investment in primary industry was 1.8 percent in both 1990 and 1991.

From 1992 to 1994, inward investment in tertiary industry increased sharply. For instance, the proportion of foreign investment in tertiary industry reached its highest level in 1993 and declined later on, while FDI in primary and secondary industries dropped significantly for the same period.

These changes indicate that FDI at the beginning mainly flows into traditional industry sectors. Later, FDI flows into tertiary industry— especially the real-estate and social-service sectors. Real estate remains a potential investment vehicle for foreign investors. Apparently, the changing proportion of investment in most parts of tertiary industry reflects the recessionary or expansionary state of the economy.

Behavior of Realized Investment

Table 11.2 indicates that the proportion of realized investments in secondary industry and the traditional industrial sector is higher than its contractual investment for the period 1997–98. However, for primary and tertiary industries, the proportion of realized investments is lower than the contractual investment. The realized investment in primary industry is small, averaging 1.4 percent for 1997–98. The proportion of realized investment is much higher, about 70.4 percent in secondary industry and 66.6 percent in traditional industry. The proportion of the realized investment in tertiary industry is low, with an average of 28.2 percent for 1997–98.

Table 11.1

Composition (%) of FDI in the Three Industries (in U.S.$)

Year	Primary Industry	Secondary Industry	Industrial	Tertiary Industry	Contractual Amount ($100million)	Total
1979–1990	2.9	60.3	36.8	403.6	100.00	100.00
1990	1.8	84.4	81.7	13.8	65.96	100.00
1991	1.8	81.5	80.4	16.7	119.77	100.00
1992	1.2	60.1	56.9	38.7	581.24	100.00
1993	1.1	49.4	45.9	49.5	1,114.36	100.00
1994	1.2	56.0	53.1	42.8	826.80	100.00
1995	1.9	69.6	67.5	28.5	912.82	100.00
1996	1.6	71.6	68.9	26.8	732.76	100.00
1997	2.1	66.7	61.6	31.2	510.03	100.00
1998	2.3	68.0	64.6	29.7	521.02	100.00
1999	3.57	66.20		30.23	412.23	100.00
1991–1998	1.7	65.4	62.4	32.9	5,318.8	100.00
1979–1999	1.76	59.56		38.67	5,722.4	100.00

Note: The above-mentioned data were picked from the sources of the Ministry of Foreign Trade and Economy Cooperation, i.e., the *National Statistics Yearbook of Using Foreign Fund*, the *China Foreign Capital Statistics*; and of the State Statistics Administration, i.e. *China Statistics Yearbook*.

Table 11.2

Composition (%) of Contractual FDI and Realized FDI (in U.S.$)

Year	Primary industry	Secondary industry	Industrial	Tertiary industry	Total amount ($100 million)
1997					
1. Contractual Investment	2.1	66.7	61.6	31.2	510.03
2. Realized Investment	1.4	71.9	68.8	26.7	452.57
3. =2−1	−0.7	5.2	7.2	−4.5	
1998					
1. Contractual investment	2.3	68.0	64.6	29.7	521.02
2. Realized Investment	1.4	68.9	64.4	29.7	454.63
3. =2−1	−0.9	0.9	−0.2	0.0	
1999					
1. Contractual investment	3.57	66.20		30.23	412.23
2. Realized Investment	1.76	66.63		31.61	403.19
1997–1998					
1. Contractual investment	2.2	67.4	63.1	30.5	
2. Realized Investment	1.4	70.4	66.6	28.2	
3. =2−1	−0.8	3.0	3.5	−2.3	

Source: See Table 11.1.

Relative Importance of Foreign-Funded Industries

Table 11.3 displays the number of foreign firms and the amount of foreign investment in the three industries for 1996 and 1998. In 1998, the number of foreign companies in secondary industry constituted 75 percent of the total, and in the industrial sector, 72 percent. The percentage of foreign firms was 2.4 percent of the total investment for primary industry and 22.6 percent for tertiary industry. For registered foreign capital, the proportion of investment in tertiary industry was a little higher—about 36.4 percent (vis-à-vis 22.6 percent).

The proportion of foreign investment (registered capital) in tertiary industry was 36.4 percent (34.8 percent) in 1996 and 37.3 percent (34.4 percent) in 1998. For the industrial sector, the proportion of foreign investment (registered capital) in industrial companies was 59.9 percent (61.3 percent) in 1996 and 59.5 percent (61.3 percent) in 1998. The results indicate the importance of foreign investment in the industrial sector, which received more than 60 percent in terms of total investment and registered capital.

The Impact of Foreign Direct Investment on the Industrial Sector

The Expansion of the Foreign-Funded Processing Industry

It is important to assess the impact of foreign investment in light and heavy industries. Table 11.4 shows the position of foreign-funded investment in the two industrial sectors. For light industry, the processing sector that takes raw materials from industrial goods, the figures show 15.6 percent in 1993, 30.4 percent in 1997, and 24.6 percent in 1998 for total value added, and 15.0, 33.3, and 29.0 percent for sales dollars for the same period. In addition, the proportion of net asset value was 13.6 percent in 1993, 26.0 percent in 1997, and 27.1 percent in 1998.

The heavy-industry raw materials and foreign processing sectors seem to have become more important over the period 1993–98. It is clear that the proportion of foreign-funded industry in processing is still much higher than that in raw materials. Digging in heavy industry is still relatively small as compared to the domestic sector.

The proportion of before-tax profit for both foreign-funded light and heavy industry has increased over time. For light industry processing,

Table 11.3

Structure of Registered Foreign-Invested Enterprises (data collected at the end of each year)

Year/number/proportion	Primary industry	Secondary industry	Tertiary industry	Industry	Total
1996					
Number of enterprises	5,748	182,464	175,020	52,235	240,447
Proportion (%)	2.4	75.9	72.8	21.7	100.0
Total investment (US$100m)	86.3	4464.7	4286.1	2602.2	7153.2
Proportion (%)	1.2	62.4	59.9	36.4	100.0
Registered capital (US$100m)	62.8	2914.2	2806.4	1437.9	4414.9
Proportion (%)	1.4	66.0	63.6	32.6	100.0
Registered foreign capital (US$100m)	42.9	1846.0	1775.5	1009.1	2898.0
Proportion (%)	1.5	63.7	61.3	34.8	100.0
1998					
Number of enterprises	5,538	170,844	164,148	51,425	227,807
Proportion (%)	2.4	75.0	72.1	22.6	100.0
Total investment (US$100m)	9.2	4,846.9	4,609.8	2,886.2	7,742.3
Proportion (%)	0.1	62.6	59.5	37.3	100.0
Registered capital(US$100m)	65.3	3.088.5	2,957.2	1,519.1	4,672.9
Proportion (%)	1.4	66.1	63.3	32.5	100.0
Registered foreign capital (US$100m)	46.5	2,012.1	1,924.6	1,078.5	3,137.1
Proportion (%)	1.5	64.1	61.3	34.4	100.0

Source: China Statistics Yearbook (1998, 1999).

Table 11.4

Position of Foreign-Funded Industry in Light and Heavy Industry of China (in RMB yuan amount)

The proportional percentage of the foreign funded industry in total Chinese industry

	Added value	Sales value	Net value of fixed asset	Fluid asset	Profit before tax
1993					
Light industry					
Raw material based on industrial goods	15.6	15.0	13.6	13.9	15.7
Heavy industry					
Digging	0.1	0.1	0.1	0.2	0.5
Raw material	0.3	3.1	4.6	3.4	2.5
Processing	9.9	9.7	9.0	7.9	13.3
1997					
Light Industry					
Raw material based on industrial goods	30.4	33.3	26.0	29.9	26.8
Heavy industry					
Digging	2.1	2.2	0.4	0.9	5.6
Raw material	9.4	8.2	12.6	8.2	9.5
Processing	21.8	24.2	19.9	19.2	30.2
1998					
Light industry					
Raw material based on industrial goods*	24.6	29.0	27.1	26.9	
Heavy industry					
Digging	0.4	0.7	0.4	0.7	
Raw material	10.2	9.6	12.2	9.3	
Processing	27.0	29.2	24.4	23.6	

Sources: Calculations based on the *Industry Statistics Yearbook* (1993, 1997, 1998.)
Notes: All of the above data come from foreign-funded industry and total industry with sole business accounting system.
The average yearly remaining sum.
Data of state-run enterprises and non-state-run industrial enterprises with annual sales value in RMB 5 million and above.
*Production includes industrial goods as raw materials.

the proportion increased from 15.7 percent in 1993 to 26.8 percent in 1997, while heavy industry processing increased from 13.3 percent in 1993 to 30.2 percent in 1997.

Promotion of Chinese Tech-Concentrated Industry

Foreign-funded firms not only possess state-of-the-art equipment, better technology, and modern management in their tech-intensive or deep-processing industries. They account for a high proportion of investment in the processing industry. The growth of foreign-funded industry stimulates the development of Chinese tech-intensive industries.

Table 11.5 displays the proportion of foreign-funded investment in Chinese manufacturing sectors. The results indicate that in 1993 foreign-funded investment amounted to 34.6 percent in electronics and telecommunication facilities, 11.3 percent in traffic communication and transport facilities, 23.9 percent in instruments and apparatus or office machines, and 9.2 percent in electrical machinery and apparatus. In 1998, however, the percentages increased to 58.6, 26.4, 49.4, and 25.5 for the same corresponding industries.

In the pharmaceutical and chemical-fiber industries, the proportion of total foreign-funded investment increased from 13.4 and 8.4 percent in 1993 to 22.9 and 42.3 percent in 1998. Similarly, for the low-tech processing requirements of the textile industry, the proportion of foreign-funded investment in the garment- and other fiber-goods–manufacturing industries also increased from 30.6 percent in 1993 to 49 percent in 1998.

Compared with the state-run and collective industries, foreign-funded investments make up a large proportion of the mechanical and electronics industry, especially manufacturing, electronics and telecommunication facilities, traffic communication and transport. According to a survey by the State Economic and Trade Commission (*Third Nationwide Industrial Survey*, published in 1998 by China Statistics Press), electronics and telecommunication facilities accounted for about 1.9 percent of added value in state-run and collective industries, while foreign-funded industry accounted for a much higher proportion—14.4 percent. Traffic communication was 5.1 percent and transport facilities were 4.4 percent of added value in the state-run and collective industry while the foreign-funded industry share was about 7.3 percent. It thus appears that foreign-funded industry with its advanced technology and equipment is pushing forward the development of the Chinese tech-gathering industry.

Table 11.5

Proportion (%) of Foreign-Funded Industry in Total Chinese Manufacturing sector (added value)

Item	1993	1995	1997	1998
Total Industry	9.2	19.5	20.6	24.8
Food processing	7.4	20.6	19.0	22.3
Food manufacturing	13.9	32.4	35.5	37.2
Beverage manufacturing	13.1	21.2	24.4	26.9
Tobacco processing	0.5	0.6	0.6	0.7
Textile industry	11.3	20.3	18.0	19.1
Garment and other fiber goods	30.6	50.0	43.7	49.0
Leather, fur, eider down goods	29.7	51.2	47.3	53.5
Lumber processing and bamboo, Rattan, palm fiber, grass	17.3	24.6	23.2	28.0
Furniture manufacturing	15.2	27.8	24.3	40.6
Paper-making and papers	11.5	15.9	17.9	23.5
Printing, copy of record media	7.0	16.5	17.3	29.2
Stationary and sports goods	28.0	40.6	42.1	61.3
Petroleum-processing and coking	0.9	0.7	3.1	1.4
Chemical material and goods	7.8	13.6	14.9	17.4
Pharmacy	13.4	25.6	24.7	22.9
Chemical fiber	8.4	10.0	15.8	42.3
Rubber goods	11.4	23.3	20.1	31.4
Plastic products	20.3	31.1	31.6	40.4
Non-metal minerals	3.8	11.7	10.7	15.4
Ferrous metal-smelting and rolling processing	1.3	4.7	2.9	4.3
Non-ferrous metal-smelting and rolling processing	4.2	10.1	9.9	9.7
Metal goods	8.6	23.6	22.9	31.9
General machinery	5.9	14.4	13.7	18.3
Special equipment	5.0	10.0	10.4	13.7
Traffic and transporting facility	11.3	23.5	23.9	26.4
Electric machinery and apparatus	9.2	14.4	23.2	25.5
Electronic and telecom facility	34.6	58.8	61.3	58.6
Instrument and apparatus and office machine	23.9	36.9	39.3	49.4
Others	14.9		33.9	42.9

Sources: Calculations based on the *Industry Statistics Yearbook* (1993, 1997, 1998), *China Statistics Yearbook* (1998), *The Third Nationwide Industrial Survey* in 1998 by China Statistics Press.

The Widening Investment Gap Among the Three Industries

The scale and proportion of foreign investment is rather small in primary and tertiary industries because most inflow of foreign investment has been concentrated in secondary industry, especially the industrial sector (1.7 and 32.9 percent respectively, as indicated in Table 11.1). From 1991 to 1998, a pattern of inward foreign investment evolved, widening the investment gap among the three industries.

For secondary industry, the proportion of inward foreign investment in the industrial sector increased 5.1 percent, from 60.3 percent in 1979–90 to 65.4 percent in 1991–98 (see Table 11.1). According to the 1998 *Third Nationwide Industrial Survey*, the proportion of output, especially from the industrial sector, rose by a large margin from 41.6 percent in 1990 to 49.2 percent in 1998, up 7.6 percent. It would be an increase of 14 percent, reaching 55.6 percent in 1998, based on 1990 price levels. The productive capability of foreign-funded industry accounts for about one-fifth of total Chinese industrial production.

By contrast, the development in Chinese tertiary industry was slow in the 1990s, due to the small proportion (32.9 percent) of foreign investment flowing into this sector. The proportion of FDI in this sector dropped 4.1 percent compared to that of the 1980s as shown in Table 11.1 (36.8 percent during 1979–90 and 32.9 percent during 1991–98).

The 1998 survey also indicated that the proportion of actual output from tertiary industry increased slowly from 31.3 percent in 1990 to 32.8 percent in 1998, a rise of only 1.5 percent. This proportion in fact dropped down to 27.9 percent in 1998, if calculated using 1998 price levels, a fall of 3.4 percent compared to 1990. Such slow development of tertiary industry widens the investment gap between the secondary and tertiary industries and leaves the Chinese tertiary industry behind that in other countries.

The inflow of foreign investment has become an important factor influencing the structure of Chinese industry. Its investment pattern is widening the gaps in the Chinese industrial structure, and stimulating the varying degrees of overexpansion in China's industrial sector. In recent years, productive capacity in some industrial sectors has not been fully operational because of funding shortages.

Policy Issues of FDI Trends After China's Entrance into the WTO

The ratio of FDI in tertiary industry is much lower than that in secondary industry, and FDI in tertiary industry is concentrated in the real-estate and social-service sectors, with 60 percent of total value in the

1980s, increasing to 70 percent in the 1990s. Moreover, FDI inflow also influenced the transportation, warehousing, telecommunications, retail, and restaurant sectors. However, FDI entry into the banking, insurance, telecommunications network, scientific, and technological sectors is still scarce up to now. Thus FDI has had much less impact on the output ratio in these sectors.

In what follows, four aspects of FDI after China's entrance into the WTO are discussed.

New Fields of Investment

The number of potential investors will probably double after China promises to speed up the opening of sectors such as communication, banking, insurance, commerce, and intermediary services, considering that more than 50 percent of total global transnational investment will be in the service industry.

Telecommunications sector

According to the WTO agreement between China and the United States, China will allow U.S. telecommunication companies to own 49 percent of investment share, which can be increased up to 50 percent two years after the date of initial investment. The European Union (EU) requires more than 50 percent stock share, reflecting the EU's concern with benefits from investment in the telecommunications market.

At present, China's telecommunications-equipment market is quite open and the production capability of foreign enterprises has reached 70 percent of total production capacity in China. Companies like Motorola of the United States and Ericsson of Sweden are all big suppliers in China's telecommunications-equipment market with high market shares. The telecommunications-service market in China has not yet been opened. Trade partners like the European Union and the United States wish China to open its telecommunications-service market through negotiations on China's entry into the WTO so that they can have first-mover advantage.

For several reasons, China insists on controlling the dominant status of its share in joint ventures at the initial opening of its telecommunications market. First, telecommunications services are closely involved with national security. Second, it is hard for this fledging industry to compete with large transnational corporations. Currently, the management and operation system of China's telecommunications industry cannot meet the requirements of the WTO. Third, the Telecommunications Bureau is not an enterprise independent from the Telecommunications Administration Department. China does not have any written telecommunications law, and many local laws and regulations lack transparency. As a result, it is necessary for China to maintain a transitional period in the primary stages of opening the market in order for Chinese companies to improve themselves and compete fairly.

Financial and Insurance Sectors

According to the agreement between China and the United States, foreign banks will be allowed to begin conducting their RMB business with Chinese companies two years after China's accession to the WTO, while the terms on insurance and proportion equity are at present only scheduled for discussion.

The finance and insurance content in the agreement excites U.S. banks and insurance companies. U.S. bankers believe that the opportunity to enter the Chinese market will be good, because it is a large one, with loans of RMB 1.1 trillion (U.S.$132.88 billion). Foreign lending institutions will eventually accept the Chinese residence deposit without limit and provide loans to individuals and companies for the first time.

Since the interest rate is still dictated by China's monetary authority, foreign banks cannot reduce the competitiveness of Chinese financial institutions in terms of price. However, the Chinese financial sector still faces severe competition from foreign banks. Given the competitive disadvantage of Chinese banks in terms of management, capital quality, and technical skills, foreign banks will make big investments in the Chinese financial sector, which will in turn significantly change the ownership structure of China's banking sector.

The agreement on insurance stipulates that foreign life-insurance companies are permitted to hold a maximum of 50 percent of the shares of a joint venture. When setting up property-insurance companies in China, foreign insurance companies can choose between investing in branches or in a joint venture. Setting up a life-insurance company in China could be done as a joint venture, and the partner on the Chinese side would thus be a life-insurance company.

China's insurance companies have a comparatively stronger competitive advantage. The opening to the rest of the world in this sector was initiated at the start of the 1980s. By the end of 1998, nine foreign insurance companies had been allowed to set up branches or joint ventures in China. Four other companies were approved by the China Insurance Supervision and Administration Committee to establish branches or joint ventures of insurance and life-insurance companies in China in 1999.

After the agreement was signed by China and the United States, more U.S. insurance companies prepared to gain access into the Chinese market in the next three to five years. Getting 1 percent of China's market share would double the business of the New York Life Insurance Company which has six million insurance policyholders. The company got a license for operating insurance on property, injury, and death in two provinces of China in September 1999 and started business at the beginning of 2000.

It is estimated that FDI in China's insurance sector will increase sharply. As a result, the competition among individual Chinese insurance companies, as well as that between them and foreign companies, will be remarkably severe. The coming of foreign insurance companies will bring new insurance technologies into China, including new combinations of insurance items and advantaged management, although it will certainly cause fiercer competition and bring heavier pressure to bear on China's insurance industry. The belief is, however, that such competition will improve market structure, ameliorate service quality, and enhance the competitiveness of China's companies and the insurance industry as a whole.

New Mode of Investment

After China's entrance into the WTO, it is expected that one popular mode of global transnational investment—mergers and acquisitions (M&A) by foreign investors on local enterprises—will be on the rise. In 1998, total world FDI was 644 billion yuan, and of this, 411 billion yuan (64 percent) was investment through mergers and acquisitions. In 1999, M&A accounted for 90 percent of total FDI with 800 billion yuan. This is a new method of investment that can have great potential in China if it is allowed.

Elimination of Some Restrictions

Some past restrictions on foreign investors will be abolished after China's entry into the WTO. Two restrictive policies are explained as follows. Domestic policy limits types of imports, while the requirement on proportions of exports forces exports. The abolition of these restrictions will attract more FDI into the marketplace in China. Furthermore, the problem of nonnational treatment of foreign investors will gradually be abolished as well. For instance, the regulations stipulating that foreign firms not be permitted to set up distribution agencies outside their places of registration will gradually be phased out.

Abolition of Tariff and Nontariff Barriers

The impact of abolishing tariff and nontariff barriers is twofold. Tariff reductions and the removal of nontariff barriers will make the import of components cheaper and easier while reducing the protection of foreign-funded enterprises. Those foreign investors who used to invest in China in order to skirt round the trade barriers may cut down their investment and shift to exports into China. Existing restricted areas will be opened up. Thus the telecommunications, finance, and insurance sectors will become important new fields for foreign investment in China.

Conclusion

Given that foreign direct investment is mainly concentrated in the industrial sector, particularly in the processing industry, one can expect to see intense competition, overproduction of consumption, and saturation of investment. Thus foreign investors need to look for new areas of investment in China, while the Chinese government also needs to further open up new investment fields in order to attract more FDI.

After joining the WTO, the Chinese government will adopt new policies: to attract FDI, loosen the limits on the scope of investment, and allow new approaches in the utilization of FDI. International investors, on the other hand, will more likely be interested in the service sector. This will stimulate improvement in the allocation of resources and in the economic structure of that sector.

12

Locational Advantages, FDI, and Technology Advance: Evidence of China

Seung H. Kim, Hongxin Zhao, and Jianjun Du

Introduction

Foreign direct investment (FDI) in China has been accelerating since the early 1980s. According to the International Monetary Fund, the amount of annual foreign investment flow into China in 1998 was only less than that into the United States. The *World Development Indicator 2000* by the World Bank reports that China took in US$43.75 billion as investment in 1998, a dramatic increase from US$0.43 billion in 1982. Issues on why China has attracted such a large amount of FDI have engrossed a number of scholars. Most scholars of China FDI base their studies upon current FDI theoretical frameworks, while others build their researches on the foundation of other disciplines and theories. Some of the studies examine why companies decide to invest into China, as most researches investigate the characteristics of China, i.e., how China can attract more FDI than all other developing countries, or what factors influence the inflow of FDI. Even more complicated, China FDI inflow is conceived differently from that of other countries because a large portion of the investment comes from overseas Chinese, particularly from Chinese in Hong Kong, Macao, and Taiwan.

These studies have helped us to understand China FDI issues, but there are a couple of weaknesses in the current research. First, a majority of the studies isolate China from international environments by taking as the only dependent variable the FDI flow into China or the regions of China. A comparison between FDI inflow to China and to other countries may reveal more valuable information that cannot be obtained from a study of an isolated single country. Second, many of the current studies are limited by the premises of certain FDI theories upon which these studies are based. Studies of this kind take on only the variables that are explained in the theories. To overcome these weaknesses, we embark on this comprehensive study. Based upon Dunning's eclectic paradigm, competitive advantage, and several other different theories, this paper tries to build a theoretical framework of competitive location advantages to attract FDI. With this comprehensive framework we then explore the relationships among location advantages, FDI, and technology advance.

This study proceeds as follows. Section two traces general FDI theories and research on FDI in China. Section three develops the hypotheses to be tested. Section four explains in detail the methodology and data used in the empirical test. The next section provides the test results and explanations of the results. The last section summarizes the study and lists the contributions and limitations of the study.

Literature Review

General FDI Theories

FDI has been extensively studied within the academic field since 1960 after Stephen Hymer's breakthrough work of imperfection market perspectives for FDI. Many theories have been developed from this point of view. Caves (1971) looks into the technology effect on FDI decisions of multinational corporations (MNC). In his view, the innovations and product differentiations caused by technology owned by MNCs give them an advantage over local companies in home and host countries. MNCs can increase their profitability by expanding their production into foreign countries and enlarging their shares in the world market. Horst (1972) and Wolf (1977) found that both firm size and technical capacity play important roles in firms' FDI. Furthermore, Horst also found that international trade and FDI are negatively related. Stephen G. Grubaugh (1987) challenged this result and found that companies invest in foreign countries to take advantage of intangible assets owned by the firms overseas and at home. Knickerbocker (1973) may be one of the first persons to look into the relationship between strategic moves by MNCs in the same industry and defensive reactions, including FDI, by an oligopolistic

MNC. Through moving operations to overseas, the MNC will be able to keep its competitive advantage. In other words, through international differentiation, MNCs can maintain the advantages they enjoy domestically. Calvet (1981) provides a comprehensive review of the progress along the market imperfection paradigm. Per this review, there are three major contributions in the area: the appropriability theory, the internalization theory, and the diversification theory.

Some early studies deal with capital markets and their relationship with FDI. In these models the markets of bank lending and foreign exchange are considered imperfect. Aliber (1970) theorizes that because of the imperfections in foreign exchange and capital markets MNCs can obtain lower interest rates in their investment than those firms in host countries. The differences between foreign exchanges may give MNCs even a foreign currency premium and may help MNCs to take advantage of devalued local costs of production factors. Froot and Stein (1989) later investigate effects of foreign exchange fluctuations on new FDI in different industries and on the increased investment input to the existing assets as a result of past FDI. Their findings show that alterations in foreign exchange affect FDI in manufacturing industries but not the expansion of existing assets.

Another theory that is often quoted in FDI research is the Heckscher-Ohlin theory or the comparative advantage theory. Though originally invented to explain international trade, comparative advantage has often been applied to FDI researches (Balassa 1986; Kogut and Chang, 1991; Nachum, Dunning, and Jones 2000). According to this theory, MNCs invest in foreign countries because these companies have comparative advantages over those in the host countries. In examining FDI and international trade from more traditional economic concepts, Robert E. Baldwin (1979) challenges the inadequacy of Heckscher-Ohlin theory, which states that a country exports its relatively abundant factors, capital, or others. His argument is that capital endowments, capital/labor intensity, and relative changes of these intensities in industries may determine overseas investment and exports. On the other hand, Raymond Vernon (1966) and his colleagues link international trade and FDI by their product life cycle theory. Vernon (1979) later refined this theory to embrace the new international environment. Though applied only to certain types of FDI, this theory distinguishes product and market differentiation and argues that the life cycle of a new product can be extended in international markets through trade first and then FDI. The saturated market where the source of the new product originated may eventually be turned into an import market for the same product. Stephen Thomsen (1993) revives Vernon's product life cycle by providing two more notions. One is that firms invest abroad to defend market share threatened by increasing competition and to free up resources for more home product development. The other is that the location of the investment is determined by a mixture of comparative advantage and government incentives. He concludes that Japanese firms' large FDI and low share of intra-industry trade accord with Vernon's hypothesis.

Some of the previous theories on competitive advantages or MNCs' ownership advantages cannot clearly explain why developed countries have significant FDI into one another, even at frequent foreign exchange fluctuations. More recent FDI theories, therefore, take a wider view of FDI. Peter J. Buckley and Mark Casson (1976), and later Alan M. Rugman (1980), look into the transaction cost reduction through internalization by MNCs in their FDI. This theory complements the previous theories on FDI in the imperfection market. According to this theory, by internalizing imperfect market factors, MNCs can keep their competitive advantages in domestic and international markets. Rugman (1981) furthers this theory and considers information or knowledge as the most important advantage MNCs possess. FDI can help MNCs to exploit the internalized knowledge or advantage in different markets.

If companies' ownership advantage is considered an important factor for companies to decide whether to invest abroad, location factors are the determinants that help MNCs that have determined to go overseas to decide on where to invest. Related to location factors are labor cost, market growth, stages of development, governmental policies and incentives for business, local competition, tariff barriers, and economic, political, and cultural environments. William H. Davidson (1980) summarizes the characteristics of a host country and their effects on FDI, and furthermore studies the role of MNCs' experiences in their investment aboard. John H. Dunning (1973, 1980, 1981, 1988) may be the first to comprehensively synthesize the existing FDI theories. Dunning draws *o*wnership advantage, *l*ocation advantage and *i*nternalization (OLI) in his eclectic paradigm of FDI. Per this comprehensive theory, if OLI exists, MNCs with the ownership advantage and internalization motivations will likely invest in the country that exhibits the location advantage so as to expand their production and markets. In short, the OLI is composed of a wide range of motivations that may determine the direction of FDI. In the eclectic paradigm, location advantage is considered a significant determinant in MNCs' FDI decision making. Dunning (1998) further explains the relationship between location choices and MNCs' FDI. In summary, the eclectic paradigm is considered one of the most established and most frequently tested FDI theories so far.

The national competitive advantage theory by M.E. Porter (1990, 1994, 1996) was not specially developed for foreign investment, but is widely quoted in FDI. Porter asserts that if a country wants to hold on strongly in international trade and investment, it must maintain economic competitiveness. Among many experts, Porter contends that labor costs, interest rates, exchange rates, and economies of scale are important determinants of competitiveness, but innovation is the true source of international competitiveness advantage. According to Porter's diamond diagram, there are four broad attributes of national competitive advantages that are carefully scrutinized by companies that intend to invest overseas: production factor conditions, demand conditions, related and supporting industries, and the environments, natural or created by the nation, in which the company is going to invest. In the same vein, Porter's competitive advantage diamond and Dunning's eclectic paradigm, both point out that a country must maintain necessary conditions to attract foreign investment.

Studies on FDI Flow into China

Studies on China FDI inflows have flourished in the last decade or so because the amount of China inflow FDI is so large that China has become number two in FDI intake worldwide. Most of the academic studies are based upon existing FDI theories and studies on the location advantage possessed by China cite the majority of these researches. These studies have proved that a number of factors influence the intake, and depending upon the theories applied, some variables have more important roles than others (for example, Luo 1998a). A detailed discussion on these researches follows.

Wei Yingqi et al. (1999) conducted a rigorous study on the regional distribution of FDI in China. They basically applied the theory of firm-specific advantages and location advantages to investigate why the FDI inflow goes to certain regions but not to others. The independent variables they used are wage rates, R&D manpower, GDP growth, infrastructure, agglomeration effect, information costs, and investment incentives. The results of their empirical test show that there is a strong relationship between regional characteristics and FDI inflow. Regions with higher levels of international trade, lower wage rates, more R&D manpower, higher GDP growth rates, quicker improvement in infrastructure, more rapid advances in agglomeration, more incentive preferential policies, and closer links with overseas Chinese attract more FDI. Their results are consistent with those provided by Tao Qu and Milford B. Green (1997), Leonard K. Cheng and Yum K. Kwan (2000), and Zhao Hongxin and Zhu Gangti (2000).

One of the noticeable features that distinguish China FDI inflow from others is that overseas Chinese, particularly those in Hong Kong, Macao, and Taiwan, invest heavily in mainland China. John Henley, Colin Kirkpatrick, and Georgina Wilde (1999) discuss the trend of China FDI inflow and note the importance of Hong Kong and the regional contribution. Rajeswary Ampalavanar-Brown (1998) and Homin Chen and Tain-Jy Chen (1998), among others, examine special cases about why overseas Chinese invest in China. The conclusions of their studies indicate that culture, legal environments, language, and relationship or ethnic linkage play significant roles in their decision to invest in China, especially in those regions where personal relationships are strong.

Thomas E. Jones (1998) investigated the importance of foreign exchange regime for FDI. He concluded that the stability policy of Chinese currency may help Asian countries to prevent another round of competitive devaluation, but the consequence is that FDI inflow to China has slowed down and foreign exchange reserves have seemingly stalled to some degree.

Cheng and Kwan (2000) investigated the effects of the determinants of FDI in twenty-nine Chinese regions from 1985 to 1995. They found that large regional markets, good infrastructure, and preferential policy had a positive effect, but wage cost had a negative effect. Education level is positively related with the FDI, but statistically not significant. In the period, FDI was heavily directed toward some regions, but the deviations wear thin through time. For those regions with comparative advantages over other regions, the previous FDI in fact contributes to domestic capital formation, export growth, and new employment opportunities or general economic development. This result is in line with others (Sun 1998).

Harry G. Broadman and Siaolun Sun (1997) investigated the distribution of FDI in China by examining the regional distribution and industrial distribution. They studied what determinants play significant roles in attracting FDI and noted that coastal areas' share has been over 90 percent of the total FDI flow into China; and up to 1995 the real estate sector related to hotels and tourism projects has been responsible for a large share of intake of FDI. Zhang Le-Yin (1994) studied the effect of location advantages on manufacturing FDI in south China. The findings from this study show the relationship between FDI and China's administrative decentralization from governmental control and/or regional active initiatives. Guangdong province has three advantages to attract foreign investment over other regions in China: They are its geographic proximity to Hong Kong and Macao, its historical and ethnic relationship and connection with overseas Chinese, including those in Hong Kong and Macao, and its relatively long tradition of dealing with foreigners.

Hypotheses Formation

When a country tries to attract foreign investment, it is up against a series of competitions. The most severe competition comes from the home country before the MNC makes the decision to go overseas. The home country tries whatever it can to keep the MNC at home. After the FDI decision is made and a target location is sought, the host country is only one of multiple choices among a number of foreign countries. As the existing FDI theories point out, MNCs go overseas to increase consumer market shares for more profits. More often than not, the competition from domestic firms and other MNCs forces the MNC to seek in foreign markets production factors to protect its market shares and enhance its competitive advantages. MNCs often match their major competitors in their overseas investment. On the other hand, countries want to attract MNCs, but only to those areas that are intended to be open to foreign companies. The host country must first possess sufficient conditions that are attractive to MNCs. Like the MNC, the host country faces a number of competitors from other countries. Only if the MNC and the host country have a good match with each other, will the FDI occur.

As pointed out above, current FDI studies on country cases, including those studying China FDI inflow, have a significant shortcoming; that is, they often ignore international environmental factors. Comparison between countries may discern the distinguishing features or relative advantages of the location. Furthermore, some of these isolated studies often cannot explain why FDI goes into one country, rather than others that have the same or similar national attractions. To correct this shortcoming, we plan to study a number of factors that are considered important enough to attract FDI according to several existing FDI theories, including Dunning's eclectic paradigm and Porter's national competitiveness. We plan first to compare China with other countries to find out why China attracts more FDI and what factors have the most influence in the process. With this goal accomplished, we then examine the effects of regional and industrial competitive attractions on FDI and distinguish what makes these regions and industries stand out from the rest. Our research framework is thus based upon this competitive-location-advantage framework, as shown in Figure 12.1.

With the above models and the literature review in the first section, we determine to test the following hypotheses regarding the location advantage of China in attracting FDI. The existing literature and theory foundations are laid out with each of the hypotheses.

H1a: Other things being equal, positive national events attract more foreign direct investment.

H1b: Other things being equal, negative national events reduce foreign direct investment.

That political instability affects FDI is not a new view, as a number of studies have proved this (Kobrin 1978; Levis 1979; Schollhammer and Nigh 1984; Nigh 1985). Companies often consider positive national events as an internal strength or ownership advantage. If companies plan to enter a foreign market, it is important that they look into the political situation of that country. Among political risks, expropriation is one of the biggest concerns—thus the largest negative factor to discourage FDI—foreign investors watch for. Juhl (1985) investigates the effect of expropriation on foreign investment. He argues that economically rational expropriation may minimize the impacts of expropriation on future FDI. Nevertheless, distorted expropriation policies may have resulted in as many as 17 million lost jobs for less developed countries through 1980.

H2: Other things being equal, Chinese from Hong Kong, Macao, and Taiwan, more than foreign investors, invest more in regions that have closer ties to their network.

Figure 12.1 **Competition Location-Advantage Framework**

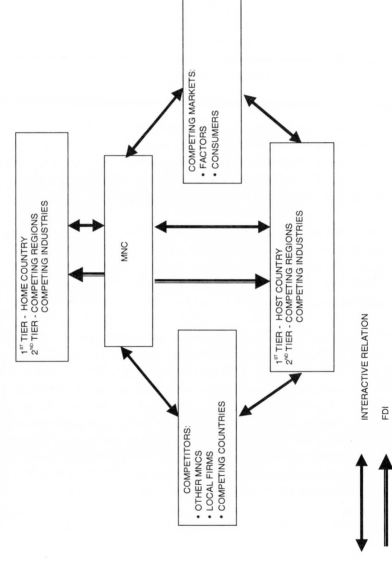

Subramanian Rangan (2000) takes a concept—"firm social networks"— to explore the response of firms to local and international economic opportunities. For historic reasons, the firm social networks are local or national, and thus the cautious response of the firms to cross-border economic opportunities. We apply this concept to overseas Chinese network relationships. Because culture, language, and personal relationships are binding among Chinese, within and outside mainland China, Chinese in Hong Kong, Macao, and Taiwan perceive the mainland as within the boundary of their social network and thus treat opportunities in China more actively than those "pure" investors.

H3: Higher economic growth attracts more foreign direct investment.

Faster national economic growth is considered a factor favorable to attracting FDI. Nicholas Billington (1999), with an econometric model, finds that the market growth variable is one of the significant determinants of location to attract FDI. Choi Chong Ju (1999) builds a model to study the relationship between global competitiveness and national attractiveness. His model asserts that expansion of market economies is a local advantage that helps to attract more FDI. Ekrem Tatoglu and Keith W. Glaister (1998) in their study on Turkey FDI found that the growth rate of Turkey's economy is a positive variable in their model.

H4: The more developed a region is, the more advanced the technology that FDI will bring in.

Stephen Young and Ping Lan (1997) investigate technology transfer to China through FDI. They found that the extent of technology transfer is limited, given that China is still at the developing stage and has only limited technological capacities. However, because of the continuing growth and increasing size of the China market, technology transfer through FDI is expected to expand. Kogut and Chang (1991) use a negative binomial regression model to estimate the effect of R&D and industry structure on Japanese companies' investment in the United States. The results indicate that Japanese FDI is drawn to the United States by the level of R&D expenditures in both countries. One significant goal of Japanese FDI is to obtain U.S. technological capability and enhance competitive advantages. Studying UK FDI, Nachum, Dunning, and Jones (2000) found that UK technological advantage and industrial structure have statistical significance in the FDI flow. Grubaugh (1987) provides the same results, though the results come from firm-level data.

H5: Other things being equal, the larger the national economy is, the more likely the economy can attract FDI.

Large market size is often considered a favorable factor in attracting FDI. Susan F. Stone and Bang Nam (1999) use what they called the gravity-model specification to estimate the bilateral flows of FDI. They note that for FDI flows into the Asia-Pacific region, the market size and income in the home country play larger roles than those in the host country. Robert T. Green and Ajay K. Kohli (1991) investigated the role of economic size and export market identifications and noted the same effect.

H6: The more stable the exchange rate is, the more FDI a country attracts.

Foreign exchange fluctuations are considered to affect FDI decisions if a company decides to invest in foreign countries. Hongmo Sung and Harvey E. Lapan (2000) studied how exchange rate uncertainty can influence the risk-taking choice and strategic FDI by MNCs. Their conclusion is that foreign-exchange-fluctuation-induced FDI can increase expected profitability and even prevent entry by a local competitor. Joshua Aizenman (1992) investigated influences of exchange-rate regimes on domestic and international investment in the presence of a short-run Phillips curve. The finding of this study shows that fixed-exchange-rate regimes encourage more aggregate, foreign and domestic, investment than flexible-exchange-rate regimes do. Therefore, the author concludes that adopting a fixed-exchange system may attract more FDI.

H7: The lower labor cost a country offers in comparison with the neighboring nations, the more likely the country will attract FDI.

Low labor cost is considered a favorite factor if it is comparatively lower while not suffering from low quality. According to the theory of minimum wage rates, lower labor costs are considered competitive and can attract capital flows across national boundaries (Neary 1985; O'Sullivan 1985). Though they examined the regions in China regarding only their ability to attract FDI, Cheng and Kwan (2000) found that FDI is more likely if lower labor costs are obvious. Nagash Kumar (1994) found that wage rates and industrial capability are important determinants for export-oriented production attracted by a country. Richard G. Harris and Nicolas Schmitt (2000) built a two-country model with both seeking FDI. They found that the one with a low labor-cost level would attract FDI if accompanied by a high level of protection on intermediate production factors or with the export promotion policy.

H8: The incentive policy to FDI has a positive effect on FDI inflow. This is true particularly within a country.

China is one of the countries that encourage foreign investment. In the early years, coastal cities of China were granted special policies by the central government to set up special economic zones (SEZ) to open to the outside world and attract foreign investment. Reality proves that up to the present these SEZs have successfully attracted much more FDI than areas that were not granted the same policies. This point has been proved by previous studies (Kohlhangen, 1977; Gastanaga, Nugent, and Pashamova 1998; Globerman and Shapiro 1999; Coughlin and Segev 2000). It is even true for different entry modes of FDI into China (Tse, Pan, and Au 1997) and for comparison between different countries in America (Hines 1996).

H9: All other things equal, the more a country invests in its infrastructure, the more FDI can be attracted. This is also true for regions in a country.

Developing countries often are cited as having poor infrastructure and thus unable to attract FDI. Infrastructure is considered hardware that can attract or discourage foreign investors. Friedrich Wu (1984) concludes from his study that underdeveloped infrastructure plus ideological ambivalence and bureaucratic foot-dragging are the reasons why China had difficulties in attracting more foreign investment. After years of improvement in infrastructure by investing significant amounts in civil construction, China has shown no problems in infrastructure, at least in the SEZs.

H10: Domestic investment will be positively related with FDI.

O'Sullivan (1985) notes that domestic capital formation is positively affected by FDI inflows. When studying location of FDI by Swedish

MNCs, Pontus Braunerhjelm and Lars Oxelheim (2000) noted that FDI in general does not replace domestic investment, but tends to do so more in the R&D-intensive industry. So according to their conclusion, it is important to disaggregate industry-level data when analyzing the effect of FDI on home country investment. Broadman and Sun (1997), on the other hand, prove that the largest share of China FDI is in the real estate sector.

H11: Lower capital costs in the host country attract more FDI.

Host countries often lower the interest rates to attract foreign investment. Aliber (1970) examined, as a part of his study, the relationship between the motives of MNCs and the imperfect foreign exchange and capital markets. The result indicates that MNCs can obtain lower interest rates in their investment than those of the host countries.

H12: Import duties are negatively related with FDI inflow.

Import duties are a source of government revenue. However, high import duties are viewed as a large barrier to local markets and are used often to protect local industries. Studies on foreign trade treat the import duty as a symbol of the openness of a country, which affects its international businesses, including FDI. The United Nations' *Incentives and Foreign Direct Investment* (1996) lists import duty reductions as one of the fiscal incentives used by nations to attract foreign investment. Dunning (1994) shows that a country is more attractive to MNCs if it imposes fewer restrictions and less burdensome requirements, particularly when such restrictions and requirements do not limit entrance into profitable industries. In financial terms, a reduction of restrictions is a reduction of financial risks and costs.

H13: Government foreign currency reserves are positively related with FDI.

H14: The higher the inflation rate in the host country is, the less FDI the country attracts.

When evaluating a country's debt payment ability and financial strength, foreign currency reserves are considered one of the most important measurements. For instance, Standard and Poor's (S&P) country sovereignty rating system takes a country's foreign currency reserves as a symbol of national financial strength. On the other hand, higher inflation rates are often considered a sign of economic problems and viewed as one of the major country risks (Dunning 1997). Higher inflation is considered a major cause for devaluation of currencies (Graham and Krugman, 1993; Froot, 1993).

Methodology and Data

We try to test what factors possessed by China and her regions or industries attract FDI into China as a whole or into regions or 2–digit industries (according to the classification system of industrial codes). Three general linear models are designed to achieve this goal. These models are expressed and explained as follows. The first model of time-series compares the effect of variables from each country that are considered important in determining FDI.

$$Y_{it} = a_i + \sum_{i=1}^{n} \beta_i X_{it} + Y_{it-j} + \Psi_i + \varepsilon_{it} \qquad t = 1, ..., m; j = 1, 2, 3 \qquad (1)$$

Where Y_{it} is the FDI in country i at year t. a_i is the intercept. b_i is the coefficient for X_{it} that is the independent variables considered having effects on the FDI. Y_{it-j} is the one-, two-, or three-year lagged FDI, which tests what effect the FDI incurred in the last years may have on the current FDI. Ψ_t is a dummy variable with value 10–1 that will be used to control special environmental influences. e_{it} is a random error term, which explains the rest of the effects that are not explained by all other variables. To apply appropriate statistical tests, these conditions must be met: mean $E\{\varepsilon_{it}\} = 10$ and variance $s^2\{\varepsilon_{it}\} = s^2$, ε_{it} and ε_{jt} are not correlated so that the covariance $s\{\varepsilon_{it}, \varepsilon_{jt}\} = 0$ for all i, j; i ≠ j.

To examine the interaction effect between lagged FDI and the other factoring variables, we will run multiple comparisons to check the significance of the interaction. We will also check the correlation between variables. Should the effects be significant, we will try either a square root or logarithmic transformation. An alternative method is that we will take the power transformations on Y_{it}, such as the Box-Cox transformation. The transformation will help us to remove the interaction effects or make them unimportant.

The next two models are for panel data, and in fact the special cases of equation (1). The second model checks the regional distribution of FDI and the effect of independent variables from each region in China. If the FDI distribution in the region is due to the effect of some of these variables, then we can compare them with the effects of the variables of other countries studied in the first model and try to explain why within China some variables play more important roles than others.

$$Y_i = a_i + \sum_{i=1}^{n} \beta_i X_i + \Psi_i + \varepsilon_i \tag{2}$$

where Y_i is the foreign investment in a region, province, or city of China, and all the other variables are the same as the ones explained for the first model.

The third model is designed to check the effects of the variables on FDI in different industries.

$$Y_i = a_i + \sum_{i=1}^{n} \beta_i X_i + \varepsilon_i \tag{3}$$

where Y_i is the foreign investment in an industry of China, and all the other variables are the same as those explained above.

Data Description

The data we use for the test come from several sources. Two of these sources are the *China Fixed Asset Investment Yearbook* (CFAIY) and the *China Statistics Yearbook* (CSY), various years up to 1997. From these sources, amounts of annual foreign direct investment from 1985 in different regions of China, including the three cities—Beijing, Shanghai, and Tianjin—are extracted. Also selected are yearly data of FDI in industries at the 2–digit level, wage data, and other related data for these regions and industries. To investigate the effect of investment by Chinese in Hong Kong, Macao, and Taiwan (HMT) and regional and industrial investment, we distinguish general FDI from this kind of FDI.

The second source is *International Financial Statistics* (IFS) by the IMF. From this source we selected and averaged the annual data for

GDP, population, interest rates, foreign debt and foreign currency reserves, exchange rates, and so forth. The third source is the *World Development Indicators* by the World Bank. The data we extracted from this source include variables for forty countries or regions from 1980 to 1998. Together, it gives us 760 country- or region-level annual observations.

The fourth source is *Tax and Financial Incentives for Business Around the World* by KPMG, an international accounting firm. In this book, various kinds of tax and financial incentives to attract investment are listed. We focus mainly on those specially set up for foreign investment. A 0–1 code is assigned, 1 for with incentives, 0 for no incentives.

The fifth source is Baeket and Campbell's list of events for emerging markets. Their list contains events from 1976 for some selected developing countries. We supplement the list with some more events because the list for some emerging countries does not contain all the periods we study. We classify the events according to the potential significance for FDI. We code an event +1 if the event has significant positive influence on FDI, –1 if the event imposes significant negative influence, and 0 if otherwise. For annual events, we summarize the total positive, negative, and no-effect events. If the score is higher than +5, a +1 is assigned to that year; if the score is lower than –5, a –1 is assigned. In between, zero is assigned.

Since our data spread over a long time span and covered forty countries, missing data were a problem. We used two methods to solve the problem. If the series missed only two or at most three years, we used the mean of nearby data or linear interpolation, depending on the location of the missing data. We used the linear trend if the trend was obvious. If a country missed very much data for that variable, we dropped that country for the test. A detailed description of the data and their sources are provided in Appendix 1.

Test Results

We first ran the multiple regression to tentatively diagnose the features of and the relationship among variables. The plots of FDI with its residual and dependent variables showed that no misspecification existed, but there were problems of non-normal distribution, collinearity, and heteroskedasticity. The histogram chart indicated that the relationship between the dependent variable and the standardized residual was tilted to the right, that is, not normally distributed. Second, the normal P-P plot and other partial P-P diagnostic plots showed non-linearity and certain patterns between the dependent variable and a few independent variables. Third, several of the collinearity statistics are quite high, indicating that unduly multiplied effects occurred due to the correlation problems. Fourth, non-stationarity for variances and means for some of the time-series data prevailed. To examine the severity of the problems revealed in the plots, we obtained an eigenvalue and collinearity index, and ran Durbin-Waston and White tests. The results showed that transformations to some variables were necessary. We took the Box-Cox power transformation on the dependent and several independent variables. The remedied results indicated that the VIF, collinearity index, and correlation values are all within the statistical acceptance range. The logarithm used also helped reduce the time trend shown in some variables for some countries. The resulting variables are accepted and explained in Appendix 1.

To test the hypothesis, we first use the function (1) for international comparison. Two statistical methods are applied. The first is the ordinary least squares (OLS), and the other is the autoregressive integrated moving average (ARIMA). A fundamental statistical method, OLS is used widely in FDI hypothesis tests. However, the restrictive requirements of an OLS regression are often violated (e.g., GDP and FDI throughout several years). The ARIMA is adopted to overcome the shortcomings of OLS. For both methods, we used logarithm-transformed data so that the results were compatible. Furthermore, one-, two-, and three-year lagged FDIs were used for each method.

The descriptive statistics of the non-lagged OLS test (OLS M_0) are listed in Table 12.1. Descriptive statistics are similar for tests of the other OLS regressions (M_1 for lagged one year and M_2 for lagged two years, and D_0 for no-lag developing country sample) and the ARIMA (A_1 for all sampled countries tested with one-year lag, one-level difference, and no moving average correction, A_2 for all sampled for one-year lag, one-level difference, and no moving average correction plus added-in yearly trend; D_1 and D_2 for emerging markets for the same tests, respectively). The statistics show that because of our previous log transformation, the correlations between variables are well below the criterion 0.8, with only a few above 0.7.

Table 12.2 reports the test results for eight models (year-three lag models are omitted due to space limitations). All four OLS models are

Table 12.1

Descriptive Statistics

	Mean	S.D.	(1)	(2)	(3)	(4)	(5)	(6)	(7)	(8)	(9)	(10)	(11)	(12)	(13)
							Pearson correlation								
FDI	20.81	2.05													
(1) EXRATE	2.16	2.94	0.04												
(2) IMDUTY	6.21	7.87	-.43*	-0.02											
(3) INCENTV	0.19	0.39	0.50*	-0.18	0.41*										
(4) MKTSIZE	11.23	0.57	0.63*	0.07***	-0.28*	-0.29*									
(5) DINVST	7.06	1.37	0.48*	-0.10**	-0.71*	-0.36*	0.44*								
(6) EVENT	0.06	0.74	0.27*	0.02	-0.20*	-0.20*	0.19*	0.22*							
(7) FXRSV	22.90	1.28	0.72*	0.19*	-0.34*	-0.48*	0.76*	0.49*	0.15*						
(8) INFLAT	1.85	1.08	-0.34*	-0.02	0.28*	0.30*	-0.42*	-0.41*	-0.20*	-0.44*					
(9) INTRST	2.61	0.55	-0.22*	0.10*	0.29*	0.07**	-0.45*	-0.39*	-0.12*	-0.38*	0.74*				
(10) INFRA	0.27	0.32	0.47*	0.06**	0.41*	0.29*	-0.24*	-0.62*	-0.14*	-0.29*	0.06**	0.04			
(11) EXPGRO	6.81	7.35	0.13*	0.20*	0.09*	-0.16*	0.04	-0.22*	0.37*	0.13*	-0.14*	-0.07**	0.18*		
(12) LBRCOST	2.76	1.16	0.18*	-0.20*	-0.55*	-0.12*	0.29*	0.76*	0.15*	0.13*	-0.16*	-0.28*	-0.46*	-0.36*	
(13) IMPGRO	6.80	11.96	0.12*	0.05	0.07***	-0.12*	0.01	-0.13*	0.02	0.09**	-0.05	-0.02	0.06**	0.38*	-0.23*

Notes: Variables are described in Appendix 1.
Significance (1-tail): *** $p < .10$, ** $p < .05$, * $p < .01$.

Table 12.2

Regression Statistic Results

Variable	OLS M0	OLS M1	OLS M2	OLS D0	ARIMA A1	ARIMA A2	ARIMA D1	ARIMA D2
EXRATE	-.114*	-.084*	-0.078*	0.004	-0.069*	-0.064*	-0.018	-0.021
IMDUTY	-0.201*	-0.198*	-0.184*	-0.190*	-0.016	-0.018	-0.019	-0.021
INCENTV	0.076*	0.089*	0.133*	0.088***	-0.223	-0.231	-0.103	-0.098
MKTSIZE	0.278**	0.321**	0.300*	0.190*	0.340**	0.362**	0.584***	0.634***
DINVST	-0.080*	-0.152**	-0.227*	-0.061	-0.228	-0.205	0.189	0.25
EVENT	0.093	0.114*	0.081**	0.057	0.021	0.016	-0.034	-0.044
FXRSV	0.400*	0.278*	0.247*	0.426*	0.491*	0.502*	0.384*	0.39*
INFLAT	-0.120*	-0.170*	-0.174*	-0.141**	-0.115**	-0.115**	-0.185**	-0.169**
INTRST	0.185*	0.153*	0.206*	0.114***	-0.032	-0.004	-0.045	-0.05
INFRA	0.270*	0.338*	0.262*	0.300*	0.483*	0.462*	0.632*	0.603*
EXPGRO	0.024	0.014	0.002	-0.068	0.030	0.028	0.029	0.035
LBRCOST	0.116**	-0.107**	0.041	-0.158**	-0.083*	-0.083*	-0.139*	-0.142*
IMPGRO	0.056**	0.117*	0.078**	0.055	0.015	0.02	0.029	0.029
CONSTANT	-4.230*	-0.505	0.922	-7.970*	0.001	0.001	0.002	0.002
AR1				-0.306*	-0.351*	-0.277*	-0.315*	
AR2					-0.141**		-0.129**	
F	87.373*	81.162*	41.244*	40.826*				
Adjusted R²	0.679	0.663	0.498	0.649				
AIC					1915.15	1902.84	1039.45	1035.15
SBC					1984.04	1976.33	1099.29	1098.97

Notes: Variables are described in Appendix 1.
ARIMA models are all run with lag used for autoregression = 1, differencing levels required = 1, and moving average correction = 0.
Significance (1-tail): ***p < .10, **p < .05, *p < .01. No year–three lag is reported.

statistically significant with $p < .01$; F values 87.373, 81.162, 41.244, and 40.826, respectively; and adjusted R^2 0.679, 0.663, 0.498, and 0.649, respectively. The results from the first no-lagged OLS model have supported most of our hypotheses. As we proposed, the exchange rate can have a negative effect on FDI. That is, a devalued currency value of a host country will cause FDI inflow drop. This confirms some previous studies. We envision that the exchange rate reflects a spectrum of host country issues, and if it is unstable or devalued, then foreign investors may be cautious about and later slow down their FDI in that country.

Import duty is also significant in affecting FDI inflows. Some predict that if import duty is heavy, some foreign companies may have to enter into that market by investing there. Our results show the opposite. The reason may be that in an internationally integrated trading system, some companies have to invest in import-controlled countries to get into the markets, but most other MNCs may see a heavy import barrier as a negative sign and thus hesitate to invest. Incentive has positive effects on incoming FDI. This is in line with the hypothesis.

The market size in this study gauges the total purchase potential, the gross national production. The test results show that a larger market is more likely to attract FDI. On the other hand, domestic investment may offset investment from overseas, as the negative significant relation between FDI and domestic investment indicates. Nevertheless, the level –.08 means that for every dollar of domestic investment, 8 cents of FDI is offset.

The next result shows that important national economic, political, and financial events do not necessarily lead to a change in FDI. The events, though not statistically significant and thus not supporting the hypothesis, show the right sign. We suspect that since "event" is measured in the combined scores of events that occurred in a year, the effects of an event may not be clear immediately in that year. In contrast, higher inflation has effects right away in the year it occurs. The result supports our hypothesis.

It surprised us that the interest rate in the host country is statistically positively significant. We envision that MNCs can access international financial markets, so a higher interest rate in the host country will not deter FDI. Infrastructure is statistically significant and positively affects the FDI. MNCs are likely to invest more in a host country where infrastructure is improved. Economic growth, here measured as export growth and import growth, is not as clear as other variables. The test shows that both growths are positively related to FDI, but only import growth is statistically significant. The last item tested is labor cost. As the test result shows, a higher labor cost negatively affects FDI. This result confirms the hypothesis.

The OLS models with the one- and two-year lagged FDI show results similar to those of the first model, except for a few differences. A few explanations on changes of the effects of the exploratory variables across the three models are warranted here. The effects of exchange rate changes on FDI will be reduced as time passes, though statistically the effects are still apparent. The import duty barrier has weaker effects on FDI in years one and two. Incentives, as expected, have strong effects on FDI in one lag (0.089) and even a stronger effect in the two lags (0.133) both with $p < 0.01$. The offset effect is equally matched in domestic investment—as years pass by, more domestic investment may offset incoming FDI. Large markets still attract more FDI in later years, but after the second year the influence is weakened. It is very interesting but understandable that the effect of significant events is even stronger in the year after the occurring year and then one more year later. Foreign reserves are often considered the result of a strong economy and sometimes the results of correct national economy policies. This has been proved in this study. In the three years tested, large national foreign currency reserves helped to attract foreign investment, though the effect diminished in later years. On the contrary, a higher inflation rate has negative effects in years 0, 1, and 2, with stronger influences showing later. The costs of capital (i.e., interest rate) continue to have positive effects in years 1 and 2. Infrastructure improvements have the strongest effect in year 1 and then taper down in year 2. It may indicate that the effect lasts well into later years. Statistically, export growth has no significant effects, but import growth has significant effects on FDI in all three years. Labor cost is one exception. It has statistically significant effects in the first two years, but not in the last year. What can be envisioned is that lower labor costs have only a short positive effect on FDI.

Considering the special characteristics of developing countries, we also ran an OLS test only on developing samples. The criteria used to select developing emerging countries are similar to those adopted by the IMF in its emerging market database (EMDB) for the year 1998; that is, roughly GDP per capita around fifteen thousand dollars. This standard was applied to countries for our last sample year, 1998. No attempt was made to change the status of those countries that exceeded that threshold in earlier years but not in 1998. The reasoning is that few countries incurred status changes, and thus no significant effect would occur in the sample population.

In this OLS D0 model, exchange rate devaluations are not statistically significant in affecting incoming FDI. Import duty is at the same significant level of negative influence. Incentive effect is similar, but the confidence level is only 90 percent. Market size effect is just at the same statistical significant level but the slope has been reduced to .190. There is no significant effect for domestic investment. We predict that compared with the developed countries, the developing countries need to increase their domestic investment to keep up with market demand and to better living conditions, and so the offset effect is reduced to non-significant. Events cast no significant effect on FDI for developing countries, either. However, foreign currency reserve has just the same significant effect. We assert that as an important mark to offset foreign debt, the heavy debt-loaded developing countries are examined closely in this benchmark. For these countries, higher inflation has even more detrimental effects on FDI. Like the other three models, this model also shows that interest rates affect FDI in the same direction, but the severity is reduced. This affirms our previous observation that MNCs may not rely less on the developing countries for financing. What surprises us most about this model is that neither export growth nor import growth has any effect on FDI. We speculate that MNCs invest in a developing country mainly because they want to enter into and occupy that market. Low labor cost is just a significant factor sought by MNCs.

We believe that the OLS results are valid because no assumptions of the OLS method were violated after the power transformations. However, to check the robustness of the results obtained, we also applied ARIMA to the same samples. The ARIMA was first applied to all sampled countries and then to the developing countries, with or without year trend.

We followed the strict requirements of typical ARIMA statistics. Autocorrelation function (ACF), partial autocorrelation function (PACF), and cross-correlation function (CCF) charts were created and examined closely to find any non-stationarity, unit root, and other possible violations. What methods should have been taken for the proper remedy were recorded and tried. The investigation showed that except for the logarithm transformation that had been taken before, the first-level differencing and autoregressions were needed to correct non-stationarity, unit root, and a few other irregularities in several variables, which had been power transformed in the OLS tests. The final test results after all corrections were made are reported in columns 6 to 9 in Table 12.2. The results show that with one- or two lags of autoregression and the first difference, the two all-sample models (A_1 for one-lag and one difference, and A_2 for two-lag and one difference) and two developing-country sample models (D_1 and D_2) produce some similar results as those in the OLS models, but differences are also obvious. The next few paragraphs briefly explain the test results, in comparison with the two lagged models of OLS.

The Akaike information criterion (AIC) and the Schwartz Bayesian criterion (SBC) both indicate that the lagged-two model, A_2, is better compared with A_1. Because the differences between A_1 and A_2 are very small, we consider both are applicable to this study. For Model A_1, with $-.306$ at 99 percent significance, AR1 indicates that for every one unit increase in the change of FDI between two and one periods back, the effect of the change on FDI between the last and the current year is negative .306. That is, if the difference between two previous periods increases, the difference for the next two periods decreases. The AR_1 for one-lag has the same explanation, while the AR_2 for two-lag in Model A_2 indicates that the effect of every one unit difference between a year and two years back on the difference between the next year and two years back is negative .141.

The exchange rate changes show the correct sign and are statistically significant at $p < .01$ level for the first two models. However, compared with OLS M_1 and OLS M_2, the effects are rather stable. Neither import duty nor incentive is statistically significant in both all-sample models, though both show the right sign. The variable market size is statistically significant, and its effect even gets enforced for the lagged-two model. Both domestic investment and significant event carry the right sign, but neither has more than 0.1 in the p value. Foreign currency reserve and inflation are both statistically significant with the right sign. Compared with the results in Model M_1 and M_2, the first variable has an even stronger effect on FDI, but the second has a lesser degree of influence. Interestingly, the cost of capital carries the right sign, though not statistically significant. Infrastructure is still statistically significant in both Model A_1 and A_2, reinforcing the importance of infrastructure in MNCs' FDI decision making. Export growth is not significant, and surprisingly nor is import growth any longer.

For ARIMA (1,1,0) D_1 and ARIMA (2,1,0) D_2, the differences from compatible OLS models are even more apparent. While the currency exchange rate change and import duty carry the same sign, neither is statistically significant and the incentive is even the opposite sign. The negative sign in incentive may indicate that in developing countries the incentive policies may not necessarily attract more FDI, but on the contrary are more likely to cause a detour. Market size has even more effect on FDI, with .584 and .634 both at the 95 percent confidence level. It indicates that a reasonable market size is a major factor in attracting FDI. As in A_1 and A_2, domestic investment and events are not statistically significant. In contrast, the foreign currency reserve shows statistical significance, meaning that a strong position in foreign currency reserves is viewed as a good sign of the host country economy and thus it can attract more FDI. Furthermore, the two inflations in D_1 and D_2 show that the higher the inflation is, the less likely it is that a developing country can attract FDI. The cost of capital in a developing country is not significant in determining FDI. The infrastructure continues its important position as a major factor of national advantage. Neither the export nor the import growth is important. In another vein, labor cost is statistically significant, with even a larger share in attracting FDI. The AR_1 for Model D_1 and the AR_1 and AR_2 for Model D_2 have effects similar to those explained in the above paragraph. In total, the AIC and SBC are smaller than the all-sample models, indicating that the special characteristics of the developing countries may require special treatments in analysis.

Since the maximum-likelihood estimation method (MLE) was used for ARIMA calculation, violations of classical assumptions are probably ignored. Generally speaking, it means that the result from MLE, in this study ARIMA, is more reliable than that of linear regression in this study OLS. However, considering that we followed all strict requirements of OLS and did all necessary corrections to any violation, and also considering the close results of the models, we do not want to rule out the validation of the results of the OLS models.

To study the effects of location advantage on FDI inflow at regional and industrial levels, we designed the second level model listed as equations (2) and (3). Up to this point, a revision of those models is warranted. The multilevel contextual and random coefficient modeling methods have been applied. For a country-level study, applying the results from the previous comparisons may help us to understand: (a) Under specific FDI related parameters, how these factors affect FDI obtained by one nation; (b) By applying multilevel modeling for a two-level study, how variances from international factors interact with parameters from industries or regions in a country. The advantages of this kind of study are obvious. For instance, previous studies only considered either national or international factors, but not interaction between these factors. The multilevel studies carried on below can easily evaluate the interaction.

The contextual method is considered a clear and easy method for capturing the effects of factors from the first level. The weaknesses are that this model cannot discover and solve the collinearity problem of the correlation between individual variables and the integrated factors carried over from the first step. Simply put, the procedure of the contextual method is to treat the parameters from the first step as the means and enter them into the model of the second step. Revised from equation (1) the mathematical model is expressed as follows.

$$\sum a_i = a + \sum c_i \underline{X}_i \tag{3a}$$

where a_i is the original intercept of equation (2), a is the fixed intercept obtained from the result of the equation (1) test, and X_t is the mean of the variable from international comparison in period t. Substituting this intercept equation into equation (2) we get:

$$Y_i = a + \sum c_i \underline{X}_i + \sum_{i=1}^{n} \beta_i X_i + \Psi_i + \varepsilon_i \tag{4}$$

where the best estimate c_i represents the between-country characteristics, and β_i is the best estimate of the interact effect within-nation. In the combined term, $\sum c_i X_i$ represents the international effect reflected in national circumstances.

For the varying coefficient modeling, the fixed parameters from the international comparison, the first step, are used as dependent variables in the simultaneous equations for coefficients for China regional investigation, the second step. The following equations show the second step models:

$$a_i = g_0 + g_1 k_i \tag{5}$$
$$\beta_i = h_0 + h_1 k_i \tag{6}$$

where a_i and β_i are the regression coefficients for intercept and slope, respectively, for new industrial and regional study models. The g_0 and g_1, and h_0 and h_1 are determined as intercept and slopes from China industrial and regional data. The k_i is the factor from the international comparison carried out above. Substituting (4) and (5) into (2), we obtained the following varying second-level model:

$$Y_i = g_0 + g_1 k_i + \sum_{i=1}^{n} (h_0 + h_1 k_i) X_i + \Psi_i + \varepsilon_i \tag{7}$$

Expanding and rearranging the above equation, we obtain:

$$Y_i = g_0 + h_0 \sum_{i=1}^{n} X_i + (g_1 k_i + h_1 \sum_{i=1}^{n} k_i X_i + \Psi_i + \varepsilon_i) \tag{8}$$

The same transformations from both the contextual modeling and the varying coefficient modeling can be applied to equation (3). The revised models are omitted in order to save space.

To test equations (4) and (8), we need to identify the independent variables that are valid for Chinese domestic situations. Exchange rates, import duties, incentives, foreign currency reserves, market size, events, and interest rates are all dropped because they affect all Chinese regions and industries. The rest of the variables that were tested in international comparison are used and their international parameters are brought into Chinese industry and region equations. A dummy variable is set at 1 for SECs and 0 for non-SECs. We classify the regions into coastal and inland for two reasons. One is the special favorable and incentive governmental policy for coastal regions, but not for inland areas. The second is that the existing literature uses the same classification (for example, Zhu and Tan 2000). Furthermore, the Chinese statistical system classifies seven general ownerships: state-owned; collectives; joint ventures; individuals; foreign wholly owned; enterprises run by Chinese from Hong Kong, Macao, and Taiwan; and enterprises of all other types. This classification is adopted, except for individuals and other groups because a substantial amount of information is missing for these two groups; besides their figures in almost all categories are very small.

For the second-level models, we first apply the multivariate method to check whether there are any significant differences among the groups. The next test is applying OLS with international parameters. All necessary statistical manipulations were closely followed, as stated above. The partial results that are interesting to us are reported in Table 12.3.

Table 12.3 shows the multivariate test results for both regions and industries. Two groups of regions are compared for means differences. The results of the Mann-Whitney nonparameter test on two independent samples show that for each category, coastal regions have statistically significant differences from those in inland areas, as their ranks are much higher than those in the latter. They prove that even within a country, different policies, economic conditions, infrastructure, and other factors also make significant differences. We ran the Kruskal-Wallis nonparameter test on k-independent samples for different ownerships. The results, shown in Table 12.3, indicate that the different ownerships are clearly different from one another in the interested areas. It is interesting to note that foreign ownership and HMT ownership are ahead of others in wages paid (more), value of fixed assets formed (larger), size of each investment projects (larger), and equipment purchased (higher value). The wages paid indicate that under the general lower wage conditions in China, compared with those of other countries, MNCs consider other things more important, such as productivity of the labor force (tested, but not reported here). The other results are indicators that FDI builds up larger projects and imposes higher value equipment, a sign of higher technology advances. It is interesting to note, and at the same time to prove our prediction, that HMT Chinese invest more in Guangdong and Fujian provinces, even more than those from overseas MNCs. The Kruskal-Wallis k-independent sample test was also run for industry-level FDI. Generally speaking, FDI is concentrated in real estate, manufacturing, and some other industries, and in terms of amount per project, is larger than domestic investments in the same industries. This is another sign that FDI helps in technology advance. The OLS results show similar results. Some of the results from the OLS are also reported in Table 12.3.

Conclusion

This study starts with international comparison and ends with China domestic industrial and regional location advantages to attract FDI. The results show that in the domestic situation, some internationally influ-

Table 12.3

Non-Parameter Statistical Results

Tests/variables	Result
Kruskal-Wallis Test (5 ownerships)	
Wage	*
Size of investment projects	*
Fixes assets formed	*
Equipment used	*
HMT investment in Guangdong, Fujian	*
Mann-Whiney Test (coastal vs. inland regions)	
Wage	*
Equipment used	*
Infrastructure	*
GDP per capita	*
Mann-Whiney Test (15 industries)	
Wage	*
Equipment	*
OLS test	
Infrastructure	0.146*
Wage	0.170
Export	−0.066
Import	0.588*
Market size	0.172*
Constant	−2/612*
R^2 squared adjusted	0.692
F	81.457*

Notes: Partial results.
*−$p<0.01$.

ential factors have similar effects, while others are reversed, such as wages. Generally speaking, the location advantages of a country, such as sufficiently large market size, lower labor costs, and good infrastructure, can attract FDI. However, put into international environments, one nation possessing such advantages must make these advantages competitive enough to prevent competition from other nations that also want to attract FDI. Otherwise, it is just another nation with potential attractions. China, in this case, according to our studies and numerous previous others, has proved to be a good and successful example.

This chapter contributes to FDI studies in several aspects. First of all, this research is another robust proof that location advantages have statistically significant effects on FDI. As is known, MNCs invest in certain foreign countries because those locations possess attractions that can help these companies compete globally, obtain more profits, increase market share, or enhance their strategic positions. Porter's national competitive advantages, Dunning's eclectic paradigm, and some other schools theorize these advantages. This chapter has proved from a number of aspects, more than most studies on location advantages, that these theories are correct, in one way or another. One special feature of this study is that there was no heavy emphasis on any single theory, but several theories were presented. This research tried to test several factors, including not only those that are not often tested, but also those that have been fully tested and have proved most influential in location advantage studies. In this way, the study is not limited to certain preconditions of these theories and is very inclusive.

The second contribution is that the chapter is the first to take the two-step multilevel methodology, international–region and international–industry. As is known, lack of sufficient and comparative data sources is a significant problem in international studies, particularly studies of developing countries. This study carefully makes international comparisons first and then further extends to region and industry studies. In this way, we avoid the noncomparable data issue that results from the one-step method adopted by almost all other previous studies.

Because a two-step method is taken, the study rigorously analyzes the factors that are influential in the international comparison but twisted by intra-country factors. This chapter has tried to identify how significant the twist may be. As the test results show, some variables, though influential in the aggregated study, are not at all obvious if taken into consideration as regional or industrial factors. From the results of this study, studies in the future may avoid mistakes by not drawing conclusions only from the characteristics of the country as a whole, but not from regions and industries, particularly in a large country like China. One closed study like this is Billington's (1999). However, his study contains no industry study and contains only seven countries and investigates fewer regional variables than this chapter does.

The last potential contribution of this chapter lies in the uniqueness of the Chinese system. As a comparative study of a number of variables in China, a socialist system, the results of the chapter may be extended to other transition economies, such as those of Russia and the East European countries. Studies of other transition economies may take a similar approach to the study of FDI in those economies.

There are several policy implications. Here we only discuss one. According to the research of *Incentives and Foreign Direct Investment*

(United Nations 1996), host countries used a number of incentives to attract foreign investment, but a majority of these incentives were ineffective or in fact twisted in application and thus could not bring in MNCs' FDI. Two points may be worthy of discussion. In today's globalized economy, almost every country has some kind of incentive policies for FDI; unless systematic policies are postulated, simply laying out some sorts of incentive policies is not sufficient. Second, the measure of incentive policies in competition is important. Our study shows that a country must improve comprehensively in its qualifications or competitive location advantages. Piecemeal regulation changes may not work well to attract foreign investment.

The study has several limitations. Because the scope of the data is limited by the integrated foreign investment, the entry modes are not identified. Some studies (for example, Rolfe et al. 1993, which concentrated on entry modes, found that different entry modes have different effects on the amount to be invested and the locations selected. More importantly, the modes of entry into a market may show the long-term or short-term strategic emphases of the companies. The second limitation of the chapter is that the study does not take into consideration the firms in the host country that interact with the foreign investors. Strategic alliances and joint ventures affect both technology transfer and the activities of the foreign investors in the host country. The third limitation is that due to the aggregated data, the study ignores investing firms' intentions, past experiences, market orientation, market knowledge, size of investment, and other factors on the company side that may affect the strategic moves of these companies (Benito and Gripsrud 1992; Rolfe et al. 1993).

References

Aizenman, Joshua. 1992. "Exchange Rate Flexibility, Volatility, and Domestic and Foreign Direct Investment." *International Monetary Fund Staff Papers* 39, no. 4: 890–923.

Aliber, Robert Z. 1970. "A Theory of Direct Foreign Investment." In *The International Corporation: A Symposium*, ed. Charles P. Kindleberger. Cambridge, MA: MIT Press, 17–34.

Ampalavanar-Brown, Rajeswary. 1998. "Overseas Chinese Investments in China— Patterns of Growth, Diversification and Finance: The Case of Charoen Pokdhand." *China Quarterly*, no. 155: 610–636.

Balassa, Bela. 1986. "Comparative Advantage in Manufactured Goods: A Reappraisal." *Journal of Economics and Statistics* 68, no. 2: 315–320.

Baldwin, Robert E., 1979. "Determinants of Trade and Foreign Investment: Further Evidence." *Review of Economics and Statistics* 61, no. 1.

Benito, Gabriel R.G., and Geir Gripsrud. 1992. "The Expansion of Foreign Direct Investments: Discrete Rational Location Choices or a Cultural Learning Process." *Journal of International Business Studies*. 23, no. 3: 461–476.

Billington, Nicholas. 1999. "The Location of Foreign Direct Investment: An Empirical Analysis." *Applied Economics* 31, no. 1: 65–76.

Braunerhjelm, Pontus and Lars Oxelheim. 2000. "Does Foreign Direct Investment Replace Home Country Investment?" *Journal of Common Market Studies* 38, no. 2: 199–221.

Broadman, Harry G., and Xiaolun Sun, 1997. "The Distribution of Foreign Direct Investment in China." *World Economy* 20, no. 3: 339–361.

Buckley, Peter J., and Mark Casson, 1976. *The Future of the Multinational Enterprise*. London: Macmillan.

Calvet, A. L. 1981. "A Synthesis of Foreign Direct Theories and Theories of the Multinational Firm." *Journal of International Business Studies* 12, no. 1: 43–60.

Caves, Richard E. 1971. "International Corporations: The Industrial Economics of Foreign Investment." *Economica* 39, no. 149: 1–27.

Chen, Homin and Tain-Jy Chen. 1998. "Network Linkages and Location Choice in Foreign Direct Investment." *Journal of International Business Studies* 29, no. 3: 445–467.

Cheng, Leonard K., and Yum K. Kwan. 2000. "What are the Determinants of Location of Foreign Direct Investment? The Chinese Experience." *Journal of International Economics* 51, no. 2: 379–400.

Choi Chong Ju. 1999. "Global Competitiveness and National Attractiveness." *International Studies of Management and Organization* 29, no. 1: 3–13.

Coughlin, Cletus C., and Eran Seveg. 2000. "Foreign Direct Investment in China: A Spatial Econometric Study." *World Economy* 23, no. 1:1–23.

Davidson, William H. 1980. *Experience Effects in International Investment and Technology Transfer*. Ann Arbor: UMI Research Press.

Dunning, John H. 1973. "The Determinants of International Production." *Oxford Economic Papers* 25, no. 3: 289–336.

———. 1980. "Toward an Eclectic Theory of International Production: Some Empirical Tests." *Journal of International Business Studies* 11, no. 1.

———. 1981. "Trade, Location of Economic Activity and Multinational Enterprises: A Search for An Eclectic Approach." *International Production and the Multinational Enterprise*, ed. John H. Dunning. London: George Allen and Unwin, 21–45.

———. 1988. "The Eclectic Paradigm of International Production: A Restatement and Some Possible Extensions." *Journal of International Business Studies* 19, no.1: 1–31.

———. 1994. *Globalization, Economic Restructuring and Development. The 6th Prebisch Lecture*. Geneva: UNCTAD.

———. 1997. "The European Internal Market Programme and Inbound Foreign Direct Investment." *Journal of Common Market Studies* 35, no. 1: 1 –30.

———. 1998. "Location and the Multinational Enterprise: A Neglected Factor?" *Journal of International Business Studies* 29, no. 1: 45–67.

Froot, Kenneth A. 1993. Comment on *The Surge in Foreign Direct Investment*. In

Foreign Direct Investment, ed. Kenneth A. Froot. Chicago: University of Chicago Press, 33–36.

Froot, Kenneth A., and Jeremy C. Stein. 1989. "Exchange Rates and Foreign Direct Investment: An Imperfect Capital Markets Approach." National Bureau of Economic Research Working Paper no. 2914, Cambridge, MA.

Gastanaga, Victor M., Jeffrey B. Nugent, and Bistra Pashamova. 1998. "Host Country Reforms and FDI Inflows: How Much Difference Do They Make?" *World Development* 26, no. 7: 1299–1313.

Globerman, Steven, and Daniel M. Shapiro. 1999. "The Impact of Government Policies on Foreign Direct Investment: The Canadian Experience." *Journal of International Business Studies* 30, no. 3: 513–532.

Graham, Edward M. and Paul R. Krugman. 1993. "The Surge in Foreign Divest Investment in the 1980s." In *Foreign Direct Investment,* ed. Kenneth A. Froot. Chicago: University of Chicago Press, 13–33.

Green, Robert T., and Ajay K. Kohli. 1991. "Export Market Identification: The Role of Economic Size and Socioeconomic Development." *Management International Review* 31, no. 1.

Grubaugh, Stephen G. 1987. "Determinants of Direct Foreign Investment." *Journal of Economics and Statistics* 69, no. 1: 149–153.

Harris, Richard G., and Nicolas Schmitt. 2000. "Strategic Export Policy with Foreign Direct Investment and Import Substitution." *Journal of Development Economics* 62, no. 1: 85–104.

Henley, John, Colin Kirkpatrick, and Georgina Wilde. 1999. "Foreign Direct Investment in China: Recent Trends and Current Policy Issues." *World Economy* 22, no. 2: 223–243.

Hines, James R. Jr. 1996. "Altered States: Taxes and the Location of Foreign Direct Investment in America." *American Economic Review* 86, no. 5: 1076–1094.

Horst, Thomas. 1972. "Firm and Industry Determinants of the Decision to Invest Abroad: An Empirical Study." *Review of Economics and Statistics* 54, no. 2: 258–266.

Hymer, Stephen. 1976. *The International Operation of National Firms: Study of Direct Foreign Investment.* Cambridge, MA: MIT Press.

Jones, Thomas E. 1998. "China Implements New Foreign Exchange Regime." *International Financial Law Review* 17, no. 12: 45–48.

Juhl, Paulgeorg. 1985. "Economically Rational Design of Developing Countries: Expropriation Policies Towards Foreign Investment." *Management International Review* 25, no. 2: 44–53.

Knickerbocker, Fred T. 1973. *Oligopolistic Reaction and the Multinational Enterprise.* Cambridge, MA: Harvard Business School.

Kobrin, Stephen J. 1978. "When Does Political Instability Result in Increased Investment Risk?" *Columbia Journal of World Business* 13, no. 3.

Kogut, Bruce, and Sea Jin Chang. 1991. "Technology Capabilities and Japanese Foreign Direct Investment in the United States." *Journal of Economics and Statistics* 73, no. 3: 401–413.

Kohlhangen, Steven W. 1977. "Host Country Policies and MNCs – The Pattern of Foreign Investment in Southeast Asia." *Columbia Journal of World Business* 12, no. 1.

Kumar, Nagesh. 1994. "Determinants of Export Orientation of Foreign Production by U.S. Multinationals: An Inter-Country Analysis." *Journal of International Business Studies* 25, no. 1: 141–156.

Levis, Mario. 1979. "Does Political Instability in Developing Countries Affect Foreign Investment Flow? An Empirical Examination." *Management International Review* 19, no. 3.

Luo, Yadong. 1998a. "Structural Changes to Foreign Direct Investment in China: An Evolutionary Perspective." *Journal of Applied Management Studies* 7, no. 1: 95–100.

———. 1998b. "Timing of Investment and International Expansion Performance in China." *Journal of International Business Studies* 29, no. 2: 391–407.

Nachum, L., John H. Dunning, and G. G. Jones. 2000. "UK FDI and the Comparative Advantage of the UK." *World Economy* 23, no. 5: 701–720.

Neary, J. Peter. 1985. "International Factor Mobility, Minimum Wage Rates, and Factor-Price Equalization: A Synthesis." *The Quarterly Journal of Economics* 100, no. 3: 551–571.

Nigh, Douglas. 1985. "The Effect of Political Events on United States Direct Investment: A Pooled Time-Series Cross-Sectional Analysis." *Journal of International Business Studies* 16, no. 1: 1–17.

O'Sullivan, Patrick. 1985. "Determinants and Impact of Private Foreign Direct Investment in Host Countries." *Management International Review* 25, no. 6: 28–36.

Porter, M. E. 1990. *The Competitive Advantage of Nations*. New York: Free Press.

———. 1994. "The Role of Location in Competition." *Journal of Economic Business* 1, no. 1: 35–39.

———. 1996. "Competitive Advantage, Agglomerative Economies and Regional Policy." *International Regional Science Review* 19, no. 1 and 2: 85–94.

Qu, Tao, and Milford B. Green, 1997. *Chinese Foreign Direct Investment: A Subnational Perspective on Location*. Aldershot, UK: Ashgate.

Rangan, Subramanian. 2000. "Search and Deliberation in International Exchange: Microfoundations to Some Macro Patterns." *Journal of International Business Studies* 31, no. 2: 205–222.

Rolfe, Robert J., David A. Ricks, Martha M. Pointer, and Mark McCarthy. 1993. "Determinants of FDI Incentive Preferences of MNEs." *Journal of International Business Studies* 24, no. 2: 335–356.

Rugman, Alan M. 1980. "A New Theory of the Multinational Enterprise: Internationalization versus Internalization." *Journal of International Business Studies* 15, no. 1.

———. 1981. *Inside the Multinationals: The Economics of Internal Markets*. New York: Columbia University Press.

Schollhammer, Hans, and Douglas Nigh. 1984. "The Effect of Political Events on Foreign Direct Investments by German Multinational Corporations." *Management International Review* 24, no. 1: 18–41.

Stone, Susan F., and Bang Nam. 1999. "Gravity-Model Specification for Foreign Direct Investment: A Case of the Asia-Pacific Economies." *Journal of Business and Economics Studies* 5, no. 1: 33–42.

Sun, Haishun. 1998. "Macroeconomic Impact of Foreign Direct Investment in China: 1979–1996." *World Economy* 21, no. 5: 675–694.

Sung, Hongmo, and Harvey E. Lapan. 2000. "Strategic Foreign Direct Investment and Exchange-Rate Uncertainty." *International Economic Review* 41, no. 2: 411–423.

Tatoglu, Ekrem, and Keith W. Glaister, 1998. "Western MNCs' FDI in Turkey: An Analysis of Location Specific Factors." *Management International Review* 38, no. 2: 133–159.

Thomsen, Stephen, 1993. "Japanese Direct Investment in the European Community: The Product Life Cycle Revisited." *World Economy* 16, no. 3: 301–315.

Tse, David K., Yigang Pan, and Kevin Y. Au. 1997. "How MNCs Choose Entry Modes and Form Alliances: The China Experience." *Journal of International Business Studies* 28, no. 4: 779–805.

United Nations. 1996. *Incentives and Foreign Direct Investment*. UNCTAD/DTCI/ 28, Current Studies 30. New York: United Nations.

Vernon, Raymond. 1966. "International Investment and International Trade in the Product Cycle." *Quarterly Journal of Economics* 80, no. 2: 190–207.

———. 1979. "The Product Cycle Hypothesis in a New International Environment." *Oxford Bulletin of Economics and Statistics* 41, no. 4: 255–267.

Wei, Yingqi, Xiaming Liu, David Parker, and Kirit Vaidya. 1999. "The Regional Distribution of Foreign Direct Investment in China." *Regional Studies* 33, no. 9: 857–867.

Wolf, B.M. 1977. "Industrial Diversification and Internationalization: Some Empirical Evidence." *Journal of Industrial Economics* 26, no. 2: 177–191.

World Bank. 2000. *World Development Indicators 2000*. Herndon, VA: World Bank Publications, Office of the Publisher.

Wu, Friedrich. 1984. "Realities Confronting China's Foreign Investment Policies." *World Economy* 7, no. 3: 295–313.

Young, Stephen, and Ping Lan. 1997. "Technology Transfer to China Through Foreign Direct Investment." *Regional Studies* 31, no. 7: 669–679.

Zhang, Le-Yin, 1994. "Location-Specific Advantages and Manufacturing Direct Foreign Investment in South China." *World Development* 22, no. 1: 45–54.

Zhao Hongxin, and Gangti Zhu. 2000. "Location Factors and Country-of-Origin Differences: An Empirical Analysis of FDI in China." *Multinational Business Review* 8, no. 1: 60–74.

Zhu, Gangti and Kong Yam Tan. 2000. "Foreign Direct Investment and Labor Productivity: New Evidence from China as the Host Country." *Thunderbird International Business Review* 42, no. 5: 507–528.

Appendix 1

Description of Variables and Data Sources

FDI   Foreign direct investment into China as a whole, a region, or an industry. The data is from *China Statistic Yearbook* (CSY), *China Fixed Asset Investment Yearbook* (CFAIY), *International Financial Statistics* (IFS) by IMF, and the World Bank's *World Development Indicators* (WDI), various years. The data is in logarithm or lagged depending on the model used.

LBRCOST   Labor cost expenses. The GDP per capita is approximated for the labor cost. Figures are from CSY, CSY, or WDI, various years. The data is in logarithm.

TRDGRO   Actual international trade growth rate, such measured as in logarithm import + export divided by GDP. Data come from WDI, CSY, and IFS, various years.

INTRST   Monetary authority lending interest rate. If this rate is not available, bank lending rates are used. Data come from IFS, various years.

INFRA   Domestic infrastructure, proxied by the telecommunication services output. Data are from WDI and CSY, various years, in logarithm.

DINVST   Domestic capital investment, measured as gross domestic fixed investment. Data are from WDI, CSY and CFAIY, various years, in logarithm.

IMDUTY   Import duty. Approximated as import duty income as a ratio of the total import value. Data are from WDI and CSY, various years, in logarithm.

MKTSIZE   Effective market size, measured as the total national public and private consumption deflated by urban population as a percentage of total population. Data are from WDI, various years, in logarithm.

GDPCAP   GDP per capita. Data from WDI, various years, in logarithm.

EXRATE Exchange rate, measured as the annual changes of the local currency to per US$. Data are from WDI, various years, in logarithm.

INFLAT National inflation rate, measured as the consumer product index. Data are from WDI, various years, in logarithm.

EVENT Events that may have effects on the dependent variable. Basic events are from Bekaert and Campbell's list of developing countries events from their Duke University website (www.duke.edu/ncharvey/country-risk/couindex.htm). Supplemental events are from various country chronologies. The coding is an annual integrated figure with +1 if the events for that year have potential positive effect on FDI inflow; −1 if negative effect; and 0 if no effect. No event codes are assigned to developed countries. The annual event score is totaled from all individual events occurring in that year. +1 is for >+5 total scores, −1 for <−5, and 0 for between.

INCNTV Incentive coding for a country or Chinese regions. If the country or region has special incentives, such as a SEZ, the code is 0; otherwise, the code is 1. Data come from KPMG *Tax and Financial Incentives for Business Around the World*, CYS and CFAIY.

AREA Area coding for Chinese regions. If the region is in East China, the code is 0; otherwise 1.

TECHADV Technological advance. Approximated with the investment amount per major new project in China. The data are from CSY and CFAIY.

Part IV

Business Environment and Policy Issues

13

United States-China-Taiwan: A Precarious Triangle

Murray Weidenbaum

Whether Napoleon really said it or not, the forecast often attributed to him is likely to be essentially correct: "China is a sleeping giant. When it wakes, it will move the world." China's 1.2 billion people combined with its record-breaking twenty years of rapid growth make it likely that the Middle Kingdom will become the second economic superpower sometime during the twenty-first century.

Nevertheless, an old Mandarin proverb states, "If you think you understand China, you don't really understand." That warning also sums up the challenges that face Americans in dealing with that fascinating national array of strengths and weaknesses. When viewed separately, each of the many aspects of policy involving China is difficult—economic, political, military, and environmental. However, when we consider the many interrelationships and then add the third part of the triangle—Taiwan—the policy challenges become increasingly complicated. Let us try to deal with this vital cluster of issues a step at a time.

Economic Relations

Let us begin with the economic relationships. Any way we look at it, China is becoming an important economic power once again. Using a

Keynote address to the Conference on the Greater China Economy, St. Louis, MO, March 25, 2000.

form of comparing national economies known as purchasing power parity, we find that the Chinese economy is now more than half as large as that of the United States and larger than Japan's. More conventional measures show China in seventh place, but coming up rapidly.[1]

China is now the ninth largest trading nation in the world. It is a major trading partner of the United States. Each year more than $70 billion worth of commerce flows between our two nations. But the term "partner," which President Clinton introduced into the public dialogue, is a misleading euphemism for a very uneven set of commercial flows. The United States imports from China more than five times the dollar amount of our exports to them. This relationship is far more out of balance than our trade with Japan.[2] Yet, unlike the case of Japan, most of the opposition to continuing normal trading relationships with China does not arise from those who believe they are hurt by the large excess of imports. Rather, it emanates from groups concerned primarily with noneconomic factors, notably the harsh treatment of religious minorities, political dissidents, and Tibetans.

Aside from low-priced clothing, toys, and electronic parts, trade with China is not a significant portion of the American economy. However, the United States is the destination of almost one-third of China's exports. Our commerce is a key way in which that nation acquires technology. Our trade also generates a substantial part of China's large accumulation of foreign currencies. China maintained a rapid rate of economic growth while financial problems were besetting East Asia in 1997 and 1998. However, serious signs of weakness are visible, notably sluggish exports, stagnant industrial production, and inefficient state industries.

Nevertheless, mainland China and Taiwan have been the two bright spots in an otherwise troubled East Asian economic scene. Despite the political difficulties, which I will cover in a moment, the economic relationships across the Taiwan straits have remained strong and substantial.

It is one of the great ironies of our time that so many of the people who fled the mainland in 1949—or their descendents—have been returning to their ancestral homes in a very special way. From Taiwan as well as elsewhere in the Chinese diaspora, they have brought with them much of the money and managerial skills that have been so essential to the economic success of China, especially in moving toward a modern capitalistic economy. Other indicators of the special nature of the cross-straits interrelationships are also impressive—the large numbers of tourists from Taiwan who visit the mainland, the rising number of telephone calls across the straits, as well as the numerous cultural and intellectual exchanges.[3]

Viewed from this side of the Pacific, the two sectors of Greater China seem extremely complementary, especially in an economic sense. The mainland possesses the land, the work force, and increasingly a major market while Taiwan provides the entrepreneurial and business skills enhanced by very substantial financial flows (over $40 billion to date). According to Li Lu, a Tiananmen Square student leader now in the United States, "[B]usiness is the ultimate force for democratic change in China."[4] Apparently, this is a compelling truth whose power frightens much of the traditional communist leadership in China. Two-way trade between Taiwan and the mainland is now running at about $25 billion a year.

In contrast, the complementarities between the American and the Chinese economies, although considerable, are not nearly so great. Of course, some Americans barely restrain their enthusiasm when they consider a market potential in excess of 1 billion customers. An example of this line of thinking was the late Ron Brown. When Secretary of Commerce, he declared, "China . . . is the pot at the end of the rainbow."[5] My own research leads me to a far more restrained conclusion. It is the rare U.S. company doing business in China that reports earning profits on its operations in that nation. Rather, they like to talk about their rosy forecasts of future sales.

A recent survey of ninety-six multinationals operating in China reported that 62 percent had overestimated the market potential and an almost equal number (61 percent) had experienced poorer profit performance than they had expected.[6] Those percentages do leave room for some outstanding successes. Procter and Gamble dominates the market for soaps and shampoos. Coca-Cola far outsells Hainan coconut juice, and Ken-de-ji is well known in the larger cities (that is Kentucky Fried Chicken to Westerners).

In contrast to the open U.S. market, numerous obstacles face American exporters to China, such as onerous licensing procedures. Compulsory registration applies to hundreds of products, typically electrical equipment and machinery. Moreover, U.S. producers of computer software, video tapes, compact discs, books, and motion pictures suffer because their products are frequently copied illegally in China. This intellectual piracy reduces potential U.S. exports to China and to the rest of the world by an estimated $2 billion a year.[7] It also is a growing source of economic and political friction. "Piracy," it should be noted, is more of a Western concept than an Asian one.

Political Relations

The political relationships between China and the United States are even more difficult to fathom than the economic. President Clinton described the state of Sino-U.S. ties as "a strategic partnership." Yet very few aspects of a true partnership are present. It is Japan that cooperates with us in a variety of important foreign policy activities, including financing a considerable portion of the Gulf War. The two nations also share a common outlook toward democracy, private enterprise, and personal freedom.

On the other hand, there is no direct basis for confrontation between China and the United States. We do not share a common border nor do we hold competing claims for territory. However, significant differences in fundamental values are clearly visible in terms of the treatment of citizens by the government, especially in regard to personal freedoms—political, economic, and religious.

The limited amount of individual liberty in China galls many Americans. Especially upsetting is the persecution of Christian groups and the jailing of political dissidents. It is difficult for the United States to accept the idea of a "partnership" with a nation that engages in such offensive practices.

On the positive side, in recent years China has relaxed the rules governing everyday life for the typical citizen. A substantial decentralization of power has taken place and greater latitude has been provided to private enterprise. The impacts of Western culture and commerce have been pervasive, especially in the larger cities.

U.S. corporations doing business in China serve to advance our human rights goals. They create safer workplaces, follow more progressive personnel practices, raise living standards, and bring in new ideas, attitudes, and ways of thinking. American companies, such as Mattel, have adopted codes of conduct requiring local subcontractors and suppliers to avoid child labor and other practices inconsistent with U.S. standards.[8] More indirectly, commercial products and advertising carry a powerful implicit message of personal choice.

Substantial portions of China's population recognize such American brand names as Coca Cola, Jeep, Head and Shoulders, Marlboro, Mickey

Mouse, and Kodak. Young women often wear miniskirts and use Western-style makeup.

The role of Taiwan adds significant complication to the Sino-U.S. political relationship. Officially, the United States recognizes the People's Republic and maintains only informal relations with Taipei. Our repeatedly stated national policy favors the voluntary unification of Taiwan with China, but also provides military support to the island in the event of force or the threat of force on the part of the PRC. To put it mildly, this is an unusual set of attitudes and commitments. Until recently, the U.S. position seemed to be reasonably workable and was consistent with the expansion of economic and cultural ties across the Taiwan straits.

The situation became murkier when important groups in Taiwan began to talk about independence and its governmental leader described relations between China and Taiwan as "state-to-state." The concern is raised a notch when the PRC states that it is "under no obligation to commit itself to rule out the use of force" in securing the reunification of Taiwan and the mainland.[9] The frank discussions I have had in both China and Taipei convince me that this is an extremely difficult and sensitive situation calling for a maximum of restraint and patience on all sides. Surely, the continuing U.S. policy of engagement with China has also established an environment in which Taiwan has flourished.[10]

When I have had background discussions with Taipei leaders, I hear about their great success in achieving personal liberty and economic expansion for the island's citizens and the strong desire to keep those hard-won gains. My informal talks with mainland officials deal with other considerations, such as national pride and strategic matters. The two sets of representatives seem to be on different wavelengths. A meeting with the leaders of one large China city was especially memorable. Perhaps a bit naïvely, I stated with some enthusiasm that our national policy was to favor the attainment of a unified China—on a voluntary basis.

The leader of the Chinese delegation promptly responded, "Tell me, when the South seceded from the Union, did you use force?" My answer frankly did not satisfy the Chinese officials, "Yes, but they fired first." In the high-tech twenty-first century that we have entered, it is possible to conjure up a new-style attack. For example, the PRC could use its large foreign-exchange holdings to shake the Taiwan currency and stock markets in order to destabilize the island's political economy.[11]

Military Relations

The military area generates great uncertainty for American policymakers. China is in the midst of a major effort to upgrade its military capability. The acquisition from Russia of destroyers with supersonic missiles is a cogent example. Is China motivated by the desire for regional hegemony? Its imperious treatment of other nations in some of the islands in the South China Sea is a source of considerable concern. The 1996 episode of China's missile testing in the Taiwan straits surely raised tensions in the region—as well as generating a strong and rapid American response.

On the other hand, the current weapon procurement effort may be interpreted as defensive in nature. China's military capability is rudimentary compared to that of the United States. Its troops are poorly equipped by our standards, and their weapons, in the main, are considered obsolete. The Gulf War demonstrated that even large stockpiles of outdated equipment are of little use against a more advanced opponent. Moreover, China currently lacks the ability to project its power over water in any substantial way. It possesses a total of about sixty surface ships and fewer than ten modern submarines.[12] So, although China presents little direct military threat to the United States, it could be a substantial destabilizing force in East Asia.

Thus, a less benign interpretation is also possible. China is procuring more sophisticated aircraft, ships, and missiles from the cash-strapped countries of the former Soviet Union. Over the past decade, it has acquired several hundred SU-27 and SU-30 fighter jets and Soveremenny-class destroyers with Sunburn missiles.[13] Ranked by explosive power, China's nuclear arsenal is reported to be the world's third largest, trailing only those of the United States and Russia. Chinese strategists may be working toward the day when their nuclear and missile forces can deter great-power intervention in the Asia/Pacific theater and their conventional forces can cow regional rivals. Such a combination would allow, indeed define, local hegemony.

At present, there seems to be little potential for extensive military action outside of an unintentional blunder into armed conflict. Taiwan quickly comes to mind in this connection, especially given the prospect of a competitive presidential election campaign. China already focuses more of its military resources on Taiwan than on any other single area. In democracies, elections can be the occasion for a barrage of wild charges and promises, which could further exacerbate tensions across the Taiwan straits. On the other hand, China's desire for a strong military establishment may be understandable when viewed in the light of its long history of defeat and exploitation by foreign aggressors. Yet, over the centuries it has played that role itself in Southeast Asia. China's rising military capability does enable it to apply pressure on the rest of the region, thus perhaps affecting the military balance between China and its neighbors.[14]

Environmental Issues

Environmental issues are a relatively new aspect of international relations and one in which American and Chinese interests could readily collide.[15] The December 1997 meeting in Kyoto on global climate change yielded a proposed treaty that would commit the United States and other developed nations to major reductions in emissions of carbon dioxide (CO_2), which are generated primarily by the use of fossil fuels. The treaty, which requires Senate approval, would effectively exempt China and other developing countries from its tough restrictions. That basic difference in national treatment generates serious political difficulties in the United States. The Senate has pledged to defeat any climate-change treaty that does not include the developing nations. Reconciling the Senate position with the Kyoto agreement will focus heavily on the role of China, a prime emitter of CO_2.

Poor countries like China believe that they cannot afford to sacrifice current income to avoid the uncertain costs of environmental damage fifty or 100 years from now. Even though air pollution is a visibly serious problem (coal generates 75 percent of its energy), China considers use of scarce resources for ecological purposes as a rich country's luxury. Thus, trying to convince that nation to limit its energy consumption while the major Western countries use five to ten times as much per person will probably prove futile—unless wealthier countries such as the United States pay the global costs of reducing fossil fuel usage.

Nevertheless, air pollution is a growing problem in the major Chinese cities. China's extreme dependence on its domestic coal supply for energy also could generate other serious problems if it turns to less-polluting sources of energy. The vast and still mainly untapped oil and gas reserves of the South China Sea are an important potential alternate source of energy. Overlapping portions of that strategic area are also claimed by Vietnam, Malaysia, Brunei, the Philippines, and Taiwan. Furthermore, all ocean shipping among those five countries and China, as well as the transport of oil from the Persian Gulf to Japan, takes place across the South China Sea.

Reconciling Divergent Interests

When asked the meaning of the French Revolution, Zhou Enlai was supposed to have replied, "It is too soon to tell."[16] In this vein, it is with some reluctance that I will try to pull together the various strands of Sino-U.S. connections. Policymakers in both the United States and China face fundamental challenges in attempting to deal simultaneously with a host of contentious economic, political, social, religious, military, and environmental issues.[17] Not all of these serious matters can be resolved soon. It would be sensible to focus on the highest priorities.

A useful starting point is to note that China's isolation is ending. Today it is more open to the influences of Western culture and business practices than ever before. Its senior officials say they want their country to be a full participant in the world economy. They acknowledge that this requires China to move to a market economy and to modernize its society. Yet China is not now a member of key international organizations, formal or informal, such as the WTO and the annual economic summits.

The United States is in a special position to aid China in its entry into the "club" of developed nations. After all, compared to European countries such as Britain, France, and Germany, the United States is one of the newer members of that club. We also have a major stake in China's success in its effort to move out of its isolationist setting. As a key Pacific power, it is to our benefit to encourage the rise of a China that interacts regularly with its neighbors and is at peace with them.

Not all American interests will benefit from China's entry into the WTO. Some investors will lose the preferential treatment now accorded to foreigners. China's pledges to open its markets to foreign distribution channels are less than firm guarantees. On the other hand, China's membership in the WTO may open the way to Taiwan's membership as a separate customs territory.[18]

In the broadest sense, China and the United States are complementary in terms of their basic economic needs and resources. We are China's leading export market as well as the most logical partner to help upgrade its technology through investment and joint venturing. In turn, China is the most promising new market for American business and agriculture.

China's huge development and infrastructure needs can provide enormous export and investment opportunities for U.S. companies seeking geographic diversification. In the important area of higher education, U.S. colleges and universities are a popular place for wealthier Chinese to send their children, especially for graduate education. Such activity has the added potential of generating personal and intellectual bridges between the two nations.

However, China's distance from the West is greater than a glance at the globe suggests. Surely, the bombing of the Chinese offices in Belgrade, although presumably unintentional on our part, was at least a temporary setback in Sino-U.S. relations, and we should be candid in acknowledging the consequences. Above and beyond such current events, central differences exist in historical experience, cultural orientation, and political and social institutions. To state the matter candidly, the rule of law as Westerners view the notion is still essentially a foreign concept in China, a special import which it seems to welcome with minimum enthusiasm. Viewed in this light, let us see how we can deal with the main issues that will either separate our two powerful nations or bring them closer.

It may be surprising for an economist to start with military rather than economic issues, but matters of war and peace are fundamental. The continued expansion of China's military power should be acknowledged as potentially destabilizing. However, the sensible response is not to try to talk Beijing out of what it thinks is a reasonable position.

Instead, we should simply but clearly note that, in terms of our vital interests, the expansion of China's armed strength provides a compelling justification for the maintenance of a substantial U.S. military presence in East Asia. The United States maintains security alliances with Japan, South Korea, the Philippines, Thailand, and Australia. Yet a China that is secure from foreign threat and can protect its legitimate sovereignty is desirable for both Asian and American vital interests. On the other hand, coercive pressure by China against its neighbors in the South China Sea or against Taiwan only serves to escalate tensions in East Asia. Alleviation of tensions requires restraint on the part of many parties. One expert in international law, for example, has urged Taiwan to "look like a state, act like a state . . . but not formally declare its independence."[19]

Our willingness to assign a significant amount of our military resources to East Asia reflects the high priority that we give to stable conditions in that region. At the same time, better relations with China may
allow the United States eventually to resume limited sales of defensive
weapons to China. No action would do more to alleviate Beijing's fear
of a policy of containment on our part.

In the area of economic policy, the United States remains the main
bulwark of the free flow of commerce and capital across the globe. Nevertheless, because we are a democracy, we respond to the concerns of
our citizens as expressed in the political process. Anyone who follows
domestic political trends in the United States knows that strong pressure
exists for devoting an increasing share of the federal budget to domestic
matters such as strengthening Social Security and Medicare. Thus, when
Chinese officials dismiss these concerns as "just domestic politics," they
demonstrate that they do not yet understand how a democracy works.

It is extremely optimistic for China to expect that we can maintain a
fully open market to their products in the face of so many adverse factors:
(1) a host of Chinese barriers to U.S. exports, (2) severe restraints on the
operations of U.S. firms in China, (3) lack of a functioning legal system
that provides local citizens as well as foreigners with essential protection of individual liberty and property, and (4) overt discrimination against
and persecution of people with whom many Americans identify.

Nevertheless, it is counterproductive for us to try to tell China what
to do under those circumstances. It is most appropriate for the United
States to clearly explain our position, motivation, and actions. We can
sincerely hope that China continues to open up its economy—including
the general use of the internet—and to achieve more of the freedoms to
which the citizens of other advanced societies have grown accustomed.
The United States should support China's entry into the World Trade
Organization—but without any special preferences. Judged strictly from
the viewpoint of American interests, the likelihood is that China will be
a more responsible world citizen operating on the inside rather than the
outside, but there are no firm assurances in such matters.

However, if China chooses not to take more enlightened positions, it
will postpone the time when it gains full membership in the global marketplace and the family of modern societies. Clearly our preference is to
welcome China into that desirable relationship sooner rather than later.

In developing closer relations with China, trade-offs are inevitable.
While private organizations emphasizing single issues are free to take

absolutist positions, it is foolish for governments to do so. Our government must balance concern for human rights against other important interests that also have significant moral aspects—such as peace, national security, and the prosperity of our citizens. The United States maintains peaceful and friendly relations with many nations that do not share our fundamental beliefs. But those relationships are not strong or enduring. A virtuous circle is possible. Closer economic and individual ties in turn can lead to improved mutual understanding—and vice versa. Thus, we should welcome the development of improved relations with China and further progress in the day-to-day interactions of our people. But we should be prepared for the possibility of more pragmatic relationships and less happy outcomes.

Notes

A version of this chapter appeared in *Challenge* vol. 45, no. 5 (September–October 2000), pp. 92–106.

1. Robert H. McGuckin and Bart van Ark, 1998, *Asia After the Crisis: Challenges for a Return to Rapid Growth.* New York: Conference Board, p. 5; Fred Hu, October 18, 1999, *China: At the Dawn of the New Millennium.* Global Economics paper no. 33. New York: Goldman Sachs.

2. It is unlikely that either Europe or Japan would have allowed a trade relationship as unbalanced as that which now characterizes the United States and China. See Barry Bosworth, "Growing Pains: Trade Frictions Erode the U.S.-Asian Relationship," *Brookings Review* (winter 1996): 9.

3. See Murray Weidenbaum and Samuel Hughes, 1996, *The Bamboo Network.* New York: Free Press.

4. Quoted in "Chinese Dissidents Find Freedom—In Business," *Business Week*, March 21, 1994, p. 126.

5. Quoted in John Maggs, "The Myth of the China Market," *New Republic*, March 10, 1997, p. 15.

6. Henry Sender, "Poor Profits Sap Foreign Investment in China," *Wall Street Journal*, October 11, 1999, p. A17; Yigang Pan and Peter S. K. Chi, 1998, "The Promises and Challenges of Direct Foreign Investments in China," *Business and the Contemporary World,* Vol. 10, no. 1: 67–105.

7. Thomas Klitgaard and Karen Schiele, 1997, "The Growing U.S. Trade Imbalance with China," *Current Issues in Economics and Finance*, May: 2.

8. See, for example, *Global Manufacturing Principles* (Los Angeles: Mattel, Inc., 1997); S. Prakash Sethi et al., 2000, "A Case Study of Independent Monitoring of U.S. Overseas Production," *Global Focus*, Vol. 12, no. 1.

9. People's Republic of China Taiwan Affairs Office and Information Office of the State Council, "The One-China Principle and the Taiwan Issue," reprinted in *The New York Times*, February 22, 2000, p. A10.

10. Robert M. Hathaway, 2000, "Dangerous Misconceptions About Taiwan," *PacNet*, February 25: 1.

11. Testimony of Gerrit W. Gong, before the U.S. Trade Deficit Review Commission, Washington, DC, February 24, 2000, p. 10.

12. *Impact of China's Modernization on the Pacific Region* (Washington, DC: U.S. General Accounting Office, June 1995). See also David Shambaugh, 1996, "China's Military: Real or Paper Tiger?" *Washington Quarterly* (spring): 19–36.

13. Gong, Testimony, p. 7.

14. Okazaki Misahiko, 1999, "A National Strategy for the Twenty-first Century," *Japan Echo* (October): 36.

15. Mark Hertsgaard, 1997, "Our Real China Problem," *Atlantic Monthly* (November): 97–112; "Pollution, Traffic Jams Blight China's Urban Growth," *World Bank News*, January 9, 1997, pp. 1–2.

16. Quoted in Martin Wolf, 1998, "Lessons of the Asian Crisis," *Berlin 1998*. New York: Trilateral Commission: 10.

17. Murray Weidenbaum, 1999, "The Future of Sino-American Relations," *Orbis* (spring): 223–235.

18. Harry Harding, *China, The WTO, and the United States*, Testimony before the U.S. Trade Deficit Review Commission, Washington, DC, February 24, 2000, pp. 2–3.

19. Michael P. Scharf, "Bridging the Taiwan Strait," *Christian Science Monitor*, December 3, 1997, p. 20.

14

International Business and Multinational Corporations in China

Xiaohua Yang, George M. Puia, and Wang Guo An

Background

When Sover S.P.A., a small Italian spectacles maker, discovered that its Chinese partner, Suzhou Spectacles No. 1 Factory, sold pirated copies of the joint venture's product in the domestic market, it proposed to liquidate its 50 percent-owned sunglass factory in Suzhou, China. The Chinese partner denied such allegations and refused to go along with the liquidation. The agreement called for unanimous approval on any dissolution by the board of the joint venture. When efforts to seek help from a high-level government bureau failed, Sover found itself stuck in the joint venture (Leung 1995).

The Sover case echoed the experiences of many other foreign firms investing in China: that is, the lack of a dynamic and effective entry strategy led to undesirable consequences. This example vividly illustrates that an inflexible entry choice can lead to unsuccessful ventures in China. Indeed, as the selection of an effective entry strategy has a major impact on the success of global expansion, it has been considered one of the most important strategic decisions that international managers make (Anderson and Gatignon 1986; Root 1987).

Throughout this article, cases will be used to illustrate concepts and provide evidence of the need for dynamic and effective entry strategies.

The choice to use cases is purposeful. Y.S. Lincoln and E.G. Guba (1985) noted that case studies and other forms of qualitative research are most effective when (1) the existing theory has not developed to a level where it can explain the current issues of the field and (2) the nature of the processes involved are holistic. Furthermore, R.K. Yin (1989) reasoned that the nature of the questions asked—for example, especially how and why questions—and the basis of the situation—for example, one in which the researcher exercises no control over the events and actions—lead to the selection of case studies as the most appropriate method of inquiry. These criteria certainly describe the current state of knowledge concerning international entry strategies, especially concerning the dynamic relationship between entry strategies and environmental determinants.

Although how to enter a foreign market has long been a concern of both practitioners and scholars (Buckley and Casson 1998; Contractor and Kundu 1998; Anderson and Gatignon 1986; Tse, Pan and Au 1997), little is known about the relationship between entry strategies and environmental determinants and how such linkage affects entry success.

Since the seminal work of H. Johanson and J. Vahlne (1977), most of the work in internationalization process has centered on comparative static analysis of entry mode choice rather than dynamic processes of change and adaptation. The earlier literature on foreign market entry has tended to treat entry choice as a dichotomy or a sequence. Thus, entry strategies were reduced to a formula, a set of rules, or a computer model. Internationalization perspective views the firm and host country as static entities and entry strategies as static activities; thus the entry choice is reduced to one mode or the other, one location or the other (Agarwal and Ramaswami 1992; Anderson 1993; Anderson and Coughlan 1987; Anderson and Gatignon 1986; Erramilli and Rao 1993; Hennart 1989; Osborn and Baughn 1990), whereas Uppsala models of market entry focus on a sequential pattern of entry into foreign markets, accompanied by progressive deepening of commitment to foreign markets (Welch and Luostarinen 1988; Denis and Depelteau 1985; Buckley and Casson 1998). While the former view assumes a more static view of the world, focusing on one transaction or one market entry at a time, the latter assumes a predictable view of the world, focusing on sequential steps of market entry. Both views neglect the dynamic interrelationship between entry strategies and environment. The existing literature is silent about how environmental determinants influence market entry, the need for creating congruency between entry strategies and environment, and how such congruency can be created to minimize risks associated with developing entry strategies.

Congruence or fit is defined as "the degree to which the needs, demands, goals, objectives, and/or structure of one component are consistent with the needs, demands, goals, objectives, and/or structure of another component" (Nadler and Tushman 1980). Congruence perspective suggests that a greater degree of fit between the environmental and organizational components will result in more effective organizational behavior at multiple organizational levels (Milliman, Von Glinow, and Nathan 1991; Morgan, 1986).

As the international business environment undergoes constant change, the firm is pressured to make strategic adjustments to maintain congruence. Given the need for firms to adjust, it is imperative that entry strategies be flexible and adaptable to fit new environments. The new model based on the congruency perspective depicts the interrelationships among entry strategies and environmental determinants. It suggests that entry strategies should be designed as ongoing, dynamic processes to allow for maximum flexibility and adaptability in order to succeed in foreign markets.

Influence of Environmental Factors on Entry Strategies

Porter's Diamond Revisited

To understand how environmental variables interact with entry strategies, one can gain some insight from Porter's (1998) "diamond of international competitiveness." Porter states that four broad attributes of a nation shape the environment in which domestic firms compete and these attributes facilitate or prohibit the creation of competitive advantage. These attributes are factor endowments, the availability of factors of production such as skilled labor or the infrastructure necessary to compete in a particular industry; demand conditions, the nature of home demand for the industry's products and services; relating and supporting industries, the presence or absence in a nation of suppliers in industries and related industries that are internationally competitive; and firm strategy, structure, and rivalry, the conditions in a nation governing how companies are created, organized, and managed and the nature of domestic competition (see Figure 14.1). Porter argues that when conditions in the diamond are most favorable, having strong local demand,

Figure 14.1 **An Extension of Porter's Diamond**

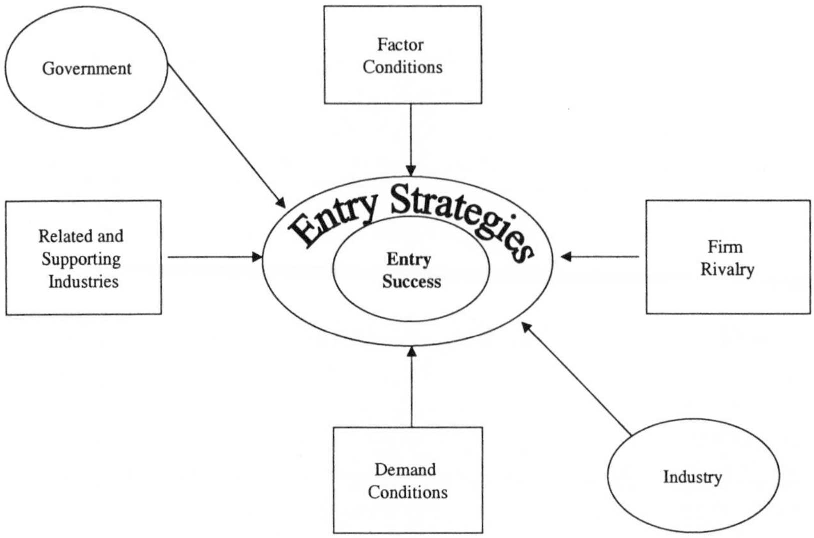

Source: Adopted from Porter (1998) and Rugman and Verbeke (1993).

qualified local suppliers, strong factor conditions, and sufficient competition to encourage competition without stifling profits—then industries and firms develop with the potential to produce the world's best products and services.

Porter also argues that the diamond is an interrelating and mutually reinforcing system; the effect of one attribute is dependent on the state of others. He further suggests that both government and chance play important roles in national competitive strategies. Government policy can detract from or improve competitive advantages. For example, government regulation can alter demand conditions and antitrust policies can change the intensity of competition. In addition, a sudden leap in technology can change industry structures and simultaneously create opportunities and threats for firms at the same time (Porter 1998). In sum, Porter's argument is that the degree to which a nation is likely to achieve international competitiveness in a certain industry is a function of the combined impact of factor endowments, domestic demand conditions, related and supporting industries, and domestic rivalry.

Porter's model focuses only on how national environmental determinants affect a nation's international competitiveness without considering how international environmental determinants interact with those four attributes. A refinement made by A.M. Rugman and A. Verbeke (1993) bridged the gap between the national-level determinants and four other geographical-level determinants: local, regional, foreign, and global. Rugman and Verbeke made a major contribution by introducing these five geographical levels into Porter's diamond. This greatly enhanced the explanatory power of Porter's diamond by recognizing that international competitiveness depends on a firm's ability to respond advantageously to influences, not just at national but at international and global levels. Indeed, today global and regional institutions are exerting much influence on international business activities. Examples include the International Monetary Fund in the Asian crisis, the World Trade Organization in reshuffling the international trading system, the European Union in creating a single currency in Europe to reduce business transaction costs and gaining bargaining power for European firms; NAFTA in creating the largest free trade zone in the world and enticing GM to move its headquarters to Mexico; and the Asian Pacific Economic Cooperation, the largest and most diverse regional economic forum in terms of its population, positioning itself to become the economic facilitator and agent for businesses in the region. As regional trade blocs become increasingly important to regional economies and business activities, firms' international expansion strategies will also be influenced by these trade bloc agreements. It is essential to include regional economic integration in any analysis of entry strategies.

Rugman and Verbeke further suggested that international competitiveness may result from mutual reinforcement and synergies among determinants at multiple levels and that a simultaneous response to critical factors at different geographical levels may lead to tensions among competing influences.

This chapter will incorporate in its analysis Porter's diamond plus government and industry and four geographical levels of analysis: local, national, regional, and global. Using the refined Porter's diamond allows us to consider the interaction between international entry strategies and environments at different geographical levels.

A New Model of International Entry Strategies

The six forces at four geographical levels in the refined Porter's diamond and their mutual interactions may create mutually reinforced en-

Figure 14.2 **A Congruency Model of International Entry Strategy**

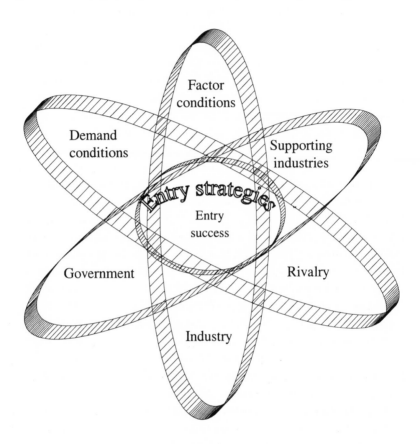

try strategies. The new model depicts such dynamic and synergistic processes as mutual shaping and mutual realignment between environmental determinants and entry strategies (see Figure 14.2).

Government

When a firm contemplates a product launch in a foreign country for the first time, it faces a number of issues, including political risk and legal restrictions at the national government level. Legal restrictions for foreign investors can limit a foreign investor's immediate options at the time, but such restrictions may be lifted at a later time. For instance, according to the *Rules for the Implementation of the Law of the People's Republic of China on Foreign-Capital Enterprises* approved by the State Council on October 28, 1990, and promulgated by Decree No. 1 of the Ministry of Foreign Economic Relations and Trade on December 12, 1990, no foreign-capital enterprises shall be established in the following sectors:

1. The press, publications, broadcasting, television, and movies
2. Domestic commerce, foreign trade, and insurance
3. Post and telecommunications
4. Other trades in which the establishment of foreign-capital enterprises is forbidden, as prescribed by the government

The establishment of foreign-capital enterprises shall be restricted in the following sectors:

1. Public utilities
2. Communications and transportation
3. Real estate
4. Trust investment
5. Leasing

The purpose of the above prohibitions and restrictions of the Chinese government is partially to safeguard China's national security, but primarily to protect its own young industries that cannot compete with those in developed countries. For example, currently when automobiles are exported to the Chinese market, the Chinese government levies astronomically high tariffs (80%–100%) in order to protect its young automobile industry. But according to the commitments China has made in its recent WTO entry negotiations with other WTO members, China will become more open by allowing foreign enterprises to invest in its domestic commerce, foreign trade, banking, insurance, and telecommunications. In four years foreign investors will be able to hold 51 percent of its shares in equity joint ventures of telecommunications. Similarly, in six years the import tariffs for foreign automobiles will be reduced from the present 80 percent to 100 percent to 25 percent. In five years foreigners can open private banks in China. In fact, in Pudong, Shanghai, foreign businessmen have begun to deal on a trial basis in the formerly forbidden or restricted trades such as foreign trade, banking, insurance, and other service trades. Subsequently the Chinese law regarding foreign direct investment will soon be amended or revised when China joins the WTO. Given potential government policy change, firms should develop entry strategies that can accommodate later strategic moves. In addition, host governments may limit the choices of entry modes and regulate the percentage of equity foreign firms can hold and the types of products foreign firms can sell. The host government tends to have greater bargaining power in more mature industries where standardization occurs, entry barriers are lowered, and oligopolistic concentration declines. For instance, the Brazilian government rejected IBM's demand for a 100 percent ownership to produce minicomputers and instead accepted Japanese and European minority joint ventures and licensing agreements (Franko 1989). However, government policies are subject to change. As countries enter higher levels of economic development, they need to expand overseas themselves. They are more likely to become conciliatory and to relax their regulatory policies. Foreign investors may then find themselves facing more options than ever before.

Shifts in entry strategies due to governmental policy changes are not uncommon. Western Electric's late nineteenth century venture into Japan provides an excellent historical example. In the early 1890s commission agents in Japan initially handled Western Electric's small business in Japan. After the government announced plans to expand the telephone system, Western Electric turned to Kunihiko Iwadare, who had briefly worked with Thomas Edison in the United States, to handle their agency needs. In 1896 Western Electric negotiated an organizational procedure and successfully bid on switchboards for Tokyo and Yokohama to be imported from the United States. Japanese law at that time forbade foreign capital in Japanese registered firms, so in October 1898 Iwadare and Takeshiro Mayeda formed Nippon Denki Goshi Kaisha to handle the Western Electric agency. In July of the following year, after the Japanese law regarding foreign capital had been changed, the firm was reorganized as Nippon Denki Kabushiki Kaisha (Nippon Electric Company, Ltd.) with Western Electric owning 54 percent of the joint venture. Initially Nippon Electric primarily imported Western Electric equipment. With a new telephone expansion program passed by the Japanese Diet in 1907, discouraging imports, Western Electric financed the construction of a switchboard factory at Nippon Electric's Tokyo plant. In 1918 a new U.S. law was passed to allow firms solely involved in export to consolidate without being threatened by antitrust action. Western Electric began to restructure its overseas operations. It transformed China Electric—the joint venture of Western Electric, Nippon Electric, and the Chinese government—into a Delaware corporation rather than a Chinese firm and established its international operations as a wholly owned subsidiary, Western Electric International (Butler 1999).

The Western Electric case points to the evidence that host governments at different levels play a major role in shaping corporate competitive strategies and at times more directly determining the type of entry strategies that firms can use. The case clearly illustrates the importance of revising entry strategies to fit the new environment in order to succeed in foreign markets.

Industry Variables

Entry strategies should also be aligned with the industry environment. Industry environmental variables are the scale of operations and entry and exit barriers. The scale of operations varies across industries and can facilitate or constrain international expansion and entry strategies (Tse, Pan, & Au 1997). For instance, the petroleum industry requires heavy investment and a large scale of operations, thus firms tend to seek partners to share costs and risks; whereas the information technology industry tends to have a smaller scale of operations and requires intellectual property protection. These firms require a high degree of control of their proprietary technology and, thus, a global strategy may better serve their needs. Information technology firms then are more likely to develop entry strategies, such as wholly owned subsidiaries, that can best protect proprietary information.

Similarly, the extent of entry and exit barriers can potentially constrain the type of entry strategies a firm adopts. Industries where heavy investment is required may present a major entry or exit barrier when considering expansion into a market or a change of entry strategies. For example, a joint venture between an Australian firm and a Chinese firm established in 1995 to produce light aircraft in Shanghai encountered major difficulties when the Asian crisis hit the market and caused sales to falter. In 1995, the market prospects for exporting light aircraft looked good and the products were considered competitive in terms of value and price. As the Asian economic meltdown developed, products from other Asian countries became far more price competitive due to their countries' currency devaluation. The change in currency values made products from this joint-venture plant very uncompetitive. The heavy investment in land, equipment, and other facilities created exit barriers for the Australian firm. Similarly, a joint venture between an Italian automaker and a Chinese automaker established to produce minivans ran into difficulties after the Asian crisis. The joint-venture plant had to be shut down due to low demand for its products, but the heavy up-front investment prohibited partners from withdrawing from the venture. This case suggests that understanding the interlinking variables of the scale of operations and the entry and exit barriers, and designing flexible entry strategies to anticipate environmental changes, is crucial for success in international markets. If these two firms had understood the potential impact of environmental determinants, they would not have locked themselves into joint ventures with large initial investments. Instead of setting up joint ventures, they could have used more flexible configurations, for example, non-equity strategic alliances. When the time is right, the firm could move to other options without incurring substantial costs. However, as different industries face different sets of variables and constraints, the process of internationalization cannot be generalized across industries (Turnbull 1987). Entry strategies should be aligned with the industry environment to ensure market entry success.

Firm Rivalry

The intensity of competition in a firm's own domestic and foreign markets tends to push firms to expand internationally. Empirical studies show that vigorous domestic rivalry is strongly associated with firms' foreign expansion strategies (Porter 1998). Such competition not only forces firms to sharpen advantages at home, but also pressures them to expand into international markets in order to grow. For example, when wine producers in France faced cutthroat competition at home and in Europe, they expanded their market into China, finding the Chinese wine market had great potential for further development. Similarly electric appliance firms (especially producers of TV sets) in China competed with one another for the lion's share of the domestic market by repeatedly reducing prices and yet they reaped only marginal profits. As a result, Haier Group Co. has aggressively pushed its products into the world market by establishing subsidiaries in many parts of the world and by registering its 516 trademarks in 128 countries and regions. Similarly, the strong rivalry in the computer industry forced firms including IBM and Hewlett-Packard to become more efficient and search for markets abroad (Porter 1998).

Furthermore, international competition can have a similar impact on domestic firms. A Swedish firm's entry into the American market forced Lincoln Electric to expand into the European market to protect its own backyard (Hastings 1999). The global expansion of the home appliance industry provides another good example. When AB Electrolux expanded into the American market, U.S. home appliance companies responded by expanding into different parts of the world. This international expansion served as way of dealing with greater global competition and an increasingly saturated home appliance market in their domestic market (Hunger 1990). Had Lincoln Electric understood how international firm rivalry would affect their business and had positioned themselves to challenge such competition by building up core capabilities for international markets over time, they might have avoided devastating failure abroad.

Factor Conditions

Factor endowment has always been considered as playing an important role in the competitive advantage of both nations and firms, although the role of factors is far more complex than what we normally understand (Porter 1998). To explore how factor conditions influence firms' entry strategies, one has to look at two geographical levels: national and global. National factor endowments allow firms to gain competitive advantages through efficient utilization of production inputs. Domestic industries grow as a result of an abundance of certain factors or are suppressed due to a lack of critical factors of production. At global or regional levels, factor endowment plays a similar role. Since the availability or unavailability of factors can either empower or constrain production, firm entry strategies must take factor endowments into consideration. Availability of skilled labor in a target market is also a crucial issue in entry-strategy decisions for industries that require labor-intensive production. For instance, electronics and textile firms prefer to establish wholly owned subsidiaries or joint ventures in foreign countries rather than export their products to where labor is abundant. Conversely, a lack of skilled labor may be an impediment to setting up wholly owned subsidiaries. High-technology companies may prefer direct exporting in the form of exclusive distribution to overcome a lack of skilled technicians and the potential loss of control of their proprietary technology. As skilled labor becomes more available, the more penetrating entry modes may become more attractive. For example, Western Electric first expanded into Japan by exporting through an export management company and then began to train Japanese technicians to handle their equipment. When Japanese laws allowed them to have equity investment in Japan, they turned their licensing agreement into a joint venture after adequate technical training was provided. As Western Electric understood how potential change in government policies could affect their business in Japan, it positioned itself to take advantage of the opportunities presented. Without realigning its entry strategies to account for host-country factor conditions, Western Electric would not have achieved market entry success in Japan.

Demand Conditions

Demand conditions and consumer behavior in the home country have great impact on the growth of industries and firms (Porter 1998). More important, demand conditions in foreign markets have a strong effect on a firm's entry strategies. The size of foreign markets determines the feasibility of gaining location economies and learning experience. Small markets may not warrant global strategic integration; however, these small markets may demand a high level of market responsiveness. Thus, firms may prefer servicing smaller markets by forming joint ventures or using licensing arrangements. As markets grow larger, entry strategies need to be revised to accommodate the new environment. In Western Electric's case, management did not initially view capital investments in Japan or China as a viable option. As demand increased due to governments' plans to invest in telecommunication systems, Western Electric developed joint ventures in these countries. From a domestic perspective, Western Electric utilized international expansion as a way to adjust production capacity during the business cycles in the domestic market. For instance, in order to maintain skilled workers during downturns in business cycles, Western Electric turned to international expansion as a solution (Butler 1999). This required Western Electric to adopt flexible entry strategies to allow for constant adjustment to their business cycle. Western Electric was successful in Japan and China because it achieved congruency between demand conditions and entry strategies.

The so-called herding phenomenon significantly swings the Chinese consumers and manufacturers' behavior. Consumers tend to look to their neighbors to keep up with trends. Chinese companies tend then to add capacity to take advantage of what they believe are attractive opportunities, often causing overcapacity. This behavior not only accelerates production adoption, but also shortens product life cycles (Yan 1998). Multinational corporations that have misaligned their strategies with demand conditions often find themselves either operating at overcapacity or missing the emerging opportunity. Under such circumstances, flexible entry strategies are of ultimate importance to allow these multinationals to gain control of their operations, make adjustments to maintain market share, and achieve profitability.

Related and Supporting Industries

The last set of environmental variables is related and supporting industries. The existence of related and supporting industries is closely associated with firms' ability to grow and thrive, for instance, truck trailer sales depend on the availability of intercity highways (Yan 1998). In the last two decades, the firms that successfully expanded internationally came from industries that had strong support from related industries, for example, auto makers supported by the tire industry and other parts producers; or the home appliance industry supported by steel, aluminum, and computer industries (Porter 1998). China is in flux and undergoing change in terms of supporting industry and infrastructure. Today, the highway system, almost nonexistent ten years ago, is sprawling across many major cities. As a result, the company that sells truck trailers had to use a different entry strategy ten years ago than the one it employs today. Companies with long-term vision that also use adaptable strategies will be able to take advantage of the changing environment in China.

From the above analysis, we derive the following three implications:

Implication 1: Firms will be likely to achieve market entry success when there is congruency between entry strategies and the environment.

Implication 2: Firms will be likely to achieve congruency if they employ adaptable entry strategies.

Implication 3: Firms with adaptable entry strategies will be more likely to achieve market entry success than those with static entry strategies.

Implications and Conclusions

Implications for Multinational Corporations in China

China's 1.2 billion population and fast economic growth has been a magnet for multinational corporations, but the results for multinational corporations have been mixed, as illustrated by some of the above cases. Although the China market is attractive in many ways, it is turbulent; there is no insurance against failure. As the case studies in this chapter have demonstrated, successful firms were those that learned to adapt their entry strategies to the changing environment as government policy evolved and market conditions changed.

Firms should constantly review their strategies and make necessary adjustments to accommodate change. When forming joint ventures, firms must be able to exit if incurring exorbitant costs. Firms should consider the option of using other forms of operations simultaneously to avoid being restricted to unattractive arrangements.

The new model suggested by this chapter provides a useful perspective on the analysis of entry strategies in China. It suggests that it is critical to view entry strategy development as a dynamic and ongoing process, rather than a static and singular event. Given the extraordinarily high costs associated with a poorly designed entry strategy, firms should design entry strategies as "flexible open systems" to allow for changes in the environment and to facilitate a maximum fit and alignment between the environment and their resources.

In order to develop effective entry strategies, firms can develop a more holistic approach by incorporating Porter's expanded diamond factors, corporate competitive strategies, and firms' core characteristics. In order to allow for simultaneous shaping and alignment, firms need to look beyond the traditional entry modes to design more flexible and adaptable entry strategies. The key is to develop entry strategies that are congruent with the environment and that allow for simultaneous adaptation.

Implications for Future Research

This chapter also provides implications for future research on entry strategies and the internationalization process. Researchers must recognize the dynamic process of market entry and treat entry strategies as "open systems," developing them as part of an evolving and ongoing process. Considerable research is also needed on the evolution of entry strategies over time. Future studies can incorporate the refined Porter's diamond variables in their analysis of entry strategies and better define "fit" between entry strategies and environment. Empirical studies are needed to test the interaction among environmental variables and entry strategies and to determine how environmental variables affect entry strategies.

References

Agarwal, S. and S.N. Ramaswami. 1992. "Choice of Foreign Market Entry Mode: Impact of Ownership, Location, and Internalization Factors." *Journal of International Business Studies* 23, no. 1: 1–27.

Anderson, O. 1993. "On the Internationalization Process of Firms: A Critical Analysis." *Journal of International Business Studies* 24, no. 2: 209–231.

Anderson, E. and A.T. Coughlan. 1987. "International Market Entry Mode and Expansion Via Independent or Integrated Channels of Distribution." *Journal of Marketing* 51, no. 1: 71–82.

Anderson, E. and H. Gatignon. 1986. "Modes of Foreign Entry: A Transaction Cost Analysis and Propositions." *Journal of International Business Studies* 17: 1–26.

Buckley, P. and M. Casson. 1998. "Analyzing Foreign Market Entry Strategies: Extending the Internationalization Approach." *Journal of International Business Studies* 29, no. 3: 539–562.

Butler, O. 1999. "An American Firm Abroad: Western Electric's Adventures in Asia." Center for Asian Business Studies lecture series, University of Queensland.

Contractor, F. and S. Kundu. 1998. "Modal Choice in a World of Alliances: Analyzing Organizational Forms in the International Hotel Sector." *Journal of International Business Studies* 29, no. 2: 325–358.

Denis, J.E. and D. Depelteau. 1985. "Market Knowledge and Export Expansion." *Journal of International Business Studies* 16, no. 3: 77–98.

Erramilli, M. K. and C. P. Rao. 1993. "Service Firms' International Entry Mode Choice: A Modified Transaction–Cost Approach." *Journal of Marketing* 57: 19–38.

Franko, L. 1989. "Use of Minority and 50–50 Joint Ventures by United States Multinationals during 1970: The Interaction of Host country Policies and Corporate Strategies." *Journal of International Business Studies* 20, no. 1:19–40.

Hastings, D.F. 1999. Lincoln Electric's Harsh Lessons from International Expansion. *Harvard Business Review* 77, no. 3: 162–178.

Hennart, J.F. 1989. "Can the New Forms of Investment Substitute for the Old Forms: A Transaction Cost Perspective." *Journal of International Business Studies* 20, no. 2: 211–234.

Hunger, D.J. 1990. "The Major Home Appliance Industry in 1990: From U.S. to Global." Midwest Society for Case Research.

Johanson, H. and J. Vahlne. 1977. "The Internationalization Process of the Firm—A Model of Knowledge Development and Increasing Foreign Market Commitments." *Journal of International Business Studies* 8, no. 1: 23–32.

Leung, L. 1995. "For China's Foreign Investors the Door Marked Exit Can Be a Tight Squeeze." *Wall Street Journal*, February 21, 1991, B1.

Lincoln, Y.S. and E.G. Guba. 1985. *Naturalistic Inquiry*. Beverly Hills: Sage: London.

Milliman, J., M.A. Von Glinow, and M. Nathan. 1991. "Organisational Life Cycles and Strategic International Human Resource Management in Multinational Companies: Implications for Congruence Theory." *Academy of Management Review* 16, no. 2: 318–339.

Morgan, Gareth. 1986. *Images of Organization*. Sage: London.

Nadler, D. and M.L. Tushman. 1980. "A Congruence Model for Diagnosing Organizational Behavior." In R. Miles (ed.), *Resource Book in Macro Organisational Behaviour*. Santa Clara, CA: Goodyear, pp. 30–49.

Osborn, R.N. and C.C. Baughn. 1990. "Forms of Interorganizational Governance for Multinational Alliances." *Academy of Management Journal* 33, no. 3: 503–519.

Porter, M. 1998. *Competitive Advantage of Nations: With a New Introduction by the Author*. London: Macmillan Business.

Root, F.R. 1987. *Entry Strategies for International Markets*. Lexington, MA: Lexington Books, D.C. Heath.

Rugman, A.M. and A. Verbeke. 1993. "How to Operationalise Porter's Diamond of International Competitiveness." *International Executive* 35, no. 4: 283–299.

Tse, D.K., Y.G. Pan, and K.Y. Au. 1997. "How MNCs Choose Entry Modes and Form Alliances: The China Experience." *Journal of International Business Studies*, 28, no. 4: 779–804.

Turnbull, P.W. 1987. "A Challenge to the Stages Theory of the Internationalization Process." In Stanley D. Reid and Philip J. Rosson (eds.), *Managing Export Entry and Expansion*. New York: Praeger.

Welch, L.S. and R. Luostarinen. 1988. "Internationalization: Evaluation of a Concept." *Journal of General Management* 14, no. 2: 34–55.

Yan, R. 1998. "Short-Term Results: The Litmus Test for Success in China." *Harvard Business Review* 76, no. 5: 61–75.

Yin, R.K. 1989. *Case Study Research*, 2nd ed. Beverly Hills: Sage.

15

Taiwan's Recent Economy and Business Environment

Elizabeth Chu

1. Introduction

Taiwan has a small geographic area and limited natural resources. It is one-sixth of the size of Missouri. Three-quarters of its land is mountainous, and only one-quarter of the land is arable. Agricultural production accounted for only 2.5 percent of real gross domestic product (GDP) in 1999. Although Taiwan does have deposits of coal, limestone, marble, and natural gas, it is not richly endowed by nature. More than 90 percent of its energy needs are met by imports aHnd its rapid industrialization has relied heavily on imports of raw materials. However, Taiwan with a population of 23 million has an ample supply of human resources.

Taiwan has shown remarkable economic growth for the past several years. This chapter briefly discusses Taiwan's recent remarkable economic performance and future challenges.

2. Economic Performance in 1999

Despite being hit by a strong earthquake, the worst ever recorded, Taiwan's economy still surpassed its targeted annual growth rate to grow by 5.7 percent. Its growth rate stands more than 6 percent in 2000. Taiwan's per capita GNP ranked twenty-fifth among economies worldwide, while its foreign exchange reserves were the third largest in the world. It is also the world's fourteenth largest trading country.

2.1 Trade

Taiwan's exports in 1999 rose 10 percent from 1998 to US$121.59 billion. As Taiwan's and Asia's economies continued their recoveries from the financial difficulties of recent years, imports to Taiwan rose by 5.8 percent to US$110.69 billion. Leading Taiwan's booming export growth was its competitiveness, global demand for new economy goods, and its domination of global production in key sectors such as foundry and contract manufacturing.

Industrial production, which has steadily increased as a share of Taiwan's exports, accounted for 98.4 percent of total exports in 1999. Taiwan's information technology production is the third highest in the world behind that of the United States and Japan.

For imports, since Taiwan has few natural resources, more than 60 percent of its total imports consist of agricultural and industrial raw materials. On the other hand, because of rising income and liberalizing economic progress in Taiwan, total imports of consumer goods grew steadily. However, due to the dampening effect of the powerful earthquake of September 1999, the share of consumer goods produced fell, while capital goods rose from 23.27 percent to 26.47 percent.

2.2 Trading Partner

The increasing trend toward regional economic integration, Taiwan's trade with countries of the Asia-Pacific region has been steadily increasing, and its trade and economic ties with those countries have been strengthening.

The United States is Taiwan's largest export destination. Taiwan exported US$35.2 billion in goods to the United States in 1999, a 6.3 percent increase over 1998. Taiwan imported US$19.1 billion worth of goods from the United States, a 5.3 percent increase over 1998. The United States is Taiwan's second largest import supplier. In general, Taiwan is the seventh largest trading partner of the United States.

Taiwan is the largest consumer of U.S. agricultural products worldwide in terms of per capita consumption. Taiwan imports apples, cherries, broccoli, pork, turkeys, corn, grapes, soybeans, potatoes, beef, dairy products, oranges, grapefruit, and sunflower oil, among other products. In addition to these imports, Taiwan is the seventh largest market for U.S.

medical equipment, and ninth largest market for U.S.-made vehicles.

Upon Taiwan's accession to the WTO, its tariffs on agricultural products will be cut from 20.6 percent to 14.1 percent in the first year after Taiwan joins. For industrial products, tariffs will be cut from 6.52 percent to 4.9 percent by 2002. WTO accession will make Taiwan's market more efficient in terms of trade.

2.3 Foreign Direct Investment

Foreign direct investment (FDI) plays an important role in the process of Taiwan's economic development, and the transfer of technology and broadening of markets that accompany such investment have made a vital contribution to the industrialization of Taiwan's economy.

Taiwan has attracted quite a lot of investment from overseas Chinese and foreign nationals. Taiwan's investment environment has been ranked one of the top countries in terms of risk, according to the Business Environment Risk Intelligence of Switzerland in its April 2000 report. Taiwan was placed first in economic growth, second in attitude toward foreign investors and profits, and third in the remittance and repatriation of capital.

Foreign investment in Taiwan is made mostly in the telecommunications industry, about 40 percent of the total foreign investment. This symbolizes Taiwan's telecommunications industry has been liberalized and drawn attention. Among all the foreign investors in Taiwan, U.S. companies have been a major player. Since 1952, U.S. investment in Taiwan has had a value of US$10.3 billion, accounting for 25.2 percent of total foreign investment in Taiwan.

Meanwhile rising prices of land and labor, growing environmental concerns, and an inadequacy of public facilities have sharply raised the production costs of Taiwan's traditional light-industrial manufactures, eroding their ability to compete with producers in the developing countries of the Asia-Pacific region. Many of these enterprises have responded by shifting their operations to lower-cost areas overseas. With the outward flow of investment, Taiwan has become a net exporter of capital. The amount of Taiwan's foreign direct investment in 1999 was US$5.2billion, making it the fourth largest foreign investor in Asia and the sixteenth largest worldwide. Forty-two percent of the investment went to the United States and about 35 percent to the PRC.

3. Taiwan's Challenge in the New Millennium

Post-earthquake reconstruction is expected to stimulate public and private investment, and should be a major driving force behind Taiwan's economic growth over the next few years.

In addition, Taiwan's 2000 presidential election has demonstrated democratic and peaceful transition of power. President Chen believes that the interests of the people is above those of any political party or individual. His policy goals are to build a modern, efficient government in Taiwan, to improve the domestic investment environment, and to allow economic development to move toward full liberalization and internationalization with fair competition.

Nonetheless, political and economic relations between Taiwan and the People's Republic of China will affect not only East Asia but also the United States and Taiwan. Under the precondition of its own national security and overall benefit, Taiwan would work to integrate the advantages of both sides of the Taiwan Straits.

Taiwan certainly would like to achieve a mutually beneficial, win-win situation if it receives a friendly response from the PRC. The continuing intimidation of Taiwan by the PRC would work against the achievement of a peaceful environment beneficial for the economies of both Taiwan and the PRC.

While on the threshold of accession to the WTO, both sides of the Taiwan Straits should demonstrate wisdom and patience in resolving the political deadlock for the sake of world peace and development.

16

Opportunities and Challenges for Hong Kong in the New Millennium

Raymond Fan

Hong Kong's Business Environment

Since 1998, Hong Kong has reduced the cost of doing business in the territory and also reformed its financial markets by strengthening its monetary system and adopting various financial reform packages. These include the opening up of the banking sector to more foreign competition and the merger and demutualization of the securities and futures markets. The Growth Enterprise Market was launched and the groundwork for various infrastructure facilities including the Science Park and the Cyberport was laid for Hong Kong to take full advantage of the new economy. Hong Kong continues to open up its telecommunications and broadcasting sectors and will see the development of a Disneyland theme park, scheduled to open in 2005.

During a recent visit in the fall of 1999, an International Monetary Fund (IMF) Staff Mission affirmed that Hong Kong's economy has recovered strongly, and the mission was upbeat about Hong Kong's economic performance this year. It forecast a 9.5 percent GDP growth for 2000, based on strong external demand. The mission projected that growth would moderate to 4 percent in 2001, reflecting partly the dissipation of the low-base effect and partly a relatively modest growth in consumption and weak investment. External demand was expected to remain strong in 2001, especially in light of better prospects for mainland China.

The mission was also supportive of the existing monetary and financial policy framework in Hong Kong, including the linked exchange rate structure, the fiscal policy, and the financial supervisory framework. It noted that Hong Kong's prudent banking practices, strong legal institutions, and effective supervision had enabled the banking system to weather the turbulence of the Asian crisis. The IMF mission also praised the upgrading of the securities regulation and financial infrastructure, including the recent merger of exchanges and clearinghouses, the proposed introduction of deposit insurance, and the move to more risk-based supervision of banks. It commended the authorities' recent efforts to raise corporate transparency and catalyze the establishment of a commercial credit reference agency.

With the economy continuing to grow, there is a return of business confidence and optimism in the market place. *The 2000 Business Outlook Survey* published by the American Chamber of Commerce (AmCham) in Hong Kong in early December showed a positive medium-term outlook for the year 2001. The survey also indicated that Hong Kong will remain the region's commercial hub and preferred location of regional headquarters of AmCham members. The fact that most AmCham member companies plan to maintain their regional headquarter and expand their operations in Hong Kong will further entrench Hong Kong's position as a regional financial and business service hub.

Similarly, UK companies in Hong Kong have also expressed confidence in the city's economy, according to a survey by the British Chamber of Commerce in Hong Kong. The survey showed that the majority of British businesses were satisfied with the standards of communications, the infrastructure, the free-port status, and the taxation system in Hong Kong.

The Asian Development Bank, in its *Asian Development Outlook for 2000*, released in September 2000, said Hong Kong's GDP should grow 8.5 percent in 2000 and 8.8 percent in 2001. The predicted high growth was based on strong external demand and strengthening private consumption.

In fact, Hong Kong's recovery was more robust than any of the projections. Hong Kong's economy has staged a strong turnaround since the onset of the Asian financial crisis in 1998. Hong Kong's economy was expected to grow by 10 percent in 2000. The forecast growth rate was raised from 8.5 percent following a growth rate of 10.4 percent in the third quarter of 2000. Combined with a growth of 14.2 percent in the first quarter and 10.9 percent in the second quarter of 2000, GDP grew 11.7 percent for the first three quarters of 2000 compared with growth a year earlier.

Hong Kong has retained its title as the world's freest economy for the seventh consecutive year in the Heritage Foundation's *2001 Index of Economic Freedom*, ranking first of 161 economies. The foundation said Hong Kong Special Administrative Region (HKSAR) spending had increased but inflation had declined, allowing its index score to remain unchanged. Hong Kong has topped the rankings since the Heritage Foundation first published its index in 1995.

HKSAR government chief executive Tung Chee Hwa said the rating signified the confidence of the international community in Hong Kong, adding that economic freedom has been a fundamental driving force for the territory's success.

The rating showed Hong Kong had a free and competitive market in which individual firms competed on their own strength in a challenging environment without government intervention. Thus the HKSAR government will not depart from the free-market principles and policies that have underpinned Hong Kong's success.

Indeed, Hong Kong's Basic Law sets out in considerable detail the social and economic policies Hong Kong is obliged to follow as a Special Administrative Region. The rule of law, an independent judiciary, a level playing field for all who do business, low taxes (corporate tax is only 16 percent and personal tax a maximum of 15 percent), and a commitment to free and open markets are all spelled out in the Basic Law. So, too, is the free flow of information, including a free press, and a clean administration. These all form part of Hong Kong's open and pluralistic society, which functions exceptionally well under the unique concept of "one country, two systems."

China's Accession to WTO: Hong Kong's Role

The granting of Permanent Normal Trade Relations (PNTR) status to China in September 2000 by the U.S. Senate was welcomed in Hong Kong. A study by the Hong Kong General Chamber of Commerce (HKGCC) showed bullish sentiments about the continued key role of Hong Kong after China enters the WTO. The study "China's Entry into the WTO and its Impact on Hong Kong Business" showed that Hong Kong will continue to play a key role, specifically as a logistics hub, a financial hub, and a digital hub.

China's WTO accession carries two important messages. First, it reinforces globalization of the world economy on which Hong Kong must leverage if the HKSAR is to maintain its position as a world-class trade and business center. Second, in order to seize the vast opportunities ahead, Hong Kong has to further develop and secure its role as a strategic partner not just to the mainland but also between the mainland and the rest of the world.

The mainland has been Hong Kong's largest trading partner since 1985, accounting for nearly 40 percent of total trade. About 90 percent of Hong Kong's re-export trade is mainland related (US$136 billion in 1999), and Hong Kong has been the largest external investor on the mainland for many years. At the end of 1999, Hong Kong's direct investment there amounted to US$156 billion, accounting for 51 percent of the mainland's total.

Hong Kong has often been described as the gateway to China. It is estimated that as a result of China's WTO accession, Hong Kong's re-export trade, involving the movement of goods to and from the mainland through Hong Kong, will be considerably boosted. Hong Kong's annual GDP growth rate will be raised by somewhere between one-half and one percent—that is, from a trend growth rate of 4 to 5 percent going up to 4.5 to 5.5 percent.

China's accession to the WTO will see increased competition and many multinationals will deal directly with the mainland. However, Hong Kong remains a unique place—politically, economically, geographically, and constitutionally. It has free and open markets, the rule of law, an independent judiciary, a level playing field for business, and a low and simple tax system: it also has freedom of speech and a free and unfettered flow of news and information, which is vital in today's global business environment.

The opening up of the mainland's services to foreign participation will provide Hong Kong companies with the opportunity to establish or consolidate their foothold in the mainland's lucrative services markets including banking, securities, insurance, tourism, distribution, and professional services. The outlook is that in the near term these sectors will be considerably boosted—and enriched—by the Chinese enterprises that are seeking to upgrade their capabilities and by governance methods to handle expanded business activities and meet foreign competition.

For Hong Kong to secure a strategic partnership with the mainland, the SAR must be able to leverage on its distinct advantages over other global players to capitalize on the opportunities presented by China's accession into the WTO. Hong Kong businessmen share a common language and culture with their counterparts on the mainland. They have a very profound knowledge of the mainland business landscape and a great deal of practical experience working with it. They also enjoy proximity and have well-established connections.

Hong Kong companies will continue to play an important intermediary function in sourcing and marketing mainland products. And given its long experience in China business, Hong Kong companies will be the ideal joint-venture partners for foreign investors, especially small- and medium-sized enterprises wishing to enter the China market. It is also likely that this role will develop gradually from one of intermediary to one of proprietor, as more and more opportunities are offered to Hong Kong investors by the further liberalization of China's economy.

Aside from playing an intermediary role, there are also other extraordinary opportunities for Hong Kong, including roles as an equity-raising hub; a regional headquarters hub; a center for mainland companies to expand internationally; a multimodal logistics hub; and a source of professional services for the mainland.

As a leading financial center in the region, Hong Kong naturally assumes the role of a major capital-raising center for China. Many mainland enterprises are expected to come to Hong Kong to raise capital for expansion and reform to meet the challenges and opportunities arising from WTO accession. There is also an increasing proportion of activities based on equity raising for local, mainland, and foreign companies. This role—which embraces private equity-finance and venture-capital activities—is inherently highly skill-intensive and will draw heavily on the depth and breadth of Hong Kong's legal, regulatory, and equities research, and financial engineering skills. As the role of equity intermediation grows in the coming years, Hong Kong's financial-services sector will be even more substantial and dynamic than it is today.

As mainland China moves to align herself with the rules and regulations of WTO, the need for professionals—whether they are accountants, lawyers, architects, or surveyors —will be enormous. Hong Kong has an abundance of quality professionals who will welcome new opportunities to participate in the growing demand on the mainland as China enters the WTO. Hong Kong's strengths stem from its position as a specialized service economy—the clustering of headquarters and headquarters-related services, its international capital-markets capability, its role as a transportation hub, and its expertise in global trading and logistics.

Hong Kong's private sector has also established good corporate governance and assumes a leading role in business deals in the region. Professional and business service providers of information technology, telecommunications, and legal, accounting, logistics and other consultancy services are bountiful in Hong Kong.

As more mainland companies begin to explore opportunities to go international, Hong Kong will play an indispensable role in enabling them to raise international capital, to develop focused strategies for targeting foreign acquisitions, and to build a prominent presence in foreign markets. In the coming decade, as more and more small- and medium-sized mainland Chinese enterprises seek opportunities to export effectively and profitably to the rest of the world, Hong Kong's clustering of global trading intermediation skills, its strength as a center for trade and finance, and above all else, its unique strengths as a logistics and fulfillment hub, will help these thousands of companies to capture export opportunities worldwide.

The conventional wisdom is that in anticipation of WTO accession, a number of multinational corporations will relocate their operations to the mainland or elsewhere in the region. The fact is that the number of regional headquarters and offices in Hong Kong has increased from 2,500 in 1999 to about 3,000 in 2000—an increase of 20 percent. The latest survey by AmCham indicates that most AmCham member companies are maintaining their regional headquarters and expanding their operations in Hong Kong.

Hong Kong's role as a headquarters hub will be broadened to address the needs of thousands of overseas medium-sized companies that aspire to go international and particularly to go into China. The tidal wave of smaller and less internationally experienced companies—the thousands of substantial companies that populate middle America and the European equivalents of Germany's *mittelstand* companies—will be seeking a headquarters location or strategic partner in Hong Kong to explore the unfolding opportunities on the mainland.

Through Hong Kong, they will be able to enter the mainland market with its huge population and expanding purchasing power. They can form strategic partnerships with Hong Kong medium-sized companies with knowledge and experience in making business deals on the mainland and knowing what kind of products the mainland market demands. Together they can enter the mainland market and be successful.

Hong Kong's hinterland—the Pearl River Delta—is growing at a dynamic pace. Over the past few years, manufacturing activities in the

Pearl River Delta have continued to expand, and there is also an increasing trend to move into high-tech sectors. More and more companies of international standing are undertaking activities in the region. The strengths of Hong Kong as a business center and the strengths of the Pearl River Delta as a manufacturing base are complementary, with a lot of room for collaboration between the two places.

As the richest region in China, Guangdong and the Pearl River Delta region will present a most attractive consumer market to both Hong Kong and other overseas companies wishing to sell their products on the mainland. As the economy of the Pearl River Delta and the entire Guangdong province continue to expand, the need for infrastructure development—whether railways, power generation and transmission, port facilities, facilities for tourism—can lead to attractive investment opportunities for Hong Kong and overseas companies alike. Thus, following the entry of China into the WTO, the formation of the regional economy shared by Hong Kong and the Pearl River Delta will gather faster momentum.

Hong Kong has enormous potential as a multimodal logistics hub. As China's trade with the rest of the world accelerates, Hong Kong faces unprecedented opportunities to intermediate this trade physically. As the total volume of exports and imports to and from China increases, the goods purchased will still need to travel from the factory to the store or to the supermarket shelf—and Hong Kong has a unique convergence of strengths to manage this movement and act as a fulfillment center for this anticipated surge in trade.

This is not something that Hong Kong will be able to make a success of on its own. The Pearl River Delta will develop into a globally significant "logistics region," combining the complementary strengths of Hong Kong, Guangzhou, Shenzhen, Zhuhai, Macau, and other dynamic townships in the delta; providing truly multimodal capabilities; and combining land, sea, rail and air transport to ensure that cargoes reach their destination with a seamlessness that will be hard to match anywhere else in the world.

This can be evidenced in its embryonic stage by a new service provided through Hong Kong International Airport at Chek Lap Kok where an exporter from any city in the United States can now have his cargo delivered on a single airway bill to a destination anywhere in China. On arrival by air in Hong Kong, and without the need for customs clearance there, the cargo is shuttled in a high-speed truck directly to Guangzhou's

Baiyun Airport, where it clears customs, and can then be delivered in the region or flown to another mainland city by a mainland carrier. The reverse flow is obviously entirely feasible.

Similarly, with high-speed cargo ferry services linking Chek Lap Kok directly with fourteen river ports along the Pearl River Delta expected to start operation in early 2001, factories on the western side of the Pearl River Delta will be able to deliver their cargoes to Chek Lap Kok in less than an hour. Such innovative, multimodal logistics services will benefit factories throughout the Pearl River Delta and will serve to strengthen Hong Kong as the best possible hub through which to conduct trade. The same, of course, has been applicable for the container-shipping sector—Hong Kong is already the largest container port in the world.

Since mainland China went ahead with reform and an open-door policy in 1978, Hong Kong businesses have been actively involved in investment and trade in the coastal provinces, developing external trade with local enterprises. Hong Kong is the largest direct investor in the mainland, as mentioned earlier, accounting for 51 percent of the country's foreign direct investment.

Hong Kong businessmen and investors have established a foothold on the mainland that is not restricted to the prosperous coastal regions like the Pearl River Delta and big cities like Beijing and Shanghai. They are also present in the developing inner and western provinces. These so-called second-tier markets accounted for 60 percent (US$111 billion) of the mainland's imports last year. Hong Kong is also the largest foreign investor in the western region.

The opening of the western region of mainland China will set in motion a series of related enterprise reforms and market-opening measures. Hong Kong is experienced in international capital financing and able to provide a wide variety of financial services. Its efficient market and monitoring mechanisms as well as its prudent banking sector can provide effective capital financing services to the western region.

Hong Kong can form an ideal strategic partnership by combining the western region's good technological infrastructures and research talents with Hong Kong's strength in financial skills, rich international marketing experience, and access to high technology. The HKSAR government strongly supports the country's long-term strategy of western development, which is instrumental in advancing national development and prosperity.

Policy Issues Important to the Development of Hong Kong

The HKSAR government recognizes that it bears the responsibility for providing leadership in terms of facilitating communication between Hong Kong and the central government, in gaining a clear understanding of how the policies of the mainland regarding WTO accession will be implemented, and in ensuring that the Hong Kong business sector has access to opportunities which flow from these policies.

On a more micro scale, Hong Kong is undertaking a number of measures to facilitate taking advantage of the opportunities and challenges presented. These include upgrading the educational system to train a generation of people with the knowledge, skills, and right attitudes necessary to take on these challenges.

The HKSAR government will spend an extra US$256.41 million on education reforms and initiatives, which will allow, among other things, essentially all junior secondary graduates to continue to study and 60 percent of senior secondary graduates to go on to tertiary education, with appropriate subsidies in both cases. These reform programs will need time to take effect, and there is going to be a careful but determined move in all spheres of activity when they relate to education.

Aside from education reforms, there is also a need to adopt an immigration policy, which attracts top quality people to work and live in Hong Kong. Effective November 1, 2000, the overseas residential requirement for overseas Chinese nationals entering Hong Kong for employment will be relaxed from two years to one. There is a need to relax the requirements that were formulated in 1990, so Hong Kong can more effectively compete with other countries and regions for quality employees. The change will allow more overseas Chinese nationals with valid People's Republic of China (PRC) passports to come to Hong Kong to help spur the economic development of Hong Kong.

Hong Kong will continue to adhere to the principle that admission will be granted only to those who possess skills, knowledge, or experience valuable to, but not readily available in, Hong Kong, and who are offered a remuneration package broadly comparable to the market rate. Applicants need to meet these requirements and to have resided outside their home country for at least one year before their applications are submitted.

To attract and retain top-quality people to the territory, the HKSAR government will continue to improve its environment to ensure that the quality of life is one of the best anywhere. Hong Kong is on track to meet the targets on reducing air pollution, as announced in 1999's Policy Address, through an aggressive air quality program. Hong Kong is now the first city in Asia to use ultra-low sulfur diesel, replacing its entire fleet of 18,000 diesel taxis with LPG vehicles. Aside from the diesel taxi replacement program to be completed by the end of 2005, there is a diesel light-bus replacement program to replace 6,000 diesel light buses with cleaner-fuel vehicles.

Since September 2000, the HKSAR government has been providing financial assistance to owners of pre-Euro light-diesel vehicles to retrofit their vehicles with particulate traps. Starting January 1, 2001, Hong Kong upgraded the requirement for all new vehicles to meet the Euro III emission standard.

Hong Kong will also cut respirable particulates from the present vehicle fleet by 60 percent by 2003 and 80 percent by 2005. Vehicle nitrogen oxide emissions will be reduced by 30 percent by 2005.

Hong Kong is also working with the Guangdong authorities to coordinate efforts in six key areas of environmental protection: improvement of air quality in the region; improvement of water quality; exchange of experiences on planning and sustainable development; improvement of water quality in the Dongjiang; conservation and other areas concerning environmental protection and sustainable development.

A consultant will complete a study in the first quarter of 2001, to trace sources of air pollution in the region. Both the Hong Kong and Guangdong province governments will then work together to tackle the problem.

The first stage of the strategic sewage treatment and disposal work is nearing completion, and the HKSAR government is now reviewing the second and third stage of sewage disposal treatment to assess its compatibility with Hong Kong's future needs.

The HKSAR government launched a "Clean Hong Kong" program at the end of 2000, as part of an effort to bring about visible and sustainable improvements on the ground through both active cleansing operations and public education and publicity efforts. The Clean Hong Kong program will last for three years and comprise four key elements. These include stepping up enforcement action against littering and dumping of waste; enhancing the effectiveness of existing laws against littering and dumping; joint efforts with local organizations to secure noticeable improvement on the ground; and public education and publicity programs to reinforce public commitment to a cleaner Hong Kong.

The HKSAR government announced the "Digital 21 Information Technology (IT) Strategy" in November 1998. "Digital 21" is a comprehensive strategy to enhance and promote Hong Kong's information infrastructure and services so as to make Hong Kong a leading digital city in the globally connected world of the twenty-first century. A broad range of initiatives has been identified and will be implemented within a specific time frame to achieve the objective of the strategy.

A key component in implementing this strategy is the development of a regulatory framework that can support and encourage the development of electronic transactions—within Hong Kong and internationally —and the provision of a secure environment in which to conduct electronic transactions. Hong Kong has established a local public key infrastructure (PKI) based on the use of digital signatures to facilitate the development of IT and e-commerce.

The government just launched the first phase of the electronic service delivery (ESD) scheme in early December 1999. Through ESD, the public will be able to obtain government services in a seamless manner under a citizen-centered approach twenty-four hours a day and seven days a week. The public can now access over sixty types of public services, including payment of government fees, submission of tax returns, voter registrations, renewal of driving and vehicle licenses, and change of personal addresses through a single portal. New services will be added from time to time.

The Cyberport project is an information infrastructure project, which aims to create a strategic cluster of leading information technology (IT) and information services (IS) companies and a critical mass of professional talent in Hong Kong. The objectives of the project include heightening the local awareness of IT, creating an international multimedia and information services center, and consolidating Hong Kong's position as an information and technology hub.

Built on roughly twenty-six hectares of reclaimed land at Telegraph Bay in Pok Fu Lam of Hong Kong Island, the Cyberport development will comprise a mix of offices and residential, commercial, and recreational facilities to support a professional community. The project will be completed in three phases, by early 2002, by the end of 2002, and by the end of 2003.

Upon full development, the Cyberport will be able to accommodate about thirty medium- and large-sized companies and one hundred small-sized companies. To date, more than two hundred companies have registered an interest in becoming Cyberport tenants. Fifteen leading IT and IS companies have signed letters of intent to become anchor tenants. These include Cisco Systems, CMGI, Hewlett-Packard, Hikari Tsushin, Hua Wei, IBM, Legend, Microsoft, Oracle, Pacific Convergence Corporation, Portal, Silicon Graphics, Softbank, Sybase, and Yahoo!

Conclusion

Building on its past success and through prudent policies aimed at the new economy, Hong Kong has steadfastly held on to its status as the prime business location in Asia. The combination of the government's determination to ensure a free economy and its commitment to provide a focused development of its business infrastructure, Hong Kong will continue to be a key player in the development of Asian and also global markets.

Editors and Contributors

The Editors

Hung-Gay Fung is Y.S. Tsiang Professor of Chinese Studies in the College of Business Administration, University of Missouri-St. Louis.

Kevin H. Zhang is Associate Professor, Department of Economics, Illinois State University.

The Contributors

Wang Guo An is Professor, College of Business, Hangzhou Institute of Electronic Engineering, China.

Kam C. Chan is Associate Professor of Finance, University of Dayton.

Gene Hsin Chang is Professor in Department of Economics, the University of Toledo.

Elizabeth Chu is Director General, Taipei Economic & Cultural Office in Kansas City, Missouri.

Louis T.W. Cheng is Associate Professor of Finance, Department of Business Studies, Hong Kong Polytechnic University, Hong Kong.

Jianjun Du is Assistant Professor of International Business, University of Houston–Victoria.

Raymond Fan is Director Hong Kong Economic & Trade Office in New York, NY.

Joseph K.W. Fung is Associate Professor of Finance, Department of Decision Sciences and Finance, Hong Kong Baptist University, Hong Kong.

Jack W. Hou is Professor in the Department of Economics, California State University.

Martin Hovey is a Lecturer in School of Accounting and Finance, Griffith University, Australia.

Seung H. Kim is Professor and Director, Boeing Institute of International Business, Department of International Business, John Cook School of Business, Saint Louis University.

Wai-Kin Leung is an Associate Professor at the Faculty of Business Administration, the Chinese University of Hong Kong, Hong Kong.

Wai Chung Lo is Professor in the Economic Department, the Open University of Hong Kong.

Changhong Pei is Professor, Chinese Academy of Social Sciences.

George M. Puia is Dow Chemical Company Centennial Chair in Global Business, College of Business and Management, Saginaw Valley State University.

Murray Weidenbaum is Chairman, Center for the Study of American Business, Washington University.

Xiaoqing Eleanor Xu, is Assistant Professor of Finance, School of Business and Administration, Saint Louis University.

Xiaohua Yang is Assistant Professor, School of Business, Bond University, Australia.

Hongxin Zhao is Associate Professor of International Business, Boeing Institute of International Business, Department of International Business, John Cook School of Business, Saint Louis University.

Index

Accounting regulations, stock market, 100
Agarwal, S., 270
Agricultural Bank of China (ABC), 14, 15, 39, 40, 64, 68
Agricultural Development Bank of China (ADBC), 44, 68
Air pollution, 263
Aizenman, Joshua, 228
Akaike information criterion (AIC), 240
Aliber, Robert Z., 220, 230
All-China Federation of Industry and Commerce, 44
Allen, F., 11
American depository receipts (ADRs), 13
Ampalavanar-Brown, Rajeswary, 223
An, Wang Guo, 269–284
Andersen, T.G., 102
Anderson, E., 269, 270
Appropriability theory, 220
Arestis, P., 57, 59
Arnott, R., 70
A shares
comparison with H-share market, 145–149
daily returns of, 150t
defined, 10
denominated in Chinese currency, 117, 118
market segmentation/integration and, 101–14, 130, 131
over-the-counter derivatives, 101
ownership structure and, 151, 152–153t
price differentials for, 11, 99–100, 117–134

A shares *(continued)*
structure and characteristics of, 143t
trading volume of, 154–155t
Ash, Robert, 165
Asian crisis period
currency plunge in, 20, 22f, 23–24
economic indicators in, 21t
joint ventures in, 277–278
Asian Development Bank, 290
Asset-management companies (AMCs), 15, 49–50
Au, Kevin Y., 229, 270, 277
Autoregressive integrated moving average (ARIMA), 234, 239, 240–241

Bai, C.E., 58
Bailey, W., 11, 99, 116, 117, 149
Balassa, Bela, 220
Baldwin, Robert E., 220
Bank of China (BOC), 14, 15, 39
Bank of Communications (BOCOM), 39, 41
Banks
central bank. *See* People's Bank of China
competition from NBFIs, 65
debt restructuring and, 49–50
foreign, 215
growth of deposits, 43t, 43
liabilities, 48t
monitoring of corporate governance, 17–18
nonperforming loans, 14–15, 46, 49
policy loans to state enterprises, 9, 42
pre-1978 monobank system, 38–40, 41t